Education,
Cultural Myths,
and the Ecological Crisis

SUNY Series in the Philosophy of Education

Philip L. Smith, Editor

Education,
Cultural Myths,
and the Ecological Crisis

Toward Deep Changes

C. A. Bowers

State University of New York Press

Published by
State University of New York Press, Albany

Printed in the United States of America

For information, address State University of New York
Press, State University Plaza, Albany, NY 12246

Production by M. R. Mulholland
Marketing by Theresa A. Swierzowski

Library of Congress Cataloging-in-Publication Data

Bowers, C. A.
        Education, cultural myths, and the ecological crisis : toward deep
    changes / C. A. Bowers.
            p.   cm. — (SUNY series in the philosophy of education)
        Includes bibliographical references (p.) and index.
        ISBN 0-7914-1255-5 (alk. paper). — ISBN 0-7914-1256-3 (pbk. :
    alk. paper)
            1. Human ecology—United States—Moral and ethical aspects.
    2. Educational anthropology—United States. 3. Environmental
    education—United States. 4. Environmental protection—Study and
    teaching—United States. I. Title. II. Series: SUNY series in
    philosophy of education.
    GF27.B69   1992
    304.2'071'073—dc20
                                                                        91-13356
                                                                            CIP

10 9 8 7 6 5 4 3 2 1

Contents

Introduction

A primary purpose of this book is to put in focus what our priorities should be in thinking about the challenges facing public school and university education in the United States and other countries that have followed Western approaches to modernization. Problems associated with ethnic, gender, and class inequities are indeed daunting, and deserve immediate attention. And the current debate over what constitutes an appropriate education for a citizenry faced with the challenges of culture shock that accompany the accelerating rate of technological innovation indeed involves important issues. Reform can perhaps mitigate such specific problems as the need for a more reliable work force and greater social equality. But if the thinking that guides educational reform does not take account of how the cultural beliefs and practices passed on through schooling relate to the deepening ecological crisis, then these efforts may actually strengthen the cultural orientation that is undermining the sustaining capacities of natural systems upon which all life depends. How our cultural beliefs contribute to the accelerating degradation of the environment, it will be argued here, is the most fundamental challenge we face. All other social and educational reforms must be assessed in terms of whether they mitigate or exacerbate the ecological crisis.

Scientifically based studies of the planet's ecosystems now constitute the major part of the environmental literature. There is also a significant literature dealing with the economic and social policy implications of the ecological crisis. With the emergence of the deep ecology movement, attention increasingly has been given to the cultural aspects of the problem. However, this book recognizes that the cultural dimensions of the ecological crisis raise profound questions for educators who play such a key role in passing on the cultural templates to the next generation. Aside from my own *Cultural Literacy for Freedom*,[1] the only other major effort to deal with the education/culture/environment connection (*Education, Modernity, and Fractured Meaning* by Donald W. Oliver, with assistance of Kathleen W. Gershman) is based on the process philosophy of Alfred North Whitehead, and thus raises a different—though no less important—set of issues.

Given the complexities in understanding the culture/thought connection, as well as the culture/ecological crisis connection (not to mention the even more difficult task of agreeing on what constitute the essential characteristics of an ecologically sustainable culture), this book must be viewed as exploratory. Formal education mediates between the past and future; it is as complex, therefore, as the different aspects of the culture that constitutes both its curricular content and its multiple pedagogical processes. Thus, only certain aspects of the education/culture/ecological crisis are addressed here.

Other issues that have direct implications for education, such as how to change the direction of the present economic and technological race between Western and Asian societies that seem to depend upon the same environmentally disruptive psychological energy that sustained the Industrial Revolution, how the current development of market economies in Eastern Europe and the former Soviet Union can be reconciled with the moral imperatives of an ecologically based social order, and how to redistribute economic and social opportunities to the poorer segments of society in a manner that fosters a sense of responsible citizenship within the larger biotic community (a problem made even more difficult by the artificial nature of urban environments), are not discussed here.

The awareness that our modern and progressive form of culture is destroying the information and food networks upon which the future depends is the beginning of a new epoch. That is, this awareness represents the beginning of cultural transformations that will be far more reaching in consequences than anything yet experienced in human history. Therefore, this book should be considered as part of the initial effort to sort out the most basic issues and relationships in the education/culture/ecological crisis. In addition to presenting the argument that the condition of our planetary habitat is the concern that should frame how we think about all other reform efforts, the other major purposes of the book are to encourage discussion around critical aspects of the cultural double bind that formal education helps to perpetuate, and to suggest cultural pathways that appear to meet the test of long-term sustainability.

The following overview of chapters will help put in focus the particular intellectual routes I have followed to clarify the nature of the double binds our current approaches to education are putting us in, and in suggesting educational reforms that reflect an ecological sensibility. Both tasks involve thinking against the grain of current orthodoxies, and thus are meant to suggest the foci of future discussions about fundamental changes in public school and university education.

The first chapter establishes a framework for considering the ecological consequences of an educational process that reinforces a set of cultural beliefs and practices formed during a period of Western history when the plenitude of the natural environment seemed to hold out the promise of unlimited economic expansion and social progress. We now see more clearly that the cultural beliefs in progress, individualism, and rational processes contributed to an upward curve in the level of demands being made on the environment. Unfortunately, the sustaining capacity of the natural systems that make up our habitat show a downward curve. The evidence of the trends moving in opposite directions is beyond scientific dispute, although there is still considerable disagreement on the long-term consequences of global warming and other changes in the planet's ecosystems.

That cultural expectations are now exceeding the long-term sustaining capacity of the environment point to the need to give serious attention to why it is so difficult to recognize the cultural patterns that are putting the biotic community in peril. This chapter helps to frame this problem of cultural self-awareness by explaining how cultural patterns become part of the person's underlying attitudes, how language encodes the thought patterns of earlier generations, and how the Cartesian view of rationality and the autonomous individual (both part of the foundations of modern consciousness) have helped to put out of focus the influence of culture on thought and to maintain the sense of separation between man and nature.

After establishing that the major crisis we face lies in evolving a form of culture that is ecologically sustainable, the second chapter takes the reader through the conservatives' arguments on the nature of the educational crisis, and what they consider as the remedy. The main focus is on the ideas of Mortimer Adler, E. D. Hirsch, Jr, Allan Bloom, and William Bennett. What is especially important about the national educational debate that their analyses helped to frame is that the disjuncture between the Western canon they want to uphold and the ecological crisis is not even mentioned. Why the conservative educational critics ignored the ecological crisis is discussed, as well as the emergence of a more ecologically responsive form of conservatism, the latter articulated by people such as Aldo Leopold, Wendell Berry, Wes Jackson, Gary Snyder, and the late Gregory Bateson. The chapter concludes with a brief overview of the educational implications of these nonanthropocentric conservatives.

Having examined how conservative critics overlooked the ecological crisis, the third chapter turns to a consideration of the liberal technocrats who are the dominant group in teacher education and professional in-service training, and the emancipatory tradition of educational liberalism. Both traditions of liberal thought within the field of education are urging reforms that do not take into account the ecological crisis. This chapter considers how the cultural beliefs and values they are advocating may contribute to deepening the crisis.

The second half of the chapter, anticipating that liberal educational critics will eventually recognize the paramount importance of the ecological crisis, addresses the question of whether the ideas of John Dewey and Paulo Freire could become the basis of an ecologically responsive approach to education. This part of the analysis is particularly important because there is a renewal of interest among both philosophers and educational theorists in the ideas of Dewey; and Paulo Freire continues to exert a powerful influence on educators concerned with the problem of social reform in Third World countries as well as in post-industrial societies. Special attention is given to how certain cultural assumptions both thinkers take for granted ignore the problem of exceeding the carrying capacity of the environment.

Chapter Four, entitled "Anthropocentrism in Textbooks," assesses the cultural values and beliefs communicated through textbooks, and how they relate to the ecological crisis. Perhaps a more suitable title for the chapter would be "You Can Have It All," which seems best to summarize the dominant cultural message in public school textbooks. Necessary qualifications about the different uses that teachers make of textbooks are considered. This is followed by an examination of cultural messages that many teachers do not make explicit because of their own taken-for-granted beliefs. The examination of elementary and secondary school textbooks is framed by the following questions: What is the image of the individual that is represented, and how is "success" understood? What is represented as having authority in people's lives, and what is the nature of power? What forms of knowledge are represented as important, and what is the basis of authority? How is community represented? What is the primary basis of human relationships—i.e. is it primarily economic and political in nature? How is the nature of tradition understood, and what forms of tradition are represented? How are humans viewed in relation to the natural environment? What is the role assigned to science and technology, and are they treated as synonymous with social progress? What are the basic human values and what is the basis of their authority in people's lives?

Writers of textbooks tend not to be aware of how they provide shared answers to these questions at a level of understanding taken for granted in their particular culture. Nor are they aware that many of these cultural patterns of thinking were formed before their culture had any inkling that individual choice and rationally based progress would, in the end, be constrained by ecological considerations. Because of the mainstream nature of these beliefs and values, most teachers are equally unaware of how textbooks reinforce different aspects of the mind set that is part of the ecological problem—even as they encourage students to be environmentally responsible citizens by recycling materials.

Chapter Five, "Toward Deep Changes in the Educational Process," has three major sections. The first summarizes why the different liberal traditions in educational thought provide an inadequate basis for learning to live in ecological balance. That we need to develop new attitudes, both toward cultural experimentation and toward conserving forms of knowing and social practices that contribute to long-term sustainability, are part of the argument. The second section presents the basic ideas of Gregory Bateson, particularly his way of viewing the person as part of a larger mental ecology that includes both the natural environment and human culture (to use older, pre-Batesonian categories). The following statement seems especially representative of his way of understanding the interdependency of humans, culture, and habitat: "In no system which shows mental characteristics can any part have unilateral control over the whole. In other words, *the mental characteristics of the system are immanent, not in some part, but in the system as a whole.*"[2] This section of the chapter also summarizes how a Batesonian way of thinking helps to illuminate the way mental characteristics of the culture are reproduced through the process of teacher decision making in the classroom.

The title of Chapter Six is "The Political and Spiritual Dimensions of the Ecological Crisis: Toward a New Sense of Balance." This chapter, like so many exploratory discussions that lie before us, considers whether the mainstream Western culture that guides and gives substance to educational practices has over valued the efficacy of the political process and under valued the importance of spiritual development. In addition to fostering technological proficiency, public education is often viewed as contributing to more effective political decision making—with an assumption that social problems are amenable to political solutions. The scope of the ecological crisis, when understood in terms of Western cultural values and beliefs, raises the question of whether the political process will be effective in getting people to live by the moral dictum articulated by Solzhenitsyn's reading of the ecological/cultural crisis: "Freedom is *self-restriction:* restriction of the self for the sake of others."[3]

To discuss the possibility that we, as members of a polyglot culture, need to explore the possibilities of inward (i.e. spiritual) development both to recover the dimensions of meaning that characterize many traditional cultures, and to live in a manner that reduces our demands on the environment, is to tread on controversial ground—particularly when discussing educational institutions that have long been viewed as having a secular mission. There are a number of people who are attempting to recover a language for think-ing about the spiritual aspects of modernity and the ecologi-cal crisis: for example, Gary Snyder, Wendell Berry, J. Epes Brown, and Robert Bellah. There are more accounts avail-able now of how traditional cultures that have evolved in more ecologically sustainable ways have also developed music, art, dance, and storytelling as a way of expressing a sense of spirituality that integrates the self with other life forms that share a common habitat. The role of the spiritual in traditional cultures in contributing to more morally (and ecologically) responsible relationships with other forms of life suggests that we may be putting too much reliance on the political process, and that we must learn from traditional cultures that, until recently, we have viewed as illiterate and backward.

This more cultural as opposed to denominational approach to developing the language of spirituality will be related to changes in the cultural orientation that can be brought about in public school and university classrooms. How traditional cultures have approached art as the making special of relationships, in contrast to the modern approach to creating objects to be displayed or sold, will serve as an example that has implications for the classroom curriculum. Special attention will also be given to classroom activities that foster a sense of connectedness, across generations and between humans and other members of the biotic com-munity. Both are required as part of a change in conscious-ness if we are to achieve genuine sustainability—which involves leaving the habitat in no less of a reduced state than what was available to the present generation.

1

The Cultural Aspects
of the Ecological Crisis

A cultural theme most middle class Americans have grown up with is that change is not only a normal aspect of existence, but that it is also progressive. The steady stream of technological innovations, from computers that exploit dimensions of time that exceed what most people can comprehend to advances in biomedicine, suggest that this aspect of our belief system is still intact. Other aspects of society appear to be breaking down—urban violence, teen pregnancies, the spread of drugs, increasing numbers of homeless and impoverished, skyrocketing national debt. Yet science continues to promise technological and thus human advancement. Change continues, but a growing body of evidence strongly suggests that our sense of living in one of the most progressive times in human history may be an illusion. The computer, for example, may be increasing our efficiency in finding solutions to certain technical problems, including how to store and manipulate the mountains of information we have come to believe necessary for effective decision making. But this form of change pales in significance when compared to changes taking place in the life sustaining capacity of our habitat.

The increasing number of reports on the changing characteristics of the planet's ecosystems indicate that over the long term they are in decline. They also suggest that in the immediate decades ahead we face the growing prospect of having to change the most fundamental aspects of our belief system and patterns of social life. The challenge will be to see through the illusions of a consumer-oriented, technologically based existence, to alter the premises upon which the belief system of the dominant culture is based, and to retain those aspects of our past cultural achievements that are compatible with a culture in equilibrium with the carrying capacity of the natural systems that make up the biosphere.

There are many dangers. One scenario of future possibilities is a continuation of the state of self-absorption that characterizes the addictive personality (and culture) until the consequences of environmental disruption lead to economic dislocation and a significant loss of human life. There are other possible scenarios, one extreme being the emergence of a fascist form of government that attempts to regulate human life according to master plans drawn up by technocratically oriented bureaucrats. The other extreme would be a widely held sense of despair and futility about the prospects of changing cultural beliefs and practices in time to avert overshooting the carrying capacity of the natural systems. With the long-term prospects appearing so bleak, people may turn to the short-term pleasures and unconcerned attitudes associated with consumerism.

Although the rate of change in the ecosystems has been accelerating in the last hundred years, the real acceleration occurred in the post-World-War-II era. Awareness within the dominant culture of human interdependence with natural systems is a relatively recent phenomena. Aldo Leopold's gentle and poetic *A Sand County Almanac* provided an analogue for living in a less exploitive relationship with the other forms of life that make up the environment. His book, calling for the development of an ethic toward the land that would supplant the tradition of viewing the environment primarily in economic and political terms, was published in 1946. Rachel Carson's *Silent Spring* (1962) provided in a way that could be understood by the general public the scientific evidence that our technological approach to the environment threatened the basis of all forms of life—including our own. By the time of Paul Ehrlich's *The Population Bomb* (1968) and Barry Commoner's *The Closing Circle* (1971), the environmental movement was gaining a wider following within certain sections of society. The point being made here is that the recognition that cultural practices cannot evolve independently of a concern for the well-being of the habitat goes back a mere forty years; and it was an awareness unevenly understood and appreciated within mainstream society. Native American cultures, of course, had evolved in ecologically responsive ways; but what could have been learned from their thousands of years of experience in adapting to the unique characteristics of their habitat was ignored because they were perceived as unenlightened and pre-modern.

The discrepancy between the view of cultural change held by the middle class and the nature of environmental change can be seen in the findings of scientists who are studying the interactive environmental systems that make life possible as we know it. The schema of understanding based on Western culture represents change as a progressive expansion of human possibilities: personal freedom and individual advancement, control over life-threatening situations, power to solve problems and direct the course of future events, and of course an expansion of possibilities for consumption. The expansion of human population (from 1.6 billion in 1900 to 5 billion in 1986) and the corresponding increase in world economic activity (from 0.6 trillion dollars in 1900 to 13.1 trillion in 1986) are indeed impressive figures. But this growth in the number of people and the scale of economic activity has also increased the disruptive impact of humans on the habitat. Here the trend line indicates a decline in the viability of natural systems.

The cultural image of progress is, in part, based on scientific-technological developments, such as the synthesizing and introduction into the environment of approximately seventy thousand different kinds of chemicals, as well as the widespread use of technologies for transportation that burn fossil fuel—to cite just two examples. The scale of human impact on environmental systems, which scientists view as accelerating over the last three hundred years—with a particularly large jump in the rate of change occurring during the last 50 years—is indeed daunting. According to the lead article in a *Scientific American* special issue (September 1989), "Managing Planet Earth," the planet since the beginning of the eighteenth century has lost forest cover equal in area to the size of Europe. And the rate of deforestation has now increased to between 70,000 and 110,000 square kilometers of land a year, which is equivalent to the combined land mass of the Netherlands and Switzerland. To put it another way, an additional one percent of the total forest cover is being lost each year, and the rate is accelerating. The concentrations in the atmosphere of methane and carbon dioxide—two chemicals viewed as contributing to the greenhouse effect—are estimated to have increased 25 percent over the last 300 years. Taking into account changes in current levels of population and economic activity, it is projected that the concentration of carbon dioxide in the atmosphere will have doubled sometime after the year 2030—which will be well within the lifetime of the children of the readers of this book. Although there is not agreement among scientists about the factors that contribute to the greenhouse effect—the influence of cloud cover, the exact inventory of the earth's carbon dioxide absorbing biomass, and so forth—there is agreement that the earth's atmosphere is warming at an accelerating rate, and that this trend will have unknown consequences on precipitation patterns, agricultural production, forest zones, and—given even just the expected rise in sea level—on human settlement.

Changes in other natural systems also show a clear downward spiral in life-sustaining capabilities. Essential sources of water, such as aquifers, are being rapidly deleted in certain parts of the world, and major rivers such as the Nile, Ganges, Mississippi, and Colorado are running at reduced flow rates as ever more demands are placed on them. The levels of acidification of lakes and soil are increasing dramatically in the Northeastern part of the United States and Canada, as well as in Europe, China, and parts of India. With more land being brought under irrigation, salinization, estimated at twenty percent of irrigated land in the United States, is becoming a problem. Other changes in the life sustaining capacities of the environment include the impact of human waste and chemicals on marine ecosystems, the accelerating of species extinction as deforestation and other land use practices reduce the amount of natural habitat, and the dumping on the environment of toxic waste (over twenty billion pounds in the United States in a single year) as well as other human garbage.

Although scientists and others studying the changes in the earth's ecosystems may disagree on the figures used to understand the interactive patterns that sustain the biosphere as a living system, and the passage of time will make obsolete much of the data currently used to understand the scope of the crisis, the direction of environmental change is unmistakable. With the possibility of the earth's population doubling within the next thirty years from 5 to 10 billion people, most of the increase will occur in Third World countries that are trying to increase their levels of economic activity in order to accommodate the increase in population and to raise living standards, the rate of environmental degradation will likely increase. The 1987 report of the World Commission on Environment and Development, *Our Common Future*, estimates that the anticipated increases in population may result in a five- to ten-fold increase in what is now a 13-trillion-dollar world economy. This may be seen as continued evidence of human progress when viewed through our cultural framework but in terms of further impact on already stressed ecosystems it has catastrophic implications.

This brief overview is not meant to be alarmist; it simply summarizes trends that are documented on a daily basis in newspapers with headlines that announce environmental problems around the world, from "Italy Copes with Summer Slime" (125 miles of coastline strangled in a mass of algae that stretches 20 miles out to sea) and "East Germany's Ghost Towns" (towns that are disappearing from the map because of practices surrounding the strip mining of low-grade, high-sulfur brown coal) to "LA Making Last-Gasp Effort to Clear the Air." Television coverage of environmental "disasters" and "catastrophes" are becoming so frequent that these words are losing their power to hold the public's attention; ozone holes, oil spills (even on the scale of the Exxon Valdez), burning and cutting the rain forest, and nuclear contamination seem like an unending succession of media events that for a brief period occupy the public's attention before being displaced by new announcements and revelations. This overview thus is related to what the scientific reports and media coverage are not dealing with—namely, the cultural and, by extension, educational aspects of the problem.

The special reports on the environment, which range from the Worldwatch Institute's yearly publication, *State of the World*, to such journals as *The Economist* and *Scientific American*, frame the problem in terms of a rationalistic approach to problem solving. This is not surprising, because the people who either carry out the studies of environmental change or summarize the data for a nonspecialist audience have largely been educated at universities in an ideology that holds human action to be based on a rational process. According to this view, information is the basis of rational thought. Thus, the reports are framed in a way that will provide rational people with the data necessary for understanding the nature of the problem, and for acting, primarily through enactment of new environmental legislation, in a more environmentally responsible manner.

The report of The World Commission on Environment and Development, *Our Common Future,* and the Worldwatch Institute's *State of the World* are typical of the way in which the environmental crisis is being presented. Both present scientific data and suggest critical areas in which new policies and legislation—both on the national and international level—are needed to guide human behavior toward a way that is more environmentally sustainable. Both reports refer to humans in terms of people, society, and governments; but references to culture (indeed, cultures) are totally lacking. The special issue of *Scientific American* on "Managing Planet Earth" contains an article "The Changing Climate," where this rationalist view of human behavior is clearly represented. Reflecting on the social significance of recent studies of climate change, Stephen H. Schneider, a leading scientist in the area of climatology, commented that,

> I am often asked whether I am pessimistic because it will be impossible to avert some global change. At this stage, it appears, no plausible policies are likely to prevent the world from warming a degree or two. Actually I see, a positive aspect: the possibility that a slight but manifest global warming, coupled with the larger threat forecast in computer models, may catalyze international cooperation to achieve environmentally sustainable development, marked by stabilized population and the proliferation of energy-efficient and environmentally safe technologies.[1]

William D. Ruckelshaus, writing in the same issue of *Scientific American,* urges that "a clear set of values consistent with the consciousness of sustainability" be articulated by national leaders.[2] Provide the data, state the issues clearly, utilize government incentives, and people will have a rational basis for changing their life styles. Again, we find the assumption that humans are rational beings when they have the right data, but no acknowledgement that people are essentially cultural beings, that the world is made of multiple cultures, and that culture makes the outcome of the political process far more problematic than is recognized by people who hold a rationalistic point of view.

Since current approaches to framing the ecological crisis are conditioning us to accept the rationalist approach to problem solving, they help to insure that the human dimensions of the crisis are never really understood at the deepest levels. The argument here is not against being rational; rather the main issue is an overly narrow view of the wellspring of human thought and behavior. The other problem with the rationalist approach is that it ignores how different cultural groups organize their way of understanding on fundamentally different assumptions and root metaphors; thus the human aspect of the ecological crisis is not simply a matter of people, societies, and nation states—those misleading metaphors of Western colonialism—but of cultural differences that cannot be easily reconciled or changed by using a political process based on the Western forms of rationalism so evident in environmental reports. The cross-cultural dimensions of the ecological crisis, while exceedingly important and complicated, are not however the main focus of this work.

Our main concern here is with the middle class culture which exerts such a dominant influence in American society, and with how the belief system of this group, which underlies so many environmentally disruptive practices, is perpetuated in the public schools and universities. Pronouncements on the necessity of other cultural groups' changing their environmentally destructive practices may help inflate our moral sense of superiority and bolster our self-image as ecologically responsible citizens. But as largely ritual behavior this diverts attention from the part of the problem that we can actually do something about. Directing our energies to bringing our own society's dominant culture into closer balance with the long-term sustaining capacities of our own environment is justified because we, along with the other Western industrialized, consumer-oriented societies, are major contributors to the problem. The technologies that support our life styles deplete nonrenewable resources and contribute to multiple forms of pollution on a scale vastly disproportionate to our percentage of the world population.

Focusing on our own situation should not, however, be taken to mean that what other cultures do about their relationship is no concern of ours. If we have learned anything in recent years it is that the ecosystems of the planet are interactive with each other. Thus, destroying the forests in one part of the world ultimately will have an influence on the precipitation patterns and changes in soil conditions in other parts of the world. Overproduction of food grains in our country, which involve the use of techniques damaging to our water supplies and soil, alter the economics in other countries with more marginal soils—forcing them to adopt even more disruptive practices. Other examples of the interactive nature of human practices and ecosystems could easily be cited. But the most immediate challenge is to address at the level of formal education our own disruptive cultural patterns—while keeping an eye on the influence that our practices and policies have on the manner in which other cultural groups use the world's commons of soil, oceans, forests, and atmosphere.

In recent years a wide variety of groups have taken on the mission of changing attitudes and social practices relating to the environment. They range from environmentalists who argue for a more responsible form of stewardship of the environment to advocates of "deep ecology." The latter is more an umbrella term covering a wide array of groups who view the ecological crisis as raising fundamental questions about our belief and value systems. The more serious "deep ecology" thinkers, such as Arne Naess, Warwick Fox, and Alan Drengson, have attempted to articulate the philosophical basis for an ecologically grounded view of self. But the American tendency toward syncretism is fully evident in the attempts of others to find the path to an ecologically enlightened form of existence in such diverse traditions as Taoism, Buddhism, libertarianism, feminist spirituality, communitarianism, Greek mythology, Christianity, Shamanistic cultures, and so forth. Often the impression is left that the pathway to ecological balance is in embracing as many of these traditions as possible.

Though somewhat less ebullient about the transformation of consciousness, the Greens are perhaps the most important social and political movement to have emerged in response to the growing deterioration of our habitat. The Greens in North America share the more comprehensive political agenda that has made them so highly visible in Western Europe and Australia. As the following statement makes plain, they see the need for a complete restructuring of society to restore the system to a smaller scale where the skills, interests, and responsibility of the individual matters again. To quote from the position paper of the Green Party of the Federal Republic of Germany:

A complete restructuring of our current near-sighted planning is necessary. We consider it mistaken to believe that our present spendthrift economy can still promote human happiness and the fulfillment of life goals. Just the opposite occurs. People have become more harried and less free. Only to the extent that we free ourselves from an overdependency on a materialistic standard of life, and make individual self-realization possible again, and recognize the limits of our own inner nature, will our creative powers be able to free themselves to form life anew on an ecological basis.[3]

Their concern with participative involvement, nonhierarchical social structures, and an ecologically and socially oriented economy, to cite just a few of their proposals for changing the basic direction of Western modernization, also involves specific proposals for changes in education. The organization of schools and a curriculum that fosters class divisions and stratified bodies of knowledge essential to furthering a technocratic society are specifically rejected.

They propose that the old competitively based model of education be replaced by an approach to education that emphasizes the following content:

— practical training for both teachers and students in handicrafts, industry, and agriculture, in order to reduce the gap between education and the working world.
— school children able to learn outside of the school, and real life situations brought into the schools. The separa-

tion between school time and leisure time must be elim-
inated. Music, theater, painting, work and play, all must
find their place in the school.
— the encouragement of thinking in terms of interrelated
systems as the ongoing goal of teaching, in order to
encourage a better understanding of social interrela-
tions, ecological cycles, and prevailing contradictions.
The school should be able to train the student to recognize the interests which lie behind social and personal
conflicts. They should be taught to solve conflicts
peacefully between people, to formulate their own concerns, and, together with others, to find effective ways
of expressing these interests.[4]

Beyond the environmentalists' recommendations on the
importance of teaching recycling in schools and avoiding
hazardous waste, as well as other common-sense practices
that accompany the annual "Earth Day" observances, the
Greens are one of the few groups to address the problem of
educational reform from an ecological perspective. With the
exception of their recommendation that students be taught
to think in terms of interrelated systems, their proposals,
however, appear to be little more than the restatement of
much of the educational thinking of the 1960s, with its
emphasis on individual self-realization in an open, nonau-
thoritarian classroom. The Greens' more coherent vision of
how different aspects of society—work and technology,
energy, agriculture, zoning and community development,
education, and so forth—must be reorganized in order to
decentralize decision making, and to replace the traditional
anthropocentrism with biocentrism, reframes the goals to be
served by these educational reforms.

But the orientation of the Greens, like the ideological traditions on which they draw so heavily, reflects the contradictions and tensions of these earlier ways of thinking—as well
as their silences. The Greens' ideal of personal autonomy
and their view of the nature of freedom raise questions
about how these traditional political ideals are to be reconciled with the Greens' nonanthropocentric view of the
human relationship to the natural world. Whether the other
aspects of their political agenda for transforming a technocratically oriented society into cooperatively based, small-

scale communities can be attained through the democratic process is also problematic. But the aspect of their thinking, as well as that of the environmentalists and most deep ecologists, that is of most concern here is the failure to consider the influence culture has on human thought and behavior.

Technology, profits, competition, multinational corporations, Taoism, and feminist spirituality are all aspects of culture. In fact, anything that humans do, including those activities and artifacts that survive over time, can be understood as representing the influence of culture. Because it is so encompassing, varied in its expression, and formative in its influence, culture is less amenable to the political process than the Greens and other environmentally conscious groups recognize. This does not mean that culture and the political process can ever be domains of human activity distinct from each other: the forms of politics are also grounded in cultural patterns and codes. And the political process—if it leads to change—involves changes within other dimensions of the culture. Recent political change brought about by the feminist movement demonstrates this point. But the lack of specific focus on the cultural aspects of the ecological crisis seems to limit remedial action to those political arenas where disagreements rooted in economic interests and ideological differences have made change exceedingly difficult and slow. Witness the time it takes to enact environmental legislation, and the compromises that must be made.

Attempts to maintain a sustainable habitat through the political process—whether in the form of demonstrations, working in the hallways and committee rooms of the legislature, or spiking trees—effectively preclude utilizing the full potential of the classroom to help ameliorate the crisis. There is no single cause for any aspect of the ecological crisis, but there are complex and interconnected cultural patterns, beliefs, and values that collectively help to introduce perturbations into ecosystems, causing them to go into decline. To put this another way, there is no single cultural cause for cutting old growth forests in the Northwest or for engineering automobiles as status symbols rather than for fuel efficiency. Practices and beliefs far from the scene of the ecological crime—so to speak—are contributing through often invisible vectors; for example, our attitudes toward packaging and reading newspapers have something to do with cutting old growth forests. It is not simply a matter of capitalism, as some extremists might argue.

The changes in some practices—like dumping toxic wastes, deforestation, depleting fisheries, and losing topsoil and ground water—require immediate attention, and this will mean utilizing the political process to enact legislation. Attempting to effect changes in these areas through the long-term process of educationally guided cultural changes would be too slow a process. But the long-term aspects of learning to live in ecological balance also require giving attention to those aspects of culture that will have an influence on the taken-for-granted beliefs, values, and social practices that people will hold in the future. To use the ongoing feminist movement as an example, it is possible to see how direct political action is being translated into legislation, and how the more long-term cultural adjustments are being worked out in the context of the classrooms as students learn to think about work in less gender-biased language and engage in other behavioral patterns that treat people on a more equitable basis. The two processes—political and educational—are going on simultaneously; while they complement each other, the processes have distinct characteristics that must be taken into account.

To consider the broader and longer-term process of bringing mainstream culture into a sustainable balance with the habitat, it is necessary that the complexity of culture must be recognized as well as why it is so difficult to be aware of this complexity. Rather than fit the discussion of how educators should respond to the ecological crisis into the controversial frameworks of the deep ecologists, Greens, and environmentalists—whose disagreements can become excuses for others' indifference—I want to propose a different approach. The focus on culture, which is the medium of the classroom, allows for more educators to become involved, and at different levels. It also addresses the symbolic dimensions of a long-term solution—which has to do with the cultural patterns, beliefs, and values that will be part of the taken-for-granted attitudes of future generations. Before we take up the more direct educational implications of this approach, it is necessary to focus more directly on the nature of culture itself and on why certain aspects of the dominant Western culture have made the formative influence of culture even more difficult to recognize. Although public school and university education, in both their curricular content and their patterns of teaching, are cultural processes, we have not really understood the special educational issues raised by the culture-language-thought connection. One of the reasons for this is connected with the specific cultural pattern of thinking now being brought into question by the ecological crisis. Thus, a deeper understanding of culture, as well as the specific cultural patterns now being recognized as problematic, may also help guide us toward a more a ecologically responsive approach to public school and university education.

Clifford Geertz's definition of culture provides a good starting point for illuminating one of the reasons culture is so difficult to recognize. The other reason, which has to do with the specific set of beliefs and assumptions that has had a privileged position in Western thought for nearly 400 years, will be taken up later. For Geertz, culture can be understood as the shared patterns that set the "tone, character, and quality" of people's lives—ranging from what is viewed as food, how it is prepared and eaten, to the categories used to understand the world and the human beings placed in it. The following explanation by Geertz points to the pervasive nature of culture in human experience: "Culture patterns— religious, philosophical, aesthetic, scientific, ideological—are 'programs'; they provide a template or blueprint for the organization of social and psychological processes, much as genetic systems provide such a template for the organization of organic processes."[5] Of course, we must recognize here that Geertz is representing culture in a highly metaphorical manner; unlike the chemical code of a gene that regulates the form that life will take, the culture that provides the patterns guiding human experience can be partly understood at the explicit level of awareness and changed as a result of thought—which may even include changes based on misconceptions. But the key point in Geertz's explanation is that the patterns that make up a culture are the largely invisible yet always present sources of authority in people's lives. Even the power of rational thought and creativity are expressed in terms of culturally shared patterns.

This brings us to a second critically important feature of culture, namely, that the patterns used by people as the basis for their experience—which range from the body's message system for communicating interpersonal relationships to the categories used to organize thought—are experienced as part of the person's natural attitudes. A way of understanding a person's attitudes is to view them as what the person takes for granted in experience. As we are here identifying an aspect of culturally based experience of which by definition, we are not aware, it may be useful to cite examples that we can recognize as the taken-for-granted foundations of our own experience. The practice of associating "up" with good and "down" with bad, adjusting interpersonal spatial distance according to social context and status relationships, designing a house, and deciding who is included in our family and community are just a few examples from the everyday world. Patterns of belief and of social interaction that are felt as immutable may be problematic in fact, as when cultural patterns of the early European explorers led them to view the New World as an economic resource to be staked out for exploitation. More recently, we have witnessed the damaging effects of technological innovations that were not anticipated because of fundamental attitudes about the progressive and ameliorative nature of new technologies. Beliefs and social practices may take a positive form, like the patterns we follow in successfully interacting with others, driving a car, and hiking on a mountain trail. It is not the unexamined nature of cultural patterns that is the problem, but the patterns themselves. The invisible nature of cultural patterns becomes a problem only when they are the source of undesirable consequences, like the cultural practice of designing automobiles to require greater use of air conditioning that results in the release of ozone-damaging chemicals into the atmosphere.

There is another dimension of given patterns that needs to be recognized. The patterns we unconsciously re-enact can be understood as lived traditions. That is, the cultural patterns—ranging from what is viewed as constituting wealth, how we organize and use space, to our sense of time, to identify just a few examples—represent past forms of understanding that have been encoded in the patterns that underlie current experience. As other members of our cultural group share these patterns of encoded knowledge, meaningful communication and social interaction is possible. If all these patterns were made explicit, judged, and improvised on a purely individualistic basis, communication would become impossible. In effect, making explicit all patterns, if it were possible, would contribute to a condition of nihilism where the authority of traditional patterns would be relativized, and values and commitment would vary in accordance with personal opinion. The critical issue here, related to Geertz's view of cultural patterns, is that even the person who is questioning all forms of authority in people's lives is being unconsciously influenced (even driven?) by cultural patterns. But this does not mean that all cultural patterns evolve in a way whereby only existentially meaningful and socially useful traditions are preserved and the outmoded ones are made explicit and so reconstituted in a way that in turn becomes the basis of experience for the next generation. There are also cultural patterns that continue to have authority in our lives even though they threaten our existence over the long-term.

For example, the distinctive set of beliefs that many people in the dominant culture associate with progress and modernity fosters mental habits particularly unsuited for recognizing either implicitly assumed beliefs or evidence that challenges the idea that change is inherently progressive. These beliefs, born in a period of self-conscious emancipation from what was viewed as the "Dark Ages," were seen as the basis of human empowerment: in overcoming illness and death, the drudgery of work, the suppression of human freedom, and the barriers to material success. The partial fulfillment of the promise has not been entirely illusory, but the essential core of these beliefs evolved in a way that lost touch with the realities of an environment that has natural limits. To make this point in a different way, the hubris of this mind set assumed that environmental limits could be transcended through the resourcefulness of human rationality.

Key aspects of this belief system still provide a basis for understanding the implications of the changes taking place in the environment. A culturally specific view of individualism, of the rational, and of the nature of language can be traced directly to the seventeenth- and eighteenth-century thinkers who laid the conceptual foundations for the evolution of modern Western consciousness. While often disagreeing on important issues relating to the nature and

source of ideas, the founding fathers of modern consciousness left a distinct and still obvious legacy. John Locke
(1632–1704) helped to establish the primacy of the individual
by arguing that the individual is to be understood as existing
prior to society: that is, as a biological entity living in a "state
of nature." Membership in society came about as a result of
the realization that the self-interest of the individual could not
be pursued on a more rational (predictable) basis in the state
of nature where there was no third party who could adjudi-
cate disputes.

René Descartes (1596–1650) also started with the individual who, through a process of radical doubt, supposedly is
then able to exercise a form of rationality free of the influence of both tradition and culture. Descartes' formulation of
thought as an inner mental process helped establish today's
dualisms of mind and body and of thought and nature. The
contemporary understanding of objective knowledge, procedural thinking, and the reduction of a thing or process to its
smallest components also have their roots in Descartes'
epistemology.

Ernst Cassirer, in summarizing the influence of
Descartes on subsequent Enlightenment thinkers, observed
that "reason is now looked upon rather as an acquisition
than a heritage. It is not the treasury of the mind in which
truth like a minted coin lies stored; it is rather the original
intellectual force which guides the discovery and determina-
tion of truth."[6] Furthermore, as the rational process was considered to be everywhere the same, involving a particular
relationship between reflection and sense data, there was
no need to account for cultural differences. The idea that
language might encode the thought patterns of a cultural
group, thus influencing the "rational process," was likewise
unimaginable to these early founders of modern consciousness.

In the course of our discussion, the terms "Cartesianism"
and the "Enlightenment" will be used as a means of identifying the historical and cultural origins of ideas and values that
now tend to be associated with a universal form of modernism. "Cartesianism" will be used when referring to those
aspects of modern consciousness that can most directly be
traced back to Descartes' mode of thinking, with its dualisms
and linear procedures of thinking. Although Descartes' legacy

has undergone important modifications, we are still, at the deepest level of our thought process, Cartesian thinkers. This can most easily be seen in the curriculum and the teaching styles that characterize the educational process from the early grades through graduate school.

The term "Enlightenment" will be used to designate the somewhat later emphasis given to the authority of reason in guiding people's lives, the belief in the inevitability of progress and, as Alexander Pope so succinctly put it, the belief that "the proper study of mankind is man." The two traditions represent a distinct cultural pathway that now seems to be increasingly problematic. Our task will be to illuminate how current interpretations of key ideas, assumptions, and values associated with modern consciousness are putting us in a double-bind, particularly in our response to the ecological crisis.

Currently, the way individualism is understood within the dominant culture varies in terms of the past socialization of different subgroups. Academics and technical experts who write on environmental issues would tend to emphasize a different, though not incompatible, set of attributes; for them, individualism would be more associated with rational self-determination than the expressive form of individualism to which many other groups subscribe. Keeping in mind that "individualism" is a metaphor that encodes different peoples' various associations, examples, and analogues of what it means to be an individual, it seems safe to say that individualism is generally associated with the idea of freedom. But "freedom" is also a metaphor that encodes different schemas of understanding, depending upon the historically formative analogues. But the most powerful analogue, which is that of the autonomous individual, suggests that freedom is a matter of choosing one's own values, one's self-identity, and future. Within the cultural mainstream, differences seem to arise more in terms of how to achieve the fullest expression of individual freedom, rather than over the deeper questions associated with freedom itself. Some argue that rationality is the basis of individual authority while others argue for a more emotive basis of individual authenticity.

In *Habits of the Heart*, Robert Bellah and his colleagues write eloquently about the consequences of making the individual self the basic social unit, and question whether this modern image, cut off from communal involvement and responsibility, can sustain either a meaningful public or private life.[7] But there are other consequences of this view of individualism that relate more to the foundations of the myth of the autonomous, self-directing individual. One consequence is that thinking of self as an autonomous individual hides the multiple dependencies upon patterns of thinking, use of technologies, and reenactment of social conventions that have been handed down from the past. To put this another way, the current image of individualism (which Edward Shils points out as being part of a Western tradition of thought) disconnects the "individual" from tradition at the level of self-understanding. But as the wheel of thought does not always have to impinge on the road of everyday reality, individuals (in being absolutely dependent upon tradition for coping with every aspect of daily life) are left in a schizophrenic condition where their view of freedom contradicts their reenactment of traditional patterns and practices. For our purposes, the important point here is that the current image of individualism does not recognize the complex nature of tradition and the authority that it has in people's lives. This is, as we shall later see, a critically important issue in any serious discussion of the characteristics of an ecologically sustainable culture.

Another consequence of associating individualism with freedom is that it prevents a deeper awareness of the dimensions of experience as influenced by culture. As discussed earlier, the way cultural patterns are taken for granted and thus not part of the person's self-awareness, helps maintain the myth of individual autonomy. One aspect of culture put out of focus by the Western emphasis on the self-directed individual is how language, with its roots deep in the past, influences thought and behavior. Language can be understood as encoding the thought processes (actually, the mental ecology) of earlier stages in our cultural history. For example, thinking of the heart as a pump encodes the earlier assumptions about the mechanistic nature of the universe; thinking of North America as "the New World" encodes the privileged European perspective (many native peoples referred to the continent as "Turtle Island"); and thinking of creativity as an original act of the individual encodes assumptions that evolved along with the Western view of modern art. What the current view of individualism obscures is that language provides the important schemata or conceptual frameworks that guide the thought process of the individual. In effect, the patterns of individual thought are culturally rooted; while this means that there is far less original thought than is now proclaimed, it does not mean that thought is entirely determined by the encoding characteristics of language. As demonstrated here, it is possible to make the underlying patterns explicit and to reconceptualize them. This may lead to minor changes in the collective conceptual mapping process. Or, as attempts to shift away from the Cartesian mind set suggest, the changes may be more profound and reach deeper into levels of cultural practice.

This brief discussion of the relationship between language and thought, where language is more deterministic in direct relation to the individual's taking its cultural formulations for granted, is related to how the myth of individual autonomy contributes to thinking about personal responsibility. The conceptual schema (what we can now recognize as part of a culturally and historically specific way of thinking) that leads to thinking of self at the same time as both self-directing and the center of an autonomous rational and moral authority, undermines the sense of being interdependent with the larger social and biotic community. Responsibility is thus viewed in terms of self-interest; and if there is any awareness of living in an interdependent world it is likely to be viewed as an unwelcomed constraint on individual freedom. The discussion of language, tradition, and beliefs (which are all different aspects of the cultural milieu that makes human life possible) points to a basic fact that is not recognized by the modern form of consciousness: namely, that, as Gary Snyder points out, life involves participation in information and food networks.

The German philosopher Martin Heidegger argues that the dualisms that reflect Descartes' influence on Western consciousness not only include separating mind from body and the mind from the external world, but also a particular way of thinking about the world. According to Heidegger, the fundamental change in our way of thinking introduced by Descartes is to conceive and grasp the world as a picture.[8] This sense of being an observer who can make separate and objective judgments strengthened other Western cultural assumptions that extend even further back in time. One of these is the anthropocentric view of the world; that is, the world is to be understood and valued only from the perspective of human needs, interests, and sense of rationality. This positioning of "man" at the apex or center of the world, depending upon which tradition of Western thought you follow, has had the effect of privileging humans as superior to other life forms by virtue of their distinctive capabilities as rational beings.

But the form of rationalism we have created over the last four hundred years of industrial development in the West has problematic characteristics other than those related just to the spectator/anthropocentric way of understanding the "external" world. When compared with the patterns of thinking among traditional peoples, which have been described as consensual in that the members reflect and act within a shared overarching conceptual framework that recognizes many traditional forms of authority, the modern rationalist thinker can be more easily recognized as operating according to a different set of norms.[9] Alvin Gouldner, the late political sociologist, has identified how these norms are based on a model that is individualistic and competitive. These norms or "rules of critical discourse" include: the justification of assertions, the use of evidence rather than the invoking of traditional forms of authority (those who represent the authority of tradition, sacred texts, communal memory, and so forth), the voluntary standing of listeners, and the competitive nature of the forum in which assertions are defended.[10] In more popular terms we have referred to these norms as providing for John Stuart Mill's open marketplace of ideas, and as a competitive arena where truth emerges because of the preponderance of evidence—only to be challenged by alternative interpretations or the emergence of new evidence.

This view of the rational process, in being based on a competitive model that locates the authority in the rational process of individuals, rejects tacit and more contextually grounded forms of knowledge. In turn, the outcome of this more context-free form of thinking is viewed as the basis for making judgments that apply universally; that is, the outcome of this rational process is regarded as valid regardless of cultural context or time frame—until overturned by a newer way of understanding.

There are several characteristics of this way of thinking that help insure the privileged standing that it now has in the Western educational process, including many parts of the world where modernization is being based on the Western model. The first has to do with the emphasis that this model of the rational processes places on presenting its claims in a supposedly open, competitive arena where argument and evidence are the basis for establishing truth claims. People educated to think theoretically (that is, to think abstractly) and who have the economic and political means to establish the evidence to support their theory are going to prevail over those people who do not possess the elaborated speech codes necessary for playing by the norms of the competitive model. Forms of authority that are grounded in experience or serve as keystones of their symbolic universe are not recognized as credible by those who uphold the norms that privilege their own patterns of rationality. A second characteristic has to do with the dynamism of this approach to rationalism. We have heard on countless occasions of the advantages for humankind from the "free marketplace of ideas"; indeed, many of the advances in technology, institutional safeguards of civil liberties, and social opportunities have their origins in the openness of the rational process

But this dynamism has another dimension that relates directly to the environmental crisis we are addressing here, and it is this dimension that has largely escaped the attention of people who give speeches and write articles and books extolling the connection between the modern view of the rational process and human progress. The continual introduction of new knowledge, and the mechanical, social, and political technologies that quickly follow, involve a continual process of cultural experimentation. That is, the innovations alter the patterns and relationships that characterize the fabric of social life. But the mind set that is oriented toward the introduction of ever-newer thinking and technology does not give much attention to the social consequences of the previous cultural experiment—unless of course the consequences, such as breakdown of a nuclear reactor or deformities resulting from a particular drug, are especially dramatic and socially visible. This tendency toward cultural experimentation is such an important and complex issue that we shall return to it when we address the implications of the ecological crisis for such long-standing ideals as academic freedom.

Reading about why our own belief system is so difficult to recognize is not nearly as exciting as being told that the moral relativism spreading across America can be traced to the influence of a couple of German philosophers or that our educational test scores have dropped to the bottom of the list for Western industrialized societies. But the hidden nature of belief systems, our own as well as those of other cultures, becomes a matter of great importance when it comes to the political challenges we face in the immediate years ahead in bringing about the changes on an international level in governmental economic policies and individual life styles necessary for reversing the disruptive effect of humans on the environment. In the past, the use or threat of military force was a basic aspect of the political process. The use of rational persuasion was also an important aspect of international politics. With the growing realization of the catastrophic dangers (and economic costs) associated with achieving political ends through military action we seem now to be left with the rationalist approach that leads to seemingly endless negotiation in order to bring about, for all the effort, only incremental changes in governmental policy. Examples of the slowness of governments to act in the face of serious environmental problems easily come to mind: the failure to address the root causes of the acid rain problem that affects Northeast Canada and the United States, the inability to address the problem of drift-net fishing in the Pacific, to cite just two examples. The international political process, in both environmentally constructive and destructive ways, is also being influenced through an increasingly internationalized media. Television coverage seems to be awakening people in living rooms around the world to the decimation of dolphins, elephants, and rain forests, and fouling of shorelines. But this grassroots political process is counterbalanced, if not overwhelmed, by the power of the media to indoctrinate people with the message that to be modern means to adopt an increasingly materialistic life style.

Aside from economic issues, which are very real, one of the reasons the international political process does not work in a way that fits the Western rationalist's expectations is the culture factor. The hiddenness of culturally specific assumptions, which influence how the constructs of another cultural group about reality, continually gets in the way of the rational process that is often upheld as the universal standard by Westerners. Ironically, it turns out that one of the least exciting things to read and think about—the constituent elements of our own belief system and why these particular beliefs cause us to ignore the cultural dimensions of the ecological crisis—is perhaps one of the most important in addressing the crisis.

We would be falling into the rationalist trap if we accepted the idea that understanding cultural differences will finally enable us to settle differences on a rational basis. The foundations of cultural belief are not rationally formulated, and thus are too deeply rooted in the person's interconnected psychology, language, and map of the world. Although more limited than rationalists would like (as perhaps a defense against the fascist tendencies in the rationalist's position), increasing cross cultural understanding is essential to facilitating communication about how issues are understood, and thus why peoples of different cultures frame the issues in such diverse and often irreconcilable ways. The solution to this problem is admittedly long-term and, again, will be only partial.

But there is a dimension to this problem of understanding how culturally based ways of thinking and acting have an adverse effect on the environment that is closer to home. This dimension has to do with changing the foundations of our own belief system, and while it may seem in the eyes of some as more defensible than setting out to change the belief systems of other cultural groups, it is no less difficult. As the ongoing feminist movement has shown, as well as other recent social changes that could easily be cited, it is possible to affect changes in people's thought and behavioral patterns at the deepest levels when the changes become a new part of taken for granted culture. And like the feminist movement, part of whose energy was focused on the belief system taught in the schools, we will direct our attention to this critical area of cultural reproduction.

Suggesting that the public schools and universities should be one of the arenas for reconstituting the conceptual foundations of a culture that is ecologically out of balance is likely to elicit the response from many educators that schools simply cannot take on any more social responsibilities. A response might be to sink further into a state of deep despair, as schools have become so politicized that they have achieved few of the social goals envisaged by social reformers. I myself vacillate between these two responses, but I cannot see that the public schools can be excluded from the crisis. The double bind of expanding cultural demands on a contracting resource base is not the sort of issue that will go away. Self-denying strategies, failure to exercise intelligence commensurate with the scope of the problem, and a diverting of energy to other political agendas (even such heavily contested ones as issues related to race, gender, and social class) will not displace the ecological crisis as the most pressing political and moral issue facing humankind.

The failure of current educational reformers, both conservative and technicist, will be taken up in the next chapter; but two of the more salient reasons for not excluding public education from the process of cultural renewal will be laid out here. Public schools and universities are only two of many institutions that pass on the culture, and they do not have the ability to influence thought and expectation to the same degree as the media. Nevertheless, they exert an important influence on what aspects of the culture are transmitted to the next generation and in determining which aspects will be understood at the explicit level of awareness and what will be part of the person's stock of unexamined "knowledge." A second reason our institutions of formal education have a special importance in the ecological crisis is that the socialization of students involves encountering in a more systematic way the language and conceptual frameworks that underpin the mainstream culture. If this conceptual framework, which also includes a sense of the moral order, is derived primarily from the period of history that produced the Industrial Revolution, we face the tragic prospect of the next generation being caught in a conceptual double bind where the ability to understand the problem will be dependent upon the same patterns of thought partly responsible for the scope of the crisis.

As the world's population begins to experience the environmental consequences of moving toward the 10 billion mark, along with the effects of economic activity associated with creating additional jobs and raising the standard of living (read: dumping more toxic waste, depleting and contaminating dwindling supplies of fresh water, and so forth), the ecological crisis will become a concern of television executives, theologians, governmental officials, and even the heads of multinational corporations. Each group, in terms of the aspects of the culture they most influence, will be faced with rethinking the most fundamental aspects of their taken-for-granted belief system. This also applies to educators—in both public schools and the universities.

2

The Conservative Misinterpretation of the Educational Crisis

Writing in *Rolling Stone*, Mark Hertsgaard cites examples of how the leading newspapers continued for years to downplay the importance of environmental issues in favor of the more traditional headliners of Cold War developments, budget deficits, and the foibles of national political figures. A story on how human activity was changing the earth's atmosphere was relegated to page 42 of the *New York Times* in 1979, but a piece with nearly identical content (now termed the "greenhouse effect") made it to page 1 in 1988. Drought, forest fires, and drying up of rivers during the summer of 1988 suddenly made the scientific reports on changes in the environment worthy of newspaper attention. This example of highly educated people ignoring a growing body of scientific evidence pointing to the very real possibility of ecological catastrophe within our own lifetime has been repeated in the recent conservative debate on the inadequacies of public school and university education.

The basic problem, as represented by such conservative advocates of educational reform as E. D. Hirsch, Jr., Mortimer J. Adler, William J. Bennett, and Alan Bloom, is that public education is failing to provide essential knowledge needed for a rational understanding of the problems we face as individuals and as a nation. The problems are myriad, ranging from a lack of factual information which prevents events and issues from being comprehended because students are unable to place them within a larger conceptual map to the nihilist condition where students are taught to substitute their own subjective response for the authority of

tradition. This manifestation of cultural malaise, which conservatives view as being hidden by the current shibboleths
of liberal ideology ("freedom," "individualism," "progress," "relevance," "empowerment," and so forth), does not include,
however, the slightest acknowledgment that the *real* crisis
has to do with the cultural beliefs and practices that are dis-
rupting the self-sustaining capacities of the ecosystems. Stated more directly, the conservative critics have ignored the
alarming reports of the negative human impact on natural
systems. Their silence on the ecological crisis, like the
silences encountered among colleagues within the academic community, is not easily understandable—particularly
among people whose conceptual style is to frame issues in
terms of a long-term perspective.

Although the ecological crisis did not cause the educational deficiencies that concern conservative critics, it does
bring into serious question their proposals for educational
reform. The ecological crisis, insofar as it has to do with
diminishing capacities within closed-loop and thus finite systems, is not like human culture, where a crisis, such as the
current budget deficit, can be deferred into the indefinite
future. Global warming will change agricultural zones and
precipitation patterns, acid rain will destroy lakes and
streams as living habitats, and the loss of topsoil will result in
lower agricultural yields. The bottom line is a diminished
capacity for sustaining life—that of humans as well as other
members of the biosphere. The recognition that ecosystems
cannot (and do not) expand their life-sustaining capacities in
response to the expanding needs of cultures (in which ideas
seem only to be limited by shortcomings in human imagina-
tion) leads to asking whether the belief system that underlies
a particular culture is sustainable over the long-term. If this
question were to be asked by conservative thinkers, their
understanding of the nature of the educational crisis and their
proposals for overcoming it would be radically different.

People who are waking up to the scope of the ecological crisis are beginning to think of practices that are sustainable in terms of the natural systems that yield the bounty
essential for survival. The analysis here of the conservative's
proposals for educational reform will be based on this question of sustainability. Thus, the primary question becomes,
"Are the beliefs and values which underpin the conserva-

tive's proposals for educational reform sustainable over the long-term, or will they contribute to the further deterioration of the habitat?" Put more simply: "Are they part of the solution to the ecological crisis, or part of the problem?"

If any generalization can be made, it is that conservative educational critics are not of one voice. But they do share a common set of concerns, a shared set of assumptions about what will resolve the crisis in public education, and they share the same silences. The pivotal issue that unites them relates to the loss of a shared political and moral community, which is to be restored through the recovery (and rediscovery) of the intellectual achievements of the past. This sense of historical continuity which separates the conservative educational critic from the technocratic liberals who are more representative of the educational establishment, with their time frame of educational problems set and resolved in the immediate present, is most clearly represented in William Bennett's defense of the study of history: "History is a source of personal identity, a means of acquiring a sense of 'connectedness' with a tradition, a community, a past. It is a way of locating ourselves in time and space, of acquiring the values and ideals by which we live our lives, and of returning to the wellsprings of our being as a people and a nation."[1] Unlike the neoromantic formulation of human freedom, which is still represented in some classrooms as fully expressed in the emotive and subjective judgments of the individual, the conservative views freedom as an achievement obtained through a reflective and appreciative understanding of history. Thus, this orientation toward the recovery of historical understanding is viewed as contributing to a responsible form of individual empowerment, and, by extension, to healing the polity.

Adler bases his argument for radical reform of the public school curriculum on the assertion that universal suffrage and universal schooling "are inextricably bound together." "One without the other," he warns, "would be a serious delusion," leading to "mobocracy."[2] Adler also believes that schooling, which is supposed to provide the foundations for the less formal education that characterizes adult life, should contribute to three general goals: moral and spiritual growth; the ability to participate as an enfranchised citizen who bears both freedoms and responsibilities; and the intellectual foundations and skills necessary for earning a living. These objectives, as viewed by Adler and the Paideia Group, cannot be met through the liberal practices of providing different educational tracks for students of differing ability and by allowing the curriculum to be determined by the student's shifting interests and sense of relevance. Adler views the former as a form of discrimination, and the latter as based upon a wrong-headed understanding of the nature of human freedom.

The conceptual confusion of liberal educators, with their batteries of tests for tracking students and their eagerness to provide course credit for trendy topics of interest, is set right by Adler's argument that "we are a politically classless society. Our citizenry as a whole, he says, is our ruling class. We should, therefore, be an educationally classless society."[3] Furthermore, the best form of education, Adler believes we know from the experience of elite private schools, should be the basis of every student's education. The curriculum thus should not have different tracks for different groups of students but be organized in a manner that will foster different abilities within the student. These include acquiring an organized body of knowledge (mathematics, history, literature, geography, etc.), developing skills for further learning (reading, writing, speaking, observing, exercising critical judgment, etc.), and establishing the foundations for appreciating, understanding, and expressing oneself in the arts. The forms of teaching should vary with the nature of its content and the skills be developed.

Aside from the fact that the liberal system of electives would be set aside, what is important about Adler's proposal is that all public school students, through a common curriculum, would encounter the same substantive achievements of the past—ideas, forms of artistic expression, and scientific discoveries that underpin the social practices of mainstream society. That Adler and the Paideia Group speak for the Eurocentric tradition, and have a gender bias as well, is not the issue to focus on here. Nor should we get sidetracked with arguments about the political naivete of assuming that a consensus for this proposal could be achieved within our often fractured and contentious communities. Rather, the real issue has to do with whether the more traditional liberal arts curriculum that Adler proposes as the basis of public school education, assuming of course that some minor and not so minor compromises could be made with other interest groups, really addresses the more fundamental problem of the mainstream culture exceeding its resource base. As the other conservative critics urge the adoption of a curriculum similar to Adler's, I will return to this issue after the other conservative interpretations of the educational crisis have been more carefully laid out.

The criticisms of E. D. Hirsch, Jr., are also motivated by a deep concern for the survival of the polity when a significant number of its citizens are ignorant of the most basic factual information about the nature and events of the world in which they live. Cultural literacy, as Hirsch defines it, means possessing the "basic information" (factual knowledge of history, geography, etc.) essential to being able to place current issues and events (as reported through the media) in a comprehensible context. This background knowledge thus enables the citizen to understand relationships, to gain insight into the deeper implications of current affairs, and generally to act in an informed and responsible manner. Hirsch makes very clear that his criticisms of public schools for failing to educate students to master a basic body of information is not based on elitism. "Literate culture," he writes, "is the most democratic culture in our land: It excludes nobody; it cuts across generations and social groups and classes; it is usually not one's first culture, but it should be everyone's second, existing as it does beyond the narrow spheres of family, neighborhood, and region."[4] To further insure that the reader does not associate cultural literacy as a concern only of conservatives, Hirsch asserts that "providing our children with traditional information by no means indoctrinates them with a conservative point of view."[5]

Hirsch buttresses his arguments for learning a body of factual knowledge on recent psychological work in the area of schema theory. As Hirsch interprets it, schema theory represents the mind as a storage area where factual information is stored—much like the data base of a computer program; Hirsch actually acknowledges his indebtedness to the field of artificial intelligence. If individuals possess a body of factual information (50,000 bits of information being the upward limit of an easily accessed schema) they can place a new event or issue within any number of patterns and relationships. The schema of background information provides the individual with the ability to situate the new within a conceptual network that can be reordered and reprioritized in many different ways. For example, if individuals possess a knowledge of historical events, issues, and people who influenced social events, current references in the media could then be more easily associated with analogous situations in the past. This ability to frame issues and events in terms of a larger context, and thus to gain perspective on them, broadens the insight and judgment of the individual.

The evidence that Hirsch presents of the schools' failure to provide students with the basic knowledge essential for cultural literacy has been backed up by other surveys, and it clearly points to a major problem. The list of misinformation and gaps in basic knowledge is as impressive in its scope as it is ominous for the well-being of the democratic process. Not knowing when the American Civil War occurred, who won, and the issues over which it was fought is only one example. Others include not knowing the name of the country on the southern border of the United States, the name of the president who presided over the New Deal (or what the "New Deal" refers to), and that Latin is not the language spoken in Latin America. A more recent study of basic knowledge possessed by college seniors further supports Hirsch's claim that students are not acquiring the basic background knowledge essential for a thinking person. For instance, a survey by the Gallup Organization funded by the National Endowment for the Humanities found that 25 percent of college seniors in the country were unable to distinguish between the words of Stalin and those of Churchill, nor to recognize the difference between the ideas of Karl Marx and those in the U.S. Constitution. The list of conceptual deficits, including both basic knowledge and discriminating judgments, as Hirsch and others document it, goes on and on.

The remedy for this crisis in public education, according to Hirsch and the other co-authors of the *Dictionary of Cultural Literacy*, is to establish a compilation of factual information—geographical names, historical events, famous people, scientific achievements, and so forth—that should be part of the schemata of background knowledge of every "culturally literate" citizen. A sense of what is included in their list (in the *Dictionary* can be grasped by what is under just part of the alphabet: "alchemy, Alcott (Louisa May), Aleutian Islands, Alexander the Great, Alexandria (Egypt), alfresco, algae, Alger (Horatio), and so on. To move to another part of the alphabet, under the letter "c" we can find Crystal Palace, Cuba, Cuban Missile crisis, Cubism, cult, cultural imperialism, Cumberland Gap. With this list in hand, public school teachers and administrators can address the task of overcoming the educational crisis fostered by low academic expectations and confusion about the appropriate content of the curriculum.

William J. Bennett's perception of the educational crisis is more synoptic in that his analysis and recommendations encompass the essential concerns of both Adler and Hirsch, but at the same time go beyond them. Bennett's concerns about the educational crisis range across the entire public-school–university spectrum, including issues related to the professionalism of teachers and the teaching of a common culture. Like Adler and Hirsch, Bennett is highly critical of the cafeteria-style curriculum that caters to what he perceives to be the shifting whims of students. He is also deeply concerned with the moral relativism he sees being fostered by the failure of teachers to teach the moral values he regards as central to Western civilization. If students are to develop a vocabulary for thinking and acting (what Bennett refers to as "moral literacy"), they must be taught by teachers who themselves possess fundamental moral character. But moral literacy itself is to be learned through the literature that provides examples of social contexts where moral values give depth and definition to character. According to Bennett, students will learn what courage means if they learn about Joan of Arc and Harriet Tubman and the Underground Railroad; *The Diary of Anne Frank* and *King Lear* provide the moral analogues for understanding kindness and compassion; respect for the rights of others can be understood by reading the Bill of Rights, the Gettysburg Address, and "Letter from Birmingham City Jail of "Martin Luther King, Jr.[6]

There is one statement by Bennett that best seems to summarize his view of the chief cause of the educational crisis, and what is needed to meet the uncertainties of the future: "In this effort of national recovery, today's generation of Americans, joining a conservative preference for the tried and true to a willingness to embrace the innovative and the bold, face their own rendezvous with destiny."[7] The tendency toward innovation in public education is often little more than movement from one fad to the next, where the substance of the innovation is mostly the popularization of some finding in other areas of the academic world that can be turned into a set of techniques. From another perspective, the nearly lockstep movement from one fad to the next (competency-based teaching, assertive discipline, right and left brain learning, cooperative learning, and so forth) suggests more the final hours of K in Kafka's *The Trial*. Bennett's criticism of the preponderance of technique over intellectual substance in public education is also meant to challenge the relativism now endemic in many educational circles, and which is given a form of legitimation by placing authority in the subjective judgments of "authentic individuals." The individual who is ideologically insulated from the voices of the past exhibits a distinctly modern form of hubris where the lessons of the past are seen as totally irrelevant to the sense of empowerment that supposedly comes from personal experience. This combination of relativism and the self-centered pride of the modern individual, when used as a basis for decision making about the content of the curriculum, the purpose and nature of learning, and what contributes to moral education, are the main targets of Bennett's comment about the nation's "rendezvous with destiny."

Allan Bloom's *The Closing of the American Mind* also is concerned with the problem of relativism, but the focus of his criticism is primarily on the dolorous condition of higher education. "This indeterminate future," writes Bloom, "or open-ended future and the lack of a binding past mean that the souls of young people are in a condition like that of the first man in the state of nature—spiritually unclad, unconnected, isolated, with no inherited or unconditional connection with anything or anyone."[8] Like Bennett, Bloom laments the loss of an intellectual and moral center that would bind the "high and low into a single body of belief." We shall not be concerned here with the validity of his claims that the seeds of nihilism, which he views as being spread across several generations of Americans, were a result of the influence of German philosophers (i.e., Heidegger and Nietzsche—with Max Weber playing a mediating role in spread-

ing the influence of the latter). The antidote to the crisis of
nihilism, where commitments, ideals, and relationships are
framed by a remissive sense of individualism, is not in what
is now the main fare of the university curriculum. Writes
Bloom:

> Because there is no tradition and men need guidance,
> general theories that are produced in a day and not
> properly grounded in experience, but seem to explain
> things and are useful crutches for finding one's way in a
> complicated world, have currency. Marxism, Freudian-
> ism, economism, behaviorism, etc., are examples of
> this tendency, and there are great rewards for those
> who purvey them.[9]

Bloom's list of "isms" now has been suplemented by decon-
structionism and post-modernism; but the point of his criticism remains essentially the same.

The antidote Bloom wants to prescribe would have universities return to being places where students undergo
experiences unavailable to them in the larger society—which
is to learn how to understand all things through the rational
process. Sidestepping the issue of how cultures are grounded in their own distinct epistemological traditions, Bloom
asserts the primacy of a common human nature as the
determinant of a curriculum that will introduce students to
history, where reason illuminated experience, served as the
basis of action, and demonstrated that the life of the mind is
the "model of true openness." Opinion, superstition, and folk
beliefs can thus be more easily exposed as false bases of
human action. To paraphrase Bloom, liberal education will
flourish again when it prepares the way for a discussion of a
unified view of nature and man's place in it, which the best
minds can debate on the highest levels.[10] Of course, the
best minds will be prepared for this task of civic leadership
through a curriculum that includes the great thinkers of the
past: Plato, Aristotle, Descartes, Locke, and so forth.

This summary of how conservative critics understand
the current educational crisis is, I think, essentially fair in the
representation of their views. I have deliberately avoided
bringing into the presentation of their ideas any of their critics' charges of elitism, sexism, or racism. These criticisms

are themselves based on complex issues that cannot fully be brought out in this discussion, and to do so now would involve going over continuous and highly acrimonious debates. But more important, it would again relegate the impact of our form of culture on the environment to the status of a non-issue. The changes in the sustaining characteristics of our habitat now pose the most fundamental challenge to humans, and accordingly the other social justice issues surrounding the proposals of conservative educational critics must be reframed. The main interest here, however, is to suggest that the ecological crisis not only brings into question the conservatives' understanding of the shortcomings of American education, but may force a reconceptualization of the guiding principles and assumptions that underlie conservatism itself.

Anthropocentrism and Other Conservative Assumptions

The conservative educational critics' disconnectedness from the nearly daily reports of how human practices are damaging the environment can be put in perspective by taking just one area of the habitat that has not received the media attention on the "greenhouse effect"; namely, our misuse of nature's topsoil. This may seem a pedestrian example in the face of the conservative's lofty rhetoric on the power of informed critical thought to displace the analogue knowledge that characterizes people deeply embedded in tradition. But when we recall that civilizations do not survive the destruction of the resource base that produces the principal foods that makes human life possible, we can see that our cultural approach to the use of "dirt" is related to a discussion of just whose history of landmark ideas and achievements is to become the basis of educational reform. A few trends may help us recognize that the epistemological tradition stretching back from the local agricultural college, on the front line in replacing folk knowledge with "rational" farm practices, back through Locke, Descartes, and Bacon to Plato, may be part of the problem.

Topsoil, the source of most foods for humans who occupy the top of the food chain, took millenia to build up. Since the introduction of the plow on the Great Plains of the Midwest, which was only a little over a hundred and fifty years ago, a third of the topsoil has been lost. What remains has been weakened through deliberate elimination of plant variety and through heavy use of fertilizers and insecticides. While the chemical assault on insects was intended to reduce crop loss, the insecticides ended up in the topsoil. It took 15 million pounds of insecticides to contain to seven percent the crop loss in 1947; in the late 1980s yearly use of chemicals was 125 million pounds, and the crop loss was thirteen percent. To cite one other example of our Western rationalist approach to the use of topsoil, the wasteful use of water for irrigation has contributed to salinization of the soil—not to mention the rapid depletion of the great Ogallala aquifer which, forty years ago, contained an amount of water equivalent to the volume of Lake Huron. At the current rate of deletion the water level of the aquifer within twenty years may be too low to pump up.

The impact of the Western mind set (although attenuated and compromised by Bloom's standards) on other areas of the environment could easily be cited. The important question in terms of the adequacy of conservatism's principal beliefs relates, in the final analysis, to the long-term sustainability of cultural practices. Concerns about the quality of human existence (aesthetic, spiritual, depth of meaning, sense of community) may seem essential aspects of this question. But with the earth's population expanding at the rate that may reach ten billion by 2020, if not sooner, the basic question is whether we can expect the ecosystem to withstand the human impact, particularly if we continue to organize our cultural practices according to the Western canon of thought advocated by the conservative educational critics. Would Bennett, Adler, and Bloom argue that the rest of the world's population will be lifted out of the thraldom of superstition and folk knowledge by adopting the essential principles of Western rationalism? Indeed, their writings strongly suggest this, without second thoughts about the characteristics of thought they champion as not having helped Western societies evolve in ecologically sustainable ways. To state the issue more directly, people who are steeped in the panoply of Western ideas (i.e., Plato, Aristotle, Descartes, Locke, Hegel, Marx, and so forth), are not the ones helping us recognize the dangers of basing cultural practices on an anthropocentric view of the universe.

The deleterious impact of human cultures on the habitat is not reducible to the evils of capitalism or even the imposition of Western ideas with modernization and progress. Pre-industrial environmental damage in China, India, and North Africa point to the fact that it is not simply a matter of throwing off Western ideas that will restore the Garden. But will the conceptual coordinates of the conservative educational critic's arguments for the restoration of American education alleviate the ecological problem, or exacerbate it? Here the issues go much deeper than whether their curriculum proposals could be modified to include, along with the Western classics that have traditionally constituted a liberal education, a course on environmental issues. Rather, the deeper questions have to do with the most fundamental characteristics of the dominant traditions within Western thought, and whether these characteristics of thought should be the basis of the next generation's way of thinking.

If we go beyond Hirsch's concern with mastery of factual knowledge, and the specific curricular proposals of Adler, Bloom, and Bennett, we find a shared set of cultural assumptions that frame how the most basic aspects of human existence are to be understood. These cultural assumptions are not only expressed by the great patriarchs of Western thought (Plato, Aristotle, Descartes, and so forth), but a strong case can be made that their contributions did not, in most instances, fundamentally alter these assumptions or even challenge them. These guiding and still evolving assumptions include an anthropocentric way of thinking of "man's" relation to the rest of the world, a way of understanding "man's" temporality, a view of the rational process as providing authority and legitimacy to human activity, and (with the emergence of the idea of progress) a sense that human possibilities must be understood in terms of an infinite horizon. The latter aspect of this mind set has been further strengthened in this century by rapid advances in science and technology, both of which further strengthen these characteristics as well as adding new dimensions, such as a highly experimental attitude toward both culture and the natural environment.

Although the conservative educational proposals would go a long way toward correcting the current deficiency in most students' historical perspective, and could even contribute to Bloom's "model of true openness" that he associates with the life of the mind, students would find little in the conservative-inspired curriculum that would enable them either to recognize or question these guiding cultural assumptions. Certainly, they would not have the opportunity to consider in any serious or sympathetic manner the belief systems of cultural groups who have attempted to live within the limits of their own habitats.

A strong case could be made that the recovery of the Western inheritance (to use a Bennett-type metaphor) as part of each student's education could be framed in terms of the ecological crisis. Students could then become aware of the historically rooted assumptions that are ecologically problematic, and they would be better able to redirect cultural practices on a more sustainable path. As this is not the intent of these conservative reformers, we must look more carefully at what is problematic about the guiding cultural assumptions that would remain largely hidden in the conservatives' more traditional approach to studying and absorbing Western culture.

Our brief discussion of the loss of topsoil—which could lead truly to catastrophic social consequences that would eclipse the conservatives' concerns about the student's ignorance of Plato's *Gorgias* or of the differences in how Aristotle and Machiavelli understood the relationship between virtue and politics—provides a useful reference point for putting in focus the guiding and largely hidden assumptions that characterize the Western mind set. Let us start with the anthropocentric view of the universe. What is essential about this aspect of Western consciousness is that it fosters a view of humans as of primary importance, with the environment as an ancillary resource to be managed (a more enlightened version of the anthropocentric position). The thoughts, needs, and spirituality of humans is thus seen against a materialistic view of the rest of the world. Anthropocentrism does not foster a sense of interdependency in which a loss of topsoil (or of forest cover, clean atmosphere, etc.) is experienced as diminishing human worth and capability. The loss of topsoil rather is viewed as a problem requiring a technological solution—just as other aspects of the biota pose technical problems in furthering "man's" needs. It is impossible to imagine Bloom, whose anthropocentricism is more stridently expressed than the others, taking seriously the comment attributed to the Sioux Indian who is purported to have said "wrong side up" when he saw the pioneer turning the prairie over with his plow to expose the soil.[11] The old Sioux did not possess an anthropocentric view where "man" could interfere with the environment with impunity. And while he was also without the Western foundations of rational thought, he knew that prairies could provide the basis of life in a way that exposed and depleted topsoil cannot, except in the short run.

An anthropocentric view, which places "man" at the center, around which everything else evolves or is subordinate, also relates to the sense of temporality that characterizes both the position of the conservative educational critics and the view of time shared within the larger dominant culture. The conservative educational critics rightly are concerned about the consequences for the social order of a self-centered form of individualism, in which the sense of temporality is largely framed by the crests and troughs of personal experience. But their curricular proposals address only part of the problem. It is, indeed, important to learn that one's own thought and actions are part of a cultural continuum that stretches into a history shaped by past events and ideas. As Hannah Arendt observed, memory is part of personal authority. But memory and the ability to reconstruct the arguments of seminal thinkers of the past, and even to use them to frame current issues, have a different significance in people's lives when the cultural view of time has been fused to the belief that change is progressive. The past does not really matter if change leads automatically to improvement. This attitude is particularly prevalent in the sciences where the past is viewed as largely irrelevant. Pointing out the problems surrounding this way of framing the dominant cultural orientation toward temporality is not too far from the position of Adler, Bennett, and Bloom, and ignores how the sense of time experienced within the dominant culture relates to the ecological crisis.

The example of using petroleum-based products to increase crop yields and to control pests, while diminishing the soil's long-term fertility, involves a sense of temporality where the wants of one generation are met at the expense of the next. Other examples are as numerous as the facets of our economy and the multiple nature of our technologies: forests are being cut, fisheries depleted, and toxic wastes accumulated and spread over the land and water with no sense of responsibility for the legacy being left to future generations. Lester R. Brown and Sandra Postel suggest that rational and moral judgments—themes close to the interests of the conservative educational critics—should be based on a consideration of whether they "diminish the prospects of the next generation."[12] On the surface the principle of long-term sustainability seems like a reasonable, even common sense suggestion. But it is a foreign way of thinking to Western-based cultures—a point strongly suggesting that the exemplary thinkers and achievers that the conservative educational critics want restored to a central place in the curriculum may not provide a basis for living in ecological balance. For example, Frederick Turner's *Beyond Geography: The Western Spirit Against the Wilderness* documents how Europeans steeped in the intellectual and spiritual traditions of Western thought viewed the plentitude of their "New World" as exploitable resources.[13] They viewed nature as a wilderness that needed to be subdued and transformed, and the native peoples—who were in many instances living in sustainable balance with their habitat—as culturally inferior. It should be mentioned that the sense of long-term temporality, which helped maintain the ecological balance worked out over thousands of years by so-called "Indian" cultures, was part of a complex metaphysics that did not separate the person from nature, nor divorce spirituality from other ways of knowing.

A third feature of the Western mind set advocated by conservative educational critics that is ecologically problematic, can be termed "living within an expanding horizon of possibilities." It is expressed in our mainstream values, attitudes, and social practices especially in the expectation that the range of consumer choices will continue to expand, that personal knowledge, wealth, and power can be indefinitely increased, and that ever-new technological solutions will be found. Growth, development, and progress are metaphors that both encode this aspect of our belief system and serve to legitimate it. Life thus becomes a quest, an adventure on an expanding plain of possibilities. This way of thinking was only fully institutionalized with the beginning of the Industrial

Revolution, and thus is new and experimental when viewed against the backdrop of human traditions stretching back beyond the Neolithic period. It still has not evolved a moral basis for self-limitation. Today, only economic and political limitations seem to count, and generally only those alternative approaches to development that appear more efficient and thus more cost effective. Contrasting ways of thinking, such as Alexander Solzhenitsyn's formulation of freedom as self-restriction, "restriction of the self for the sake of others," suggest weakness of character and even betrayal of the Western humanist tradition. While his views may appear archaic, they nevertheless bring back into focus the current trends in which cultural demands on the habitat are rising and the sustaining capacities of the natural systems are declining. His observation also points to the possibility that the shift from an expanding horizon of possibilities to some form of self-limitation (as persons and as a multicultural society) must be based on a moral (i.e., spiritual) way of understanding, rather than on a form of rationality too easily bent to finding technological solutions to environmental limits.

A fourth feature of the Western mind set that would be strongly reinforced by the conservative educational proposals is a view of rationality that is difficult to criticize because it has contributed to so many advances in the quality of social life. But it has also contributed to putting the entire ecosystem at risk. Through the example of Socrates and the scientist conservative critics have articulated two forms of expression—as reflecting on the nature of the human condition (What is knowledge? What is virtue?) and on the scientific method of inquiry. Both approaches give theory a privileged status as a guide to human action. Hirsch, yielding to more contemporary fashion in learning theory, represents the rational process as recognizing connections and meaning in the patterns of information. But the difference that separates Hirsch from the other conservative educational reformers is minor compared to the fact that their outlook on the rational processes embodies the misunderstandings and prejudices about the nature of rationalism that have been the hallmark of the dominant epistemological traditions in the West.

At issue here are the silences and prejudices that led the most "rational" cultures in human history to ignore the fact that the habitat—soil, atmosphere, plants, animals—is an essential part of human life, and that when it is being destroyed human life is also being threatened. These are also the silences and prejudices overlooked by Bloom, Bennett, Adler, and Hirsch. The rational process, as they represent it, is not, first of all, free of cultural influence. As mentioned earlier, all thought is metaphorical: its schema of understanding grows out of the root metaphors of the culture, it understands new dimensions of experience in terms of the already familiar (analogic thinking), the nonproblematic aspects of language which serve as the building blocks of thought are the iconic metaphors (e.g., individualism, intelligence, mankind) that encode earlier stages of analogic thinking. To put this another way, language encodes the earlier stages of a cultural group's metaphorical thinking. Thus, the thought process of the individual is always influenced by the tacit conventions of the language. What are some of the conventions that give the Western approaches to rationalism its distinctive character (some might say "hubris")? Part of the answer is to be found in the previous discussion of anthropocentrism, short-term temporality, and the infinite horizon of possibilities. The intellectual geneology of a "man"-centered universe, and the accompanying assumptions that the future represents a progressive advance over the present and that the continued expansion of human choices (increasingly understood as conveniences) and power is limitless, have framed (and reframed) how the nature and purpose of the rational process has been understood.

But there are other distinguishing Western characteristics that the conservative educational critics tend to ignore. These include a tendency to represent human experience as a theoretical problem, to approach the process of knowledge construction and validation as a competitive process that occurs on a level playing field (that is, free of influence by unequal power), to view its purpose as emancipation from the irrational in tradition (and often from tradition itself), and, since the time of Descartes, to separate the knower from the known (where the world to be known, in Heidegger's words, is "conceived and grasped as a picture").[14] In the last century, these tendencies have led to a distinctive mutation where the rational process has been reduced to a matter of technological problem solving, where efficiency, predictability, and hierarchical control are the guiding values.

These distinctive characteristics of Western forms of rationalism have been criticized for contributing to nihilism, to the cultural imperialism associated with the modernization process spreading around the world, and to the ecological crisis. The criticisms are, in part, valid, for reasons we will take up later as part of the discussion of how the ecological crisis may force conservative thinkers to reconceptualize their guiding assumptions and principles.

The dimension of Western thought that would be studied and used as a model of human achievement in the type of classroom envisaged by Hirsch, Adler, Bennett, and to a lesser extent Bloom has to do with the nature of scientific thought, its achievements, and its contribution to the development of socially useful techniques. The National Endowment for the Humanities *50 Hours* report, which mirrors the thinking of conservative educational critics, makes compelling recommendations for incorporating courses on science into the university curriculum: to learn the nature of scientific discovery and demonstration, to learn the fundamental concepts of science, to understand how theory influences the direction and nature of research, and how, in turn, theory is refined by the results of experimental observation. To quote Lynne V. Cheney, the author of the *50 Hours* report, "Our ability to make everyday decisions wisely is diminished when we do not comprehend scientific principles and the technologies built upon them."[15] In one sense, she is entirely correct. But there is a dimension to the Western approach to science and technology that is ignored in the *50 Hours* report as well as in the writings of Adler, Hirsch, Bloom, and Bennett. It is in this area of silence that questions arise about the possibility that our cultural orientation toward the nature and uses of science and technology (not identical—though now more interdependent) may be contributing to deepening the ecological crisis. This suggestion may sound both outlandish and irresponsible, but before the suggestion is dismissed out of hand we need to consider more carefully the problematic aspects of science that go largely unnoticed in academia and in public discussions.

When the ideology that surrounds and legitimates the process of scientific research and the transformation of scientific findings into technologies is carefully considered, it quickly becomes obvious that it still incorporates the anthropocentrism (now expressed as "stewardship") of the Western mind set, as well as the other characteristics of short-term temporality, the expanding horizon of possibilities, and a view of the rational process that is presumed to be culturally neutral. Ecologically oriented sciences are, of course, revising this guiding ideology—but unfortunately they do not represent the scientific mainstream. One of the consequences of this ideology is lack of a basis for self-limitation by which the discovery of new knowledge is held in check because of the recognition that it might be used in a manner detrimental to human life or to the environment. The atomic bomb and the lethal wastes from nuclear facilities are an example of the failure to exercise self-limitation in the face of moral and political concerns. As we begin to understand the long-term effects of the nearly seventy thousand chemical compounds that have been introduced into the environment, we might begin to reflect more seriously about which scientific discoveries are beneficial and which are detrimental to life. This reflection appears to have begun on the fringes of the scientific community as recent advances in the area of biotechnology create the danger of upsetting the balance of ecosystems.

The aspects of science and technology being addressed here have to do with what can be called the "culture connection." All cultures are concerned with the problems of explanation, prediction, and control; the Western approach to solving these problems through use of the scientific method points to the connection between culture, science, and technology. But the culture–science connection can be seen more clearly by taking into account how scientists explain the nature and purposes of their research. The following statements were made by Leroy Hood, a professor at the California Institute of Technology, who as a molecular biologist is working on the task of mapping the 3 billion nucleotides that make up the human genome. This research is being done "so that we have a book that has all the information that's responsible for *constructing* a man.... In a sense the *hardware* for making a man is 23 pairs of chromosomes. But what's the nature of *software* that actually takes the material and constructs a man?" The role of a protein is described as folding itself "into a *three-dimensional machine*, and each *machine* does a different kind of thing." According to the Cal Tech professor, in 15 to 20 years scientists will be able to determine "just exactly what your probabilities are for any one of a number of diseases," and will have the ability to remove the cells that cause problems. "We'll design preventive medicine," he assures the interviewer, "that will never let you get sick." Keeping people from aging will be "the last of the problems solved."[16]

The issue here is not whether Professor Hood spoke for the scientific community, but the way in which the values and assumptions of his culture influenced his way of understanding and justifying the purpose of scientific research. His metaphorical images, "constructing a man," "software that actually takes that material and constructs a man," "three-dimensional machine," as well as the ideal of eliminating all diseases and even aging itself, reflects the orientation of his larger culture to representing life in mechanistic terms and to viewing the extension of human life as a set of scientific-technological problems to be worked out. How the ecosystems are to survive the population increase resulting from people not becoming ill, aging, and dying is not addressed. Nor is there any sense of uncertainty about the scientist's ability to play God in the construction of a new mechanized Garden of Eden. It is the consequence of this presumption that we somehow have a "neutral," culture-free science and technology that needs to be put in focus here, as this presumption also relates to a set of issues that have been ignored by the conservative educational critics.

The conceptual orientation of the scientific community toward the continual discovery of new knowledge, which is increasingly used as the basis of new technological developments, is generally understood as the highest expression of human progress. But the outcome of scientific knowledge can also be understood as involving an ongoing experimental relationship between the culture and the ecosystems. That is, the outcome of scientific knowledge, which may for example take the form of DDT, computers, or genetically modified bacteria, involves introducing into the culture of traditional human patterns and processes and into natural systems—as in the cases of DDT and genetically engineered bacteria—a new element that may have profound effects. Unlike the scientific process itself, where an experiment requires careful and thorough observation, there is seldom any forethought given to the long-term consequences of introducing new technologies into the culture. The experimental relationship of science and technology to the culture is more like the momentary excitement of a promiscuous relationship—the attention of the scientist and technologists is short-lived (solving an immediate problem) and does not take into account long-term consequences of the changes that they introduce into the culture. The culture into which scientifically based technologies are introduced involve tacit forms of knowledge (traditions), belief systems, values, and other not easily quantified phenomena that do not lend themselves to the scientist's way of understanding a laboratory experiment. Yet I suspect that it is not these more complex and hidden forms of knowledge that cause the scientists to ignore the impact of their discoveries upon the fabric of culture, but rather the long-held belief that science is culturally neutral.

Science continues to influence culture in another way that does not have anything directly to do with the introduction of culture-altering technologies. Briefly, this influence can be understood most easily as the delegitimation of traditional forms of cultural knowledge (including moral judgments) that do not meet the criteria of a more popularized understanding of the scientific materialist view of knowledge. The evocative power of the scientist's way of knowing is, in effect, used metaphorically as the framework of understanding for other areas of cultural life. People who are dealing with moral, political, and traditional relationships, following the model of science, attempt to establish the authority of their arguments and decisions by claiming the right to determine what constitutes relevant evidence and to assess it in terms of their own "rational" understanding. The emphasis on the use of measurable evidence (what has been called the "mathematization of experience") further erodes traditional forms of authority. Liberal ideology has also been a powerful influence on the culture's slide into nihilism where the authority of shared traditions are being increasingly replaced by supposedly autonomous individuals who associate consciousness-raising with freedom.

Scientists readily acknowledge that their way of knowing cannot deal with moral issues, and the more reflective ones would be critical of the spread of scientism into all areas of cultural practice. But in the face of their achievements, as well as their failure to help the larger public obtain a proper perspective on the legitimate domains of science, science contributes to the further secularization of the culture—which includes a materialistically reductionist way of understanding both the cultural and natural world, an instrumental approach to problem solving, and the relativizing of traditional forms of authority.

Two additional points need to be made about the influence of science and technology on culture. The first is that an increasingly nihilistic culture will not have the shared moral norms that set the limits within which human wants are understood and met. This is a critically important issue related directly to the continuing upward curve in the use of natural resources and the downward curve in the sustainability of natural systems upon which all life depends. The other issue relates more directly to the failure of Hirsch, Adler, Bennett, and Bloom to recognize that our approach to science and technology is deeply embedded in a cultural orientation made problematic by the ecological crisis, and that serious reflection on the Janus nature of science and technology should be made a central part of their proposals for educational reform.

Unless the deteriorating condition of the environment is taken into account, what we are likely to learn from the various curricula proposed by the conservative educational critics will be made largely irrelevant by the scale of social disruptions that will follow from the further divergence of the culture-habitat trendlines. The study of Western traditions in thought and scientific achievement is supposed to provide students with answers to such perennial questions as, "Where have we come from?", "Who are we?", "What is our destiny?" In effect, the conservative view of the curriculum serves to frame the challenge of "Know Thyself" within a historical perspective but the "self" that is to be known is understood in rationalistic terms that still view all the foundations of human life as based on earlier cultural achievements. If the conservatives had recognized that the deepest foundations of human life, and of cultural achievement, are rooted in the health of the ecosystems, their educational proposals would indeed become highly relevant to addressing the crises that lie ahead.

The complex set of questions surrounding the problem of humans living in ecological balance requires that the past be studied with great care. Who were the thinkers and what were the cultural events that led to the hierarchical systems that elevated certain forms of knowledge over others, some types of human activity over others, and all humans over nature? How has the relationship of individual to community been understood over the course of recorded history, and were there times in Western history when community was understood in inclusive terms that encompassed all life forms within the bioregion? How have questions of social justice and quality of cultural attainment been influenced by environmental conditions? How have Western religions represented human-environment relationships?

These are indeed broad questions, but even their general nature points to how the reading of Plato, Aristotle, Locke, and so forth, could be reframed from the anthropocentric position that characterizes the thinking of the conservative educational critics to one that recognizes that human knowledge is, in the last analysis, dependent upon a responsible use of the larger information network that constitutes the natural world. There is also a need to study other cultures that have evolved in more ecologically balanced ways. The question of why we have had a prejudice against learning from traditional peoples (generally referred to as "primitive") could also lead back to a critical look at such culture direction-setters as Plato, Descartes, and Marx.

The educational proposals of Adler, Hirsch, Bloom, and Bennett involve a double bind, in that their curricular reforms would further strengthen the very characteristics of the Western mind set associated with the upward curve in human demands on a finite environment. Given their indifference to the sources of this double bind, it would be reasonable to ask if the form of conservatism represented in their writings provides a viable framework for understanding and responding to the problems we now face. To put the question another way: Has the emerging ecological crisis made obsolete those dimensions of conservatism that ignore the problem of long-term sustainability? Still another question relates to what an ecologically responsive form of conservatism would be like, and what its educational implications would be.

Emergence of an Ecologically Responsible Conservatism

The alternative to a form of conservatism still rooted in Enlightenment assumptions that are now, quite literally, being buried by the waste products of the culture based on these assumptions is not liberalism, with all of its mutations. Liberalism also is based on an anthropocentric view of the world, and shares with conservative educational critics the other aspects of the Western mind set discussed earlier: a view of time that discounts the need to conserve in the present for the sake of future generations, a sense of life as infinitely expanding in opportunities, belief in the authority of rational processes, and so forth. Liberalism, in its many variations on these themes, differs from the conservatism of Adler, Bloom, and Bennett in that it has little appreciation of history and no tolerance for the type of hierarchy (liberals would call it elitism) valued by these conservatives—which is not to say that liberals find repugnant all hierarchical arrangements. Promoting an increasingly technologically oriented social order, and attempting to provide for the emancipation of those who are either left out or psychologically overwhelmed by the leviathan technocratic liberals have created, seem to keep the two mainstreams of liberalism in tension with each other.

The alternative thus is not to be understood in terms of the old left-right political continuum, where liberalism is understood as the alternative to conservatism. Instead, the alternative to the ecologically indifferent conservatism of Adler, Bloom, and Bennett is to be found in a new group of thinkers whose literary geneology goes back to such American writers as Henry David Thoreau and John Muir. But the most distinctive features of the new form of conservatism that may better serve us through the years of adjustment that lie ahead have been laid out in the writings of such thinkers as Aldo Leopold, Wendell Berry, Wes Jackson, Gary Snyder, Gregory Bateson, and Eric Havelock, to be discussed. Their more ecologically responsive conservatism also has room for more traditional conservative thinkers who have not been directly concerned with the condition of the habitat, including Michael Oakeshott, T. S. Eliot, and Shils.

The conceptual coordinates of the anthropocentric conservatives do not, from the ecological conservative's point of view, meet the test of long-term sustainability. But the central concern of this new ecologically oriented conservatism is with not just mere survivability—but it should be added without that nothing else really matters. Wendell Berry, Gary Snyder, E. F. Schumacher, and Wes Jackson—to cite just a few of the ecological conservatives—also address the problem of restoring a greater sense of community self-sufficiency, responsibility for raising the quality of human activity, and a more spiritualized sense of awareness. A brief overview of the conceptual framework of these ecological conservatives may help put the conservatism of Adler, Bloom, and Bennett in perspective. It will also provide a basis for discussing the forms of education that not only contribute to ecological sustainability but also to healing the distortions in human expectations caused by the hubris of anthropocentric thinking.

The basis of human life, from the ecological conservative's point of view, is not found in the exercise of rationality that privileges humans over other forms of life. Rather it is in recognizing that humans are members of the larger biotic community. Using the metaphor of "mental" to refer to the information exchanges that occur as different parts of an ecological system interact, Gregory Bateson observes that "in no system which shows mental characteristics (where a "difference which makes a difference" involves information exchanges) can any part have unilateral control over the whole. In other words, *the mental characteristics of the system are immanent, not just in some part* (like the rational individual) *but in the system as a whole.*"[17] The information that sustains the life of a natural system, according to Bateson, is not always understood, because of the metaphorical frameworks that encode earlier stages of human thought. In spite of this narrowing and even distortion in understanding, Bateson maintains that the total self-correcting unit is not the autonomous rational man, but "a flexible organism-in-its-environment." Or as he put it, "The unit of evolutionary survival turns out to be identical with the unit of mind."[18]

Wendell Berry makes the same point about interdependence being the most critically important aspect of human life. Although we can only live by eating other forms of life, we must, according to Berry, recognize both the limits and dangers involved: "past a certain point in a unified system, 'other life' is our own." He writes,

The definitive relationships in the universe are thus not competitive but interdependent. And from a human point of view they are analogical. We can build one system only within another. We can have agriculture only within nature, and culture only within agriculture. At certain critical points these systems have to conform with one another or destroy one another.[19]

And Aldo Leopold, writing in *A Sand County Almanac*, urges us to recognize that ethics (a possible "kind of community instinct in the making") should be an integral aspect of how humans understand their relationship to the land.[20]

The ecological conservatives' rejection of the Great Chain of Being which placed rational man at the top of the biotic pyramid, and even of the more contemporary notion of "stewardship," carries with it a view of community that involves the recovery of attitudes, values, and abilities that appear obsolete in a consumer-oriented society. Referring to a community where people have a sense of place and past, E. F. Schumacher writes that "the home-comers base themselves upon a different picture of man from that which motivates the people of the forward stampede."[21] The negative attitudes of the people of the "forward stampede" toward work has led to an overemphasis on the development of technologies that have undermined human capacities and relationships, and also threaten the habitat. For Schumaker, as well as Berry and Snyder, part of the healing of ecological damage will be achieved only as we recover a deeper sense of the interconnection between work and community—the latter being understood in the enlarged sense of human-to-human and human-to-habitat relationships, as well as in terms of a sense of responsibility to both the achievements of past generations and the needs of future ones. Schumacher views work as contributing to the further development of a personal skill or ability, to meaningful social relationships, and to the creation of objects or performing activities that are socially useful.

Berry expresses essentially the same conservative view when he warns against the "grotesquery—indeed, the impossibility—of an idea of community wholeness that divorces itself from any idea of personal wholeness." The latter he defines as the uniting of "workmanship, care, conscience, responsibility"; and he considers these qualities to be best nurtured in a "communal order of memory, insight, value, work, conviviality, reverence, aspiration." This community, moreover, must keep in focus human necessities as well as human limits; this is to be achieved, in part, by continually clarifying for its members "our inescapable bonds to the earth and each other."[22] This view of the relationship between work, community, and character also characterizes the writings of Gary Snyder.

The ecologically minded conservatives have a far more complex view of the nature of knowledge, and thus of the rational process, than the conservative educational critics. The difference can be put in perspective by using Bloom's model of the intellectual community, which he considers "exemplary for all other communities." The highest expression of the rational process is in the act of knowing—that is, in seeking truth. As Bloom put it in the concluding section of *The Closing of the American Mind*: "The real community of man, in the midst of all the self-contradictory simulacra of community, is the community of those who seek the truth, of the potential knowers, that is, in principle, of all men to the extent the desire to know."[23] Hirsch, Adler, and Bennett urge the democratization of this rational process because the polis, as they view it, will survive only as the rational processes of all citizens are based on shared intellectual traditions. Conservative educational reformers all share a view of the rational process that equates knowledge with mental processes occurring in the heads of individuals. That is, the rational process is individually centered, with the safeguard being a knowledge of the intellectual achievements of the great thinkers of the past.

The ecological conservatives, as well as more traditional conservatives like Oakeshott and Shils, provide a very different view of knowledge and thus of the myriad dimensions of thinking. Echoing Edmund Burke's statement that "the nature of man is intricate; the objects of society are of the greatest possible complexity,"[24] they recognize a dimension of knowledge that is as antithetical to the views of Hirsch, Adler, Bloom, and Bennett as it is pervasive in human experience. The two conservative thinkers who have not written on the state of the ecosystem, Oakeshott and Shils, provide the most accessible way of recognizing the tacit forms of knowledge upon which most human experience is based. Oakeshott refers to these tacit forms of knowledge in his distinction between "practical knowledge" and "Rationalism." Although he associates "Rationalism" with technical knowledge, which involves explicit and context-free procedures of thinking that can be traced back to Descartes, and thus is more narrow than what Bloom and the other conservative educational critics have in mind, it is his understanding of practical knowledge that is important to us here. Practical knowledge (or tacit knowledge) is the basis of what a good cook, artist, or teacher does. According to Oakeshott, "practical knowledge can neither be taught nor learned, but only imparted and acquired. It exists only in practice, and the only way to acquire it is by apprenticeship to a master—not because the master can teach it (he cannot), but because it can be acquired only by continuous contact with one who is perpetually practicing it."[25] Thus its essential features include its contextual nature, its analogue form of representation (as opposed to propositional knowledge), and its unification of the body and mind in the act of performance.

What Oakeshott calls "practical knowledge" is very close to Shils' way of understanding "living tradition." Briefly, living traditions include everything that is handed down from the past to the present. These practices, patterns of thinking, and objects (often technologies) involve the utilization of tacit knowledge. That is, the reenactment of traditions—which range from organizing thoughts in a subject-verb-object pattern or laying out space in rectangular patterns, to using our body to send messages about our relationships to others—involves the utilization of earlier mental processes that have been encoded in the traditions we now take for granted. The use of words is a particularly good example of how encoded knowledge from the past becomes part of our tacit way of understanding and performing.

Although practical knowledge and traditions are a pervasive part of human experience, the key issue identifying the foundations for a more ecologically responsive conservatism is that Oakeshott and Shils, in their respective ways, help us to recognize that knowledge (and now, information) can be understood as encoded in the larger cultural environment of material objects as well as in the more symbolic processes, and thus cannot be reduced to the intentional and explicit mental activity of individuals, as the conservative educational critics represent it.

Ecologically oriented conservatives, however, go much further than Oakeshott and Shils. For example, Bateson acknowledges that humans interpret the meaning of the information exchanges that make up an ecological system (at least the information exchanges they are aware of) through the metaphorically based schema encoded in their language, but he also emphasizes that the entire system of which the individual is a part must be understood as possessing mental characteristics. Bateson's expansion of mental processes to include the entire interactive environmental system of which the individual is only a part is difficult to understand, particularly for the person who has been culturally conditioned to view the mind as the distinguishing feature that separates humans from the natural world, indeed, as the principle justification for elevating humans over nature. Gary Snyder makes Bateson's point in a slightly different way:

Perhaps one of its most interesting experiments at the point of evolution, if we can talk about evolution in this way, is not man but a high degree of biological diversity and sophistication opening to more and more possibilities. Plants are at the bottom of the food chain; they do the primary energy transformation that makes all the life-forms possible.... Since plants support the other life-forms, they became the 'people' of the land. And the land—a country—is a region within which the interactions of water, air, and soil and the underlying geology and the overlying (maybe stratospheric) wind conditions all go to create both the microclimates and the large climactic patterns that make a whole sphere or realm of life possible. The people in that realm include animals, humans, and a variety of wild life.[24]

Another dimension of the anthropocentric conservative's view of knowledge is put in perspective by Wendell Berry's argument that the rationalist form of knowledge, which highlights the authority of abstract and critical reflection, contributes to a nomadic form of existence. Ideas and values become the center of the individual's reality, and they can, like other private possessions, be transported to new environments as the old ones become uninhabitable or are viewed in terms of limited opportunities. For Berry and the other ecologically minded conservatives, knowledge is what connects individuals to where they live—that is, the place that is their life-sustaining habitat. As Berry puts it, "Without a complex knowledge of one's place, and without the faithfulness of one's place on which such knowledge depends, it is inevitable that the place will be used carelessly, and eventually destroyed."[27]

Valuing tacit forms of knowledge, as well as recognizing that the natural world is a complex network of information essential to sustaining the different forms and processes of interdependent life, radically separates what might be called the ecocentric conservatism of Berry, Bateson, and Snyder from the anthropocentric conservatism of people like Bloom and Bennett. Forms of tacit knowledge and the taken-for-granted reenactment of traditions would be viewed by the latter as yielding to folk knowledge, myth, and other nonrational ways of understanding which are to be banished by the power of rational thought. Bloom and Bennett would also find the argument that knowledge should be rooted in a deep awareness and appreciation of one's habitat (place) as both parochial and stultifying. And the warning by Wes Jackson and Wendell Berry that we have no real way of assessing the value of the new knowledge that is being created or discovered, because we are largely unaware of the knowledge and information that is disappearing, would be incomprehensible to people who subscribe to Adler, Bloom, and Bennett's view of rational process. Examples include both the loss to the information chains that constitute an ecology when species disappear and the intuitive forms of understanding that are built up over generations of living on the land. But the real test, to rework Hirsch's metaphor of culture literacy, is whether the forms of knowledge associated with land literacy (being able to decode the information systems of one's place) are more essential to the long-term sustainability of the culture. Viewed over the long-term, the forms of knowledge that Adler, Bloom, and Bennett want to restore as the source of individual empowerment have existed for only a brief period of human history. Thus, along with the scientific-industrial revolution that it made possible, it must be viewed as highly experimental. It should also be kept in mind that intelligent experiments are only possible when there is a margin of security; when that margin is insufficient for the society to cope with the consequences of a failed experiment, the experiment itself becomes an expression of ignorance.

There are two other distinguishing features of an ecologically centered conservatism that separate it from the conceptual foundations underlying the conservatism of Adler, Bloom, and Bennett. The first has to do with technology, and the second has to do with the preeminence of literacy over orality. Both relate directly to the problems of a culture that is ecologically unsustainable, and both represent areas of silence in the conservative discourse that is the basis of educational reform proposals of Adler, Bloom, and Bennett. Let us first briefly consider the importance that the ecologically oriented conservatives give to the question of technology.

The position of the anthropocentric conservatives like Bloom and Bennett is that technocrats are intellectually too narrow. Armed with a knowledge of past cultural achievements (i.e., a knowledge of Plato, Shakespeare, Rousseau, and so forth), they would be able to understand the geneology of ideas and events, and they would perhaps be more interesting conversationalists. But the paradoxical combination of viewing technological innovations as both culturally neutral and as evidence of the progressive nature of change would remain unchallenged by exposure to these liberalizing studies. By way of contrast, the ecologically oriented conservatives—Schumacher, Berry, Snyder, and the others—view unlimited technological development as a major cause of environmental deterioration. Instead of learning about the life processes that make up a habitat, and fitting into the larger web of relationships with as little disruption as possible—both essential conditions of long-term sustainability—reliance on technology has led to a relationship of domination and short-term exploitation of the habitat. It has also resulted in the increasing specialization of knowledge essential to technological advance, with the result that the experts who gain the power to introduce technological innovations into the culture/habitat relationship do not have the broader knowledge essential for understanding the long-term consequences of their experiments.

A reading of Schumacher, Berry, and Jackson, for example, suggests a different conservative approach to technology. The linchpin of their thinking is to subordinate technology—its type, function, and goals—to the larger concerns of an interdependent biotic community. They would also want to connect the choice of appropriate technology to the broader questions relating to the cultural traditions of the community. In effect, their form of conservatism, as it relates to technology, would involve using technology to supplement or only slightly modify the workings of natural systems. The use of natural predators over pesticides, solar power over massive hydroelectric and nuclear sources of power, and organic and multicrop farming over petroleum-subsidized monocrop agriculture are just a few examples. With regard to technology, their conservatism involves the decentralization of knowledge, the reunification of knowledge with context, the nurturing and refinement of human skills that are essential to the continuity of the community, and, perhaps most important of all, a recovery of the Burkean attitude that change should be based on "a disposition to preserve, and an ability to improve."[28]

The tendency of the conservatism represented in the thinking of Hirsch, Adler, Bloom, and Bennett to equate rationality with the traditions of literate culture is based on a prejudice that puts their form of conservatism in a double bind. Aside from granting the literate mind superiority over the supposed "backwardness" of traditional and primal cultures, which has limited our ability to recognize the characteristics of cultures in balance with their habitats, the emphasis on literacy as a basis of human knowledge fosters the mental habits and social patterns integral to modern consciousness and anomic individualism. The argument here is not that literacy, by itself, causes a particular mind set; rather it is that, given the presence of other cultural assumptions and values, literacy contributes to certain qualities of mind and, by extension, to a particular form of social life.

A summary of characteristics fostered by alphabetized literacy include separating the word from the body (reification of the word), analytical and decontextualized thinking, association of knowledge with sight, thought as an interiorized activity of an individual, and the emergence of an abstract "public." When orality is the dominant mode of communication, different tendencies are reinforced, again; the presence of other cultural traditions amplify these tendencies. These tendencies include the use of a broader range of contextual (including nonverbal) cues and thus a greater sensitivity to relationships, a more participatory (less sender–receiver) model of communication, greater sensory involvement in the formation of knowledge, the use of memory as a basis of authority, the use of analogues drawn from a shared and lived experience as the information storage cells of community memory.

In not taking into account the interactive patterns of a living culture, the anthropocentric world view, with its orientation toward individualism and continual change, is reinforced by the practice of putting knowledge into print form. The fixed and supposedly objective nature of a text allows for the person to become an analytic thinker who can compare one account with another. The fluidity of the oral tradition, on the other hand, makes a participatory relationship the norm, and what is being shared and modified ever so slowly through the re-telling process is the knowledge that has evolved in the process of communal survival. The literate person, writing for an audience that may come into existence at some future time, presents abstract and thus highly experimental ideas, which can be reflected upon by people who experience a similar sense of autonomy (disconnectedness) from the authority of communal tradition. They too can become rational seekers of universal (abstract) truths, while living lives based on cultural norms that go unrecognized because of the privileging of abstract thought.

The connection between the kind of knowledge stored and shared in an oral tradition and the vitality (and sustainability) of a community is an often unrecognized dimension of the ecological crisis. This is not to suggest that all oral cultures are models of good ecological citizenship. Rather, what it suggests is the need for conservatives to recognize that orality involves a sense of time and human relationships, as well as forms of knowledge, essential to stable communities, and that the morally and conceptually stable (as opposed to static) human communities are more likely to exist in a sustainable balance with the environment. This recognition should not lead to eliminating literacy, but to finding a balance with oral traditions.

Educational Implications

The conservative's sensitivity to the shaping power of the past touches on one of the givens of the human situation in a way that the liberal representation of the autonomous individual does not. As discussed earlier, thought is partly organized by the schema of understanding encoded in the language—and this encoding process, in aspects of our language, goes far back into our collective history. Thus, the recommendation that education provide students the opportunity to examine the origins and continuities of cultural practices in the arts, philosophy, government, sciences, and so forth makes perfectly good sense. Indeed, the past does illuminate the present. But it can also reproduce the same misconceptions—like the hubris of the anthropocentric view of the world and the notion that rational thought is free of cultural influences.

Bloom summarizes what appears as the central point in the proposals of the conservative educational critics: "Knowledge is the goal; competence and reason are required by those who pursue it. The disciplines are philosophy, mathematics, physics, biology, and the science of man, meaning a political science that discerns the nature of man and the ends of government. This is the academy."[29] Although Hirsch stresses more the acquiring of factual knowledge, the conservative view of education seems to come down to reading the seminal works of the past: Dante, Chaucer, Machiavelli, and the rest—to cite part of a list of readings suggested by Cheney in *50 Hours*. The curriculum may be broadened to take into account non-Western cultures and the achievements of women; but it is essentially the same type of curriculum that one could expect to find in elite private colleges and public schools in the heyday of industrial expansion.

The educational implications of the ecologically centered conservatives stand in sharp contrast to the rational geometry of power that characterizes the thinking of Hirsch, Adler, Bloom, and Bennett. The educational differences reflect the differences in their root metaphors: For the ecologically centered conservative, the person must be understood as living in an interdependent community (the biota), while the pre-ecological conservatives view man as empowered through the development of a rational capacity. The difference, for example, can be seen in Bloom's total indifference to the forms of knowledge that have to do with his place—the varied forms of soil, animal, and plant life that exist either around his boyhood home or the land he traversed in his journey to the University of Chicago. Frederick Turner's account of some of the 200 species of plants that once existed in the virgin prairie, and are now found in a small patch of restored prairie, is instructive. He does not simply see a field of grass infested with weeds, but a multiplicity: "the towering bluestem and Indian grass in the damper hollows; the twisted awns of the drier stipa; the feathery offset florets of the side oats grama," not to mention the downy flax, coneflower, and Turk's cap lily.[30] Bloom's discussion of relationships has to do with the more traditional social categories of race, sex, and love. Along with the other conservative educational critics, he does not even mention the characteristics of his place, his environment. This is primarily because, as a product of the education he advocates for others, he feels independent from the ecosystem that provides the air he breathes, the water he drinks, the food he eats, and the soils under the cement slabs he now walks upon. These aspects of life are simply taken for granted.

The acceptance of interdependency leads to a very different set of curriculum proposals. Interdependency, along with a concern with long-term sustainability, would make the study of Western civilization an imperative. But the study of other cultures would also be important to the ecologically centered conservatives. The study would be framed by questions that relate to bringing our cultural practices back into balance with the habitat. The questions might include: What are the geneology and consequences of our practice of viewing theoretical (propositional) knowledge as superior to other forms of knowing? Where did we get the idea that "man" is the highest expression of creation, and that the environment must be understood in terms of domination, ownership, and, perhaps "stewardship"? When did the idea of change as inherently progressive come into our thinking? Who were the thinkers who influenced our way of thinking about work and technology? The point is not to establish an official list of ecologically oriented questions, but to connect the study of the past to the central issues of our time.

These questions, like the study of Western civilization itself, can still leave students disconnected from their own environment. The students' own place, their bioregion, can also be used as the basis for understanding the past. Who were the earlier inhabitants of the bioregion and how did their traditions (mythologies, technologies, social practices) reflect their understanding of their habitat? Ron and Suzanne Scollon, two social linguists who have lived among traditional (primal) cultures, point out that there are still people who remember the knowledge of the old ways encoded in the narrative traditions of earlier peoples.[31] The recovery of the oral traditions through the bearers of communal memory should also be an essential part of the curriculum. There are living witnesses of the dramatic transformation of natural environments into the infrastructure of the mechanized society that we now associate with being modern. Their stories are part of the collective memory that need to be told as part of the education of the next generations.

But getting the past into perspective is not the only concern of the ecologically responsive conservative. Learning about one's place is also an essential aspect of good environmental citizenship. The Scollons help to frame how a knowledge of place, one's habitat, can be approached in nonanthropocentric and nonexploitive terms. The questions that would shape the curriculum include: What is the nature of the soil where you live? How deep is it, and what are the forms of animal and plant life that it supports? What animals and plants have disappeared from the land, and why? What is the source of your water, and where does the sewage go? What are the sources of energy you use? How do the political divisions of the bioregion influence the health of the natural systems? What technologies are used in the bioregion, and how have they influenced the soil, water, and air, plant and animal life?[32]

The ecologically responsive conservative would also want to see a more relational approach taken to other aspects of the culture, including an understanding of the many dimensions of work and other aspects of community life where experience and mentoring are important aspects of passing on (and improving upon) the cultural heritage. The arts, in all their forms of expression, would also be a central part of their curriculum, as it is in this area of human activity that achievement can serve to develop the spiritual dimension of the person and community without exacting a physical toll on the environment.

Unlike the conservatism of Hirsch, Adler, Bloom, and Bennett, which has its roots in nearly twenty-five hundred years of Western rationalism, the foundations of the conservatism that will help us survive in the future are not recognized and thus not understood either by the general public indoctrinated in public schools or by mainstream intellectuals who now build their lives on the mythic structures learned in our universities. Even the ecologically responsive thinkers being identified here with this new (actually, ancient) conservatism have not fully addressed the educational implications of the new thought patterns that make interdependency and long-term sustainability the chief organizing principles of a culture. The suggestions here are thus to be taken as preliminary extrapolations of a crisis situation that has been incorrectly framed by the conservative educational critics.

3

The Liberal Impasse:
Technocrats and Emancipators

Having seen how conservative educational critics have overlooked the ecological crisis, we must now turn our attention to the question of how educational liberals understand the main challenges facing the public schools. The basic question is whether they have recognized the impact of cultural practices on the habitat. The answer can be found by considering their proposals for educational reform both at the level of classroom practice and in teacher education. This sounds like a simple and straightforward task. But when dealing with the ideological aspects of public education, that is, the set of guiding ideas and assumptions, it becomes very complex—especially when dealing with educational liberalism. One of the reasons for this is that educational liberalism does not represent a single, conceptually unitary set of ideas. There are at least two distinct traditions of educational liberalism, and the problem of explicating what they stand for is made even more difficult by the fact that these traditions are antagonistic toward each other—to the point where one group uses "conservative" as the pejorative term for describing the other. Thus, before we can consider whether the reform proposals of educational liberalism take into account the ecological crisis, we need to sort out the different traditions and archetypal expressions of educational liberalism, to find what they share in common and what their distinguishing characteristics are.

The two main traditions can be identified as those of the technocratic liberals and of the emancipatory liberals. The latter, over the years, has included variations on the main theme of emancipation: the neo-romantic educators who promoted freedom and self-realization through an open classroom, the neo-Marxists who began as structuralists, evolved into Critical Theorists concerned with the cultural roots of class differences and false consciousness, and now have become the advocates of critical pedagogy. John Dewey and the followers who emphasized different aspects of his theories on the nature of learning and the school/society relationship—the child-centered and the social reconstructionists—are also part of the emancipatory tradition in educational liberalism. But now they are primarily of historical interest. The technocratic educators encompass a wide range of educators, part of a tradition influenced by the behaviorist principles of B. F. Skinner, the approach to scientific management pioneered by Frederick Winslow Taylor, and more generally the epistemological framework associated with Cartesianism. In terms of approaches to classroom practices and approaches to educational reform, the terms "classroom management," "mastery teaching," "effective schools," "learning styles," "curriculum alignment," "site-based management," and so forth, are representative of the mind set that characterizes technocratic liberalism in education.

It is important to identify the basic tenets of liberal thinking that the technocratically oriented educators share with the emancipatory tradition in educational liberalism. Starting from the same basic set of shared deep assumptions, they quickly separate into distinct interpretations of educational liberalism by emphasizing different aspects of liberal thought. The shared tenets include a view of change as linear and as a manifestation of the progressive nature of social development. For the technocratic educator, "competency-based teaching" represented a progressive step beyond the previous set of techniques; its displacement by still newer techniques and procedures (e.g., cooperative learning, accountability-based curriculum, outcome-based programs) is thus viewed as the inevitable expression of progress. This also means that these techniques, which provide an abundant livelihood for a vast number of consultants who are the camp followers of the public schools, will be replaced by still newer and even more powerful teaching techniques.

As we shall see later, the assumption that change is inherently progressive is also a hallmark of the emancipatory

educators. Typical of this conceptual orientation is the recommendation by one of the leading spokespersons for what
is now called "critical pedagogy." Teachers, as he put it,
should "encourage students to develop a *pedagogical negativism*—to doubt everything, and to try to identify those forms
of power and control that operate in their own lives."[1] John
Dewey's efforts to base everyday decision making on the scientific method, Carl Roger's argument that the freedom of
students is best nurtured when they take responsibility for
what and how they learn, and, to cite a more contemporary
example, Paulo Freire's argument that a truly emancipatory
approach to education must be based on the premise that "to
exist, humanly, is to name the world, to change it,"[2] also
become conceptually coherent positions to take only when
the progressive nature of change is taken for granted. If
change was not viewed as inherently progressive, these
educational thinkers surely would have urged a more cau-
tious attitude toward the relativizing of all traditions except
those authorized by the critically reflective individual or, in
the case of Rogers, the emotive response of the student.

A second characteristic of the liberal mind set shared by
both technocratic and emancipatory educators is the representation of the student as an atomistic individual. The technocratic educators, in their interpretation of the scientific
method as only taking seriously data associated with what
can be "objectively" observed, tend to reduce the atomistic
students to their behavior, which is further reduced to that of
an "educational outcome" or "product." Given this reductionist
way of thinking about the student, the challenge, in terms of
professional knowledge, is to understand the variables in the
classroom that cause one set of outcomes to occur rather
than another. The technocratic educators' efforts to perfect a
science of education that provides increased certainty about
the explanation, prediction, and control of "behavioral outcomes" in the classroom thus insures that a more complex
view of the student, particularly one that takes into account
the influence of language and culture on the student's way of
experiencing the everyday world, does not emerge.

In spite of John Dewey's efforts to formulate a view of
intelligence as social in nature, the current spokespeople for
emancipatory education share the technocratic view of the
student as an atomistic individual. In fact, the process of

educational emancipation—through critical reflection or emotive release, depending upon the particular emancipatory educators—is supposed to further empower and contribute to the self-realization of the student as an autonomous individual. Put another way, the purpose of education is to enable the student to achieve greater autonomy from outside forms of authority. This maximizing of individual freedom is spelled out in Maxine Greene's statements on freedom, which is to be understood as "a surpassing of a constraining or deficient reality," which involves a critical understanding and a courage to respond to "the ambiguities of various kinds, layers of determinateness," expressed in the "free act...undertaken from the standpoint of a particular, situated person to bring into existence something contingent on his/her hopes, expectations, and capacities."[3] This view of the free, authentic individual continually struggling against the social processes that make life determined (what Freire refers to as "limit situations"), as we can see, requires the cultural assumption that such change is inherently progressive.

A third tenet of liberalism shared by both technocratic and emancipatory educators is that the rational process is one of the distinctive attributes of the individual, and that it is this rational activity that enables the individual to be self-directing. The technocratic educators tend to reduce thinking on the part of students to the manipulation of data, or to moving to different levels of rational performance depending on the question-asking strategy or data-inputting process—to use their jargon. Even with the argument that an individual possesses multiple forms of intelligences, as Howard Gardner suggests, the technocratic response is to develop teaching strategies for each form of intelligence.

The emancipatory educators start with the same assumption that thought, reflection, intelligence, whatever we want to call mental activity, is carried on in the head or mind of the individual. But they differ with the technocratic educators over how to stimulate the individual's thought processes, as well as what constitutes real thinking. Unlike the technocratic educator, who accepts observation and data as the means of knowing and representing everyday reality, the emancipatory educator starts from the assumption that the "real," what the individual encounters as real and is thus the basis of thought, is a social construct. As a social construct, it represents the interests of a controlling group, which may be an economic class advantaged by a particular representation of reality or it may be the heritage of some past interest group. "Reality," in the mind of the individual, can thus be a false reality because it is based on the social representations that serve special interests.

When students uncritically accept this socially constructed reality (thinking about casual relations, one's role as a man, the nature of property, how to understand success, etc.), they are viewed by the emancipatory educators as in a state of false consciousness. By contrast, the technocratic educators have no understanding of false consciousness or that the categories and patterns of thinking are socially constructed; thus they are untroubled about the possibility that classroom socialization, where students acquire the content and learn the "strategies" of a thinking person, may be contributing to individual self-alienation and to a state of false consciousness. As we shall later see, the emancipatory educators view as their primary responsibility the fostering of the individual's powers of critical reflection on the received representations of reality. The main point to be emphasized here is that the goal of the emancipatory educators is to empower the individual, and this ability to think critically—to demystify the "layers of determinateness," to use Maxine Greene's phrase—is the basis of individual self-determination.

It it no great intellectual feat to recognize that the basic coordinates of the liberal's conceptual map are not alien to the world view of the conservative educational critics discussed in the previous chapter. The view of change as progressive (along with the expanding horizon of human possibilities), and the assumption that the individual is the basic social unit and center of rational activity (which also underpins the anthropocentric view of the universe), are perhaps best understood as essential characteristics of the dominant mind set in the West. Less than fundamental differences in interpretation and emphasis, it could be argued, have led, when extrapolated far enough, to what appears on the surface as distinct ideological traditions, like Marxism and capitalism, liberalism and conservatism, and technocratic and emancipatory education.

It may be that these shared conceptual starting points

prevented both technocratic and emancipatory educators from recognizing that the trend of a technocratic–consumer-orientated culture are moving in the opposite direction from sustaining the habitat. From the emancipatory liberal's point of view, conservatives would be expected, given their backward orientation, not to recognize the dominant events of our times. As Maxine Greene puts it, "We have taken note of the forms of evangelism and fundamentalism, the confused uneasiness with modernism that so often finds expression in anti-intellectualism or an arid focus on Great Books."[4] But the question that must be asked here is why leading spokespeople for the emancipatory tradition in educational liberalism—Paulo Freire, Ira Shor, Henry Giroux, Maxine Greene—have been so at ease with those aspects of modernism that are the greatest threat to the rest of the biotic community. It is the technocratic liberals, using an industrial model as the metaphor for understanding both the purposes and processes of education, who could be expected to misread the signs that suggest that the immediate years ahead will be quite different from what is suggested in the image of the "Information Age." But why have the educational theorists who represent themselves as role models living on the cutting edge of progressive change been totally silent?

To obtain a clearer sense both of what the two groups of educational liberals are advocating as the direction for educational reform and of the relevance of their way of thinking to understanding and responding to the ecological crisis, it will be necessary to examine more closely the ideas, values, and assumptions dealt with more generally up to this point. We shall also see more clearly the special challenges that the two main traditions of educational thought, having evolved in different directions, pose for redirecting public education in a more ecologically responsible direction.

Technocratic Liberalism

Aldo Leopold begins *A Sand County Almanac* with a personal admission: "There are some who can live without wild things, and some who cannot. These essays are the delights and dilemmas of one who cannot."[5] This sensitivity led him to write about the need for a "land ethic." In 1962, Rachel Carson began the second chapter of *Silent Spring* with what should have been at that time a self-evident statement: "The history of life on earth has been a history of interaction between living things and their surroundings." She then went on to document the extent and consequences of chemical contamination of water, ground, and air—which we can now see as minor compared to the release into the U.S. environment of 22 billion pounds of toxic chemicals in 1989. Farley Mowat, noticing a rapid decline during his own lifetime in species of marine and bird life in the Gulf of St. Lawrence and along the Atlantic seaboard, set out to document the bounty of natural life of the region before the arrival of the first Europeans. The destruction of whole species, and the vast diminuation of most others in the region, led him to wonder about the cultural roots of what he calls modern man's "biocidal course."

It would be easy to add the names of other people who, reaching large audiences, are helping to break the web of Western beliefs and practices based on an exploitive relationship with the environment. It is also easy to document increased exposure of environmental issues in the press and on the television over the last ten years. The growing threat to the environment, in effect, has been a topic of widespread awareness for well over a decade now.

Yet the technocratic educators who largely dominate the way of thinking within the mainstream of public education, and who thus exert the greatest influence on educational reform, have never acknowledged in their articles and books that there is such a thing as a natural environment. It is difficult to believe that in their personal lives they have had fundamentally different environmental experiences from those that led Leopold, Carson, and Mowat to alert a culturally sedated public: smog, polluted water, soil erosion, clear-cut hillsides, and declining animal, bird, and fish populations are difficult to ignore, even for academics. The ability of formal education, even at the doctoral level, to create conceptual blinders is another matter. But instead of looking for causal explanations of why the direction-setters in education have ignored the ecological crisis, we shall turn instead to a consideration of the school culture they are now creating. Their language, thought patterns, and ability to transform new ideas from diverse fields into classroom techniques will be our main concern, for these dimensions of their influence will help illuminate the extent of the challenge we face in redirecting public education.

The search for better technique continues to be the Holy Grail of the educational establishment. Professors of education, who too often frame the educational issues in terms of the research methodology they learned in graduate school, continue to exercise control over such critical areas as how to think about the process of education and what constitutes significant reform. As both creators and legitimators of professional knowledge, they exercise enormous influence on the education of teachers, as well as on the burgeoning field of professional development. This influence can be understood as having two dimensions. One is their socialization to a technological mind set which leaves teachers as a vulnerable audience for a seemingly unending series of educational innovations that could be more properly viewed as short-lived fads. The other influence is harder to identify because it has to do with areas of silence in the education of teachers. Basically these are understandings that cannot be articulated within the limited thought patterns and language of a technocratic way of thinking—culture, the formative influences of language, social justice issues, environmental concerns.

Another key group within the educational establishment creating the illusion of keeping teachers on the cutting edge of an ever-increasing field of professional knowledge are the disseminators who conduct the workshops and in-service sessions for teachers. Yet they too maintain a collective silence on issues relating to the nature of the culture passed on through the various classroom techniques. As professors of education or private consultants, their professional role is to monitor developments in other fields (molecular biology, business management, social psychology, cognitive science, etc.), as well as to be barometers of the latest movements in pop psychology. Their self-assigned task is to translate for teachers the ways these new and often untested ideas and values can be incorporated into the classroom. Thus, the implications for the classroom of the most recent findings, for example brain research, provide an opportunity for a workshop or conference keynote address that will leave teachers with new techniques and the feeling that they are part of the forward march of scientific knowledge. But much of their translation and dissemination work is not, as we shall see, derived from these areas of inquiry, but instead represents the sharing of techniques derived from educational research.

Not all of what the professors of education and disseminators of in-service knowledge do is wrong-headed. The main concern here is with how their almost complete domination of crucial aspects of public education limits the opportunity for other concerns that do not fit their ideological orientation to be taken seriously by classroom teachers. Put another way, by the time classroom teachers encounter all that these two groups in the educational establishment think essential for an effective teacher, there is little time, energy, or interest left for responding to other concerns. There is simply too much to learn with too few opportunities to question whether it is really worth learning. And as we shall see, what teachers are left with in the way of professional education does not include other theoretical frameworks that would enable them to see this professional orthodoxy from a more critical perspective. And simply the exhaustion of teachers faced with an ever-growing cornucopia of classroom techniques and research findings on aspects of teacher effectiveness becomes especially critical when we begin to consider the classroom implications of the ecological crisis.

Educational research that most directly influences the preparation of teachers has been focused on classroom variables presumed essential for understanding the teacher's effectiveness. Some of the research findings reflect efforts carried on for over a decade, while other findings represent inquiry into relatively new topics of concern. The summary of findings in the 1986 *Handbook of Research on Teaching* (third edition) is a testament to how much can be learned about the process of teaching and learning in just one setting, the classroom. It also suggests how this "science of education" can be misdirected by academics who are unconsciously influenced by an ideology more suited to an industrial model of production.

The amount of knowledge we now have on the classroom can be seen in the number of areas listed in the *Handbook* as carved out for research, and the number of published articles and books in each area (indicated in parentheses): Teachers Thought Processes (158), Student's

Thought Process (131), Teaching of Learning Strategies
(103), Teacher Behavior and Student Achievement (219),
Teaching Functions (75), Classroom Organization and Management (312), Classroom Discourse (172), School Effects
(121), Adapting Teaching to Individual Differences Among
Learners (183). To this list must be added the more specific
topics of teaching creative and gifted learners, bilingual students, and the handicapped, each involving the same close
scrutiny on the part of researchers. With the exception of the
topic of classroom discourse, which was written by an
applied linguist, the research articles and books represent
the student as a culture-free individual, language as a neutral
conduit through which objective information or individual
ideas are passed (a sender-receiver model of communication), and the rational process as free of cultural influence.
Given the paradox of such massive research findings on
teacher effectiveness being coupled with the continuing
record of poor school achievement, when measured against
other countries that have not even started to develop a science of education, we have to ask how all this knowledge
about the classroom is influencing the education of teachers. The answer to this question, unfortunately, will not
leave us hopeful about this part of the educational establishment providing leadership in developing a more ecologically
responsible approach to the cultural transmission process in
the classroom.

Although there is growing awareness among a small
number of professional educators that culture and language
are the most fundamental aspects of the classroom, the
mainstream approach to teacher education continues to find
in this massive collection of data on classroom variables the
patterns that fit the now discredited nineteenth-century
industrial model of production. The teacher's role is represented as that of a manager, and the students are viewed as
material to be shaped into predetermined form by the teacher's use of proper "inputting" strategies. Clear and precise
instructional objectives, the establishment and consistent
enforcement of rules governing student behavior and intellectual performance, measurement of learning in terms of
student behavior, knowledge of and skill in the use of a
broad range of teaching strategies, and consistent use of
reinforcement as the key element of classroom manage-

ment are how the teacher's role is being represented in the mainstream methods of teaching. These concerns, in themselves, are not necessarily the problem, as most of them, when carried out by teachers who possess a broader perspective on the educational process, can be viewed as common-sense practices. The problem arises when these become the *only* concerns of the teacher.

But some of the people who have looked closely at the accumulation of research findings communicate a sense of uncertainty about what it all means. The authors of the chapter in the *Handbook* summarizing the findings of the 219 articles and books dealing with "Teacher Behavior and Student Achievement," for example, sound a note of caution about the results of this massive effort:

> The data reviewed here should make it clear that...what constitutes effective instruction...varies with context. What appears to be just the right amount of demandedness (or structuring of content or praise, etc.) for one class might be too much for a second class but not enough for a third class. Even within the same class, what constitutes effective instruction will vary according to subject matter, group size, and the specific instructional objectives being pursued.[6]

This frank admission about the uncertainties in one of the domains of the science of education, unfortunately, does not seem to have affected those who are carving out lucrative professional careers in the area of teacher in-service training.

The disseminators of "professional development" promise teachers the latest in successful classroom techniques and educational trends. Perhaps more important, their approach to professional development is packaged so as to insure a minimum burden on the teacher's time, energy, and depth of intellectual involvement. Workshops are often presented in an hour, or over a two-day period squeezed into a weekend.

Aside from both the faddish nature of many of these workshops and their questionable effects on teacher performance when measured against the added costs to school districts, what is distinctive is the vast array of topics and techniques represented as essential to improving the teacher's ability. The Association for Supervision and Curriculum Development, which is one of the larger professional organizations, sponsored in a seven-month period a total of 45 workshops for teachers at different sites around the country. Each workshop dealt with a different technique that claimed to enhance the teacher's performance. The titles of the workshops, as well as the benefits the teachers should derive from them, are illuminating: "Implementing Tactics for Thinking in the Classroom (learn thinking skills and strategies); "Mentor Teacher and Peer Coaching" (learn observation and conferencing techniques); "Learning Styles Models" (help students become "self-accepting, confident, and successful learners"); "Instructional Implications of Brain Research" (how to transform "a heterogeneous group of gifted, underachieving, urban adolescents into successful learners"); "Implications of 'Multiple Intelligences' Theory for Schools and Classrooms" (developing a curriculum that "nurtures all seven categories" of intelligence); "Site-Based Management" (learn to develop a school-based short- and long-range plan); and so on.

Dissemination of techniques as part of the teacher's professional development is also carried out by more small-scale entrepreneurs, some of whom are earning large sums of money. School districts provide lists to teachers and administrators of the professional development workshops available in their region, and many workshops are sponsored within the district. All of them promise teachers the skills and strategies needed for more effective teaching. The promise of more power and relevance (two apparently conflicting goals) is never accompanied by an opportunity to think critically about the conceptual underpinnings of the new techniques. The workshops are both too short in duration and too filled with practical tips to allow this. Besides, it does not serve the interests of the disseminators to have the teachers reflect seriously on what they are learning or the simulations they are being taken through. The more appropriate ambience is that of shared enthusiasm for the teacher's empowerment obtained through the mastery of the new techniques.

A short workshop on study skills may help demonstrate how the seeming abundance of helpful strategies precludes adopting a critical perspective that might lead to questioning either the real merit of what is being presented or addressing more educationally and socially significant issues. A workshop based on the book, *Making the Grade*, covers 80 skills that will improve students' classroom success, as well as help them "be a winner throughout life." That most of the skills are simply a matter of common sense that most students pick up as a natural part of school socialization and personal problem solving is not the important issue. For example, Skill 18 is, "Write your lecture notes on binder paper," Skill 32 is "Read at your normal rate of speed," and Skill 80 is "Avoid becoming distracted by what other students do during the test."[7] No one can argue with these suggestions, although some may wonder if they should be represented as "skills." Others may wonder whether teachers need to be devoting their time and intellectual energy to learning what each of the 80 skills are. It is almost like taking an activity such as eating and breaking down each movement, aspect of awareness, and relationship into a separate skill. Skill 1, Make sure you are the right person in the right room at the right time; Skill 3, Make certain that your body is aligned with the chair before sitting down; and Skill 18, Establish visual contact with the serving spoon and the dish of food. There is, of course, the possibility that making some of these practices and expectations explicit would be helpful. But the real meaning of this workshop, which is so representative of professional development and in-service training, is the filling of the teacher's noninstructional time with talk about classroom techniques.

Furthermore, many of the techniques are not only trivial, but based on fundamental misconceptions. For example, one of the current fads at workshops and conferences for classroom teachers is to provide techniques for teaching "thinking." At just one conference, teachers could attend sessions on "Inventive Thinking," "Creative Thinking," "Critical Thinking," and the "Structure of Intellect." Each involved breaking thinking into subcategories ("comprehension," "divergent thinking," "memory," "forecasting," "decision making" and so forth), with classroom techniques appropriate to fostering each form of thinking. The "Inventive Thinking" approach also represented communication as a process of "marketing," which is a highly simplified and ideologically loaded way of thinking about communication. But the representation of thinking as a culture-free process and the goal of education as engendering rationally autonomous individuals were the most serious problems. One prominent speaker told the teachers that their task was to enable children to learn, think, and produce other forms of knowledge that do not mimic the past; that is, the students should not, ideally speaking, "replicate known knowledge." As stated at another session, "Learning at its best (is) self-directed investigation and discovery." Hearing that the goal of the teacher is to produce autonomous thinkers seemed to uplift and invigorate the audience. But a problem related directly to how the dominant belief system contributes to our exceeding the sustaining capacities of our habitat, was that few of the teachers had the knowledge necessary to recognize that they were being given a totally erroneous way of thinking about thinking, that the basic explanations and teaching techniques were based on an ideological orientation that has its roots in the anti-tradition thinking of the Enlightenment, and that the ideal expressed in the aphorism "good schools increase individual differences" is both culturally naive and politically irresponsible. The complex relationships between culture, the metaphorical nature of language and thought, and the manner in which the student individualizes the cultural forms learned at both the explicit and implicit level, was beyond the grasp of people caught up in a collective messianic journey through the remnants of an outworn ideology.

The vast number of techniques being promoted as essential to professional growth also has another effect, namely, the fostering of a nihilistic attitude where everything begins to be seen as of equal value. Without a deeper knowledge that allows issues, trends, and techniques to be put into a more reflective perspective, each technique loses its distinctness and special merit, particularly when teachers begin to realize that each year brings new disseminators with even more "advanced" techniques and learning skills. What may have been found useful from a previous workshop, like individualized instruction or performance objectives, disappears from the list of workshop topics as the new topics are added. The danger for the teacher is to appear professionally outdated. The steady flow of new techniques, in effect, relativizes the merit of what has gone before; and what endures is merely the expectation of change. It also becomes part of a professional hypnosis where the events in the larger world beyond the classroom are not and cannot be fully grasped as related to what goes on in the classroom. This is particularly the case when social and environmental events cannot be related to the technique. How does the teacher connect the loss of forest cover with classroom techniques derived from brain research, or the warming of the earth's atmosphere with "Proactive Classroom Management"? There is a connection between events in the larger world and the classroom, but it is, in part, in the one aspect of education that none of these techniques addresses—the content of the curriculum. In effect, the culture of beliefs and practices transmitted through the curriculum is the one part of mainstream professional development that is never addressed.

Emancipatory Liberals

While technocratic thinking in education goes back to the turn of the century, there has also been a tradition of emancipatory thinking about the purpose of schooling with its roots in the writings of John Dewey, and for some, of Karl Marx—although they would be less willing now to acknowledge the lineage of their thinking than a few years ago. Unlike the technocratic educators, whose vision is limited to solving specific classroom problems (some real and others apparitions of their ideological orientation), those in the emancipatory tradition pride themselves as theorists who understand the larger context of education. They also view themselves as the chief spokespeople for keeping alive a vision of social justice and individual emancipation. Like Diogenes, who walked around in broad daylight with his lighted lamp in search of justice, emancipatory educators use their theory to illuminate the relationship that both bind and blind. Given their broader perspective on the context and purpose of public education, one might expect them to address how the ideas and values embedded in the curriculum, as well as the emphasis on technique, are further deepening the ecological crisis. Surprisingly, the emancipatory tradition in educational thought continues, like the conservative educational critics, to ignore this problem.

Why they remain silent about immediate and long-term threats to world habitat is a question that we shall address here. We shall also be concerned with whether their way of framing the problem of educational change will, in itself, become an obstruction to the process of radical thinking that must be undertaken. One of the ironies of discovering that the sustaining characteristics of natural systems—a finite and fragile habitat—have limits that cannot be stretched to meet ever-growing human demands upon them is that ideologies previously viewed as progressive may now represent reactionary positions. In effect, the ecological crisis has turned topsy-turvy the privileged status of our most progressive and modernizing ideologies. To be a radical thinker in education should now mean returning to the original meaning of the word: to think about the most basic foundations of our cultural existence. Before this process can be started, it is first necessary to examine the arguments of the educators who are in the emancipatory tradition of liberalism.

Criticisms of the educational theorists who view themselves as the chief guardians and interpretators of critical thought are often open to misinterpretation. Thus the attempt to understand why the emancipatory tradition of educational liberalism has ignored the ecological crisis should not be translated into the binary categories where issues are understood in either-or terms. Many aspects of this emancipatory tradition should be taken seriously; for example, at the most general level its concern with the connections between education and political processes seems essential. It also has important things to say about aspects of the teacher-student relationship. Thus our concern here is to examine only those aspects of such thinking that prevent them from contributing to the discussion of the changes in education that will contribute to an ecologically sustainable form of culture.

The two thinkers who have had the greatest influence in shaping the distinctive discourse of critical pedagogy are John Dewey and Freire. Both developed a theory of education in response to what each perceived as the fundamental problems of their time. For Dewey, the educational challenge was to provide people from diverse cultural backgrounds and social classes a common basis for problem solving, thus ensuring the promise of a truly democratic society that could be shared by all segments of society. Freire was motivated essentially by the same social vision, but initially focused his attention on the problem of developing an approach to literacy that would enable the poor to become their own agents of social change. The social divisions and inequities in early twentieth-century America and the problems of illiteracy in Third World countries helped to establish the framework for thinking about the emancipatory potential of education carried on by the followers of Dewey and Freire. The challenge for us is to understand how two theories of education that were intended to address such important social issues could be inadequate for thinking about the ecological crisis.

Sorting out why these two theories of education tend to foster a cultural orientation that is ecologically problematic should not be interpreted to mean that the social concerns of Dewey and Freire are no longer important, or that their approaches to ameliorating the problems are now without merit. Rather, it is now a problem of understanding how social justice issues, like political empowerment through education, can be achieved in more ecologically responsible ways. Teaching people a method of participatory decision making that is based on the scientific method of problem solving, or a literacy program that fosters an anthropocentric view of the world, may be emancipatory in terms of a pre-ecological state of consciousness. But when viewed in terms of a more inclusive view of community, one that includes other life forms and natural systems with whom humans share an interdependent existence, this becomes more problematic.

It is ironic that the two thinkers who most shaped the emancipatory educator's way of understanding the process of critical thought did not themselves recognize how the thought process reproduces the epistemic orientations of a language/cultural community. For example, the relationship between a cultural group's root metaphors and how the resulting process of analogic thinking is encoded in our use of such iconic metaphors as "individualism," "freedom," "technology," "community," was, unfortunately, not understood by Dewey. In *Knowing and the Known*, co-authored with Arthur F. Bentley in 1949, Dewey attempts to explain the role of language in a transactional relationship that connects humans with the evolving patterns of the natural world. The challenge, given his understanding of transactions as "primary life processes in their environment," was to use language in a manner that avoided the imposition of previously formulated categories and ways of understanding. That is, Dewey was taking the position that the encoding (storage) function of language impedes the ability to be knowing participants in the transactional relationships that make up the living world. Writes Dewey:

> ...we recognize no names that pretend to be expressions of "inner" thoughts, any more than we recognize names that pretend to be compulsions exercised upon us by "outer" objects.... We tolerate no finalities of meaning parading as "ultimate" truth or "absolute" knowledge, and give such purported finalities no recognition whatever under our postulation of natural system for man in the world.[8]

The culture-language-thought connection is thus rejected by Dewey, even as he himself is dependent upon the use of a metaphorical language that encodes the analogic thought processes of a post-Newtonian understanding of the natural world, which can also be understood as a cultural root metaphor.

Nor does Freire, with his more sophisticated recognition of the political nature of language, fully grasp the deep nature of a metaphorically based language and thought process. Both thinkers set themselves the task of explaining how forms of critical rationality could emancipate individuals (for Freire) and social groups (for Dewey) from traditional patterns of thinking that serve to maintain an inequitable system of power and privilege. In effect, Dewey and Freire built their theories on the foundations of culturally specific root metaphors that evolved out of the struggle to overturn metaphorical constructions of pre-modern and (for Dewey) pre-scientific thinking. As the followers of Dewey and Freire also lack an understanding of the metaphorical basis of language and thought (even critically reflective thought) and an awareness of the culturally specific mind set encoded in the root metaphors that frame their vision of education and society, it is necessary to explicate the most basic assumptions of Dewey and Freire.

This project in symbolic (metaphorical) archeology will provide an understanding why the educational goals of emancipatory educational theorists appear reactionary in relationship to the ecological crisis. Their view of the emancipatory potential of critical thought, which reflects the Enlightenment vision still taken for granted by a large number of people who have the potential of becoming an alternative voice to that of the technocratic educators now dominating teacher education, frames legitimate social justice issues in terms of the very root metaphors that have kept us from recognizing that genuine human progress cannot be based on the continued exploitation of the natural environment. To put it more succinctly, emancipation from exploitive relationships that leads to ever greater freedom for the individual or even freedom for the social group, when based on the root metaphor that validates every change and choice as progressive, will likely result in even greater demands being made on the environment. The need to live in balance suggests that Alexander Solzhenitsyn's view of freedom as "self-restriction" ("Restriction of the self for the sake of others") may be a more ecologically responsible way of thinking. Why the followers of Dewey and Freire continue to follow an ideological pathway that views as reactionary Solzhenitsyn's view of freedom, as well as the belief systems of traditional cultures that have evolved in more ecologically sustainable ways, will become clearer as we turn to the deep cultural beliefs Dewey and Freire took for granted.

John Dewey: (1859–1952)

Dewey left a complex and sophisticated legacy that educators have never quite fit into the realities of the American classroom. He adamantly opposed all forms of dualisms: separation of the knower from the known, intelligence from experience, individual from social group, humans from the natural world, and the present from the past and future. His understanding of how thinking occurs gave rise to a number of phrases that are distinctly Deweyian: the spectator view of knowledge (which he rejected), the method of intelligence (which he thought could be applied to all moral, political, and educational issues), education as growth, and many more. In addition to fusing together the scientific method of problem solving with democratic decision making, which Dewey viewed as the ideal of education as a "reconstructing, trans-forming" process of growth, he also viewed individual intelligence as part both of the natural world and of a larger communal process of problem solving. The complexity of Dewey's position seemed to invite various groups of educators who shared part of his agenda for social/educational change to appropriate various aspects of his thinking. But the appropriated parts represented a distortion of his position, leading him, in the late 1930s, to rebuke his followers for oversimplifying his ideas. With the current attempt to use Dewey's ideas as a basis for an emancipatory form of classroom education, it is important to identify the constructs that characterize his position. These constructs are epistemological orientations that, as I shall argue, were intended to fulfill the promise of the scientific and democratic progress Dewey considered to be jeopardized by the class divisions fostered by capitalism and outmoded traditions of intellectual and moral authority.

If one leaves culture out of consideration when thinking about the ecological crisis, Dewey's ideas appear as a solid and ecologically sound basis for educational reform. As Thomas Colwell points out, the metaphor of nature so integral to Dewey's thinking about the interdependent systems that constitute a habitat was also central both to his theory of knowledge and to his view of education as a process of growth.[9] Dewey continually represented human capacities, previously regarded as separating "man" from nature, as potentialities of the natural world. The errors of a non-naturalistic understanding of human capacities, as he saw it, included a spectator view of knowledge, dependence upon transcendental values, and an approach to education that expected to fill the minds of students with ready-made ideas that, at best, had only an incidental relationship to the vicissitudes of experience.

One of the most important tasks Dewey set for himself was to present a naturalistic interpretation of human experience, including the processes of thinking, valuing, and doing. This warning against relying upon knowledge previously encoded in language reflected his attempt to align the use of language with his naturalistic position. At a time when he was most actively engaged in formulating the social, political, and educational implications of his naturalistic understanding of human intelligence, Dewey wrote that, "The intelligent activity of man is not something brought to bear upon nature from without; it is nature realizing its own potentialities in behalf of a fuller and richer issue of events." Furthermore, "intelligence within nature means liberation and expansion, as reason outside of nature (the spectator view of knowledge) means fixation and restriction."[10] Not only does he view human intelligence as a naturally evolved capacity, like being bipedal, he also associates it with the individual's ability to recognize possible courses of action in an otherwise problematic set of interactions and patterns that constitute experience. As Dewey put it, "to assume that anything can be known in isolation from its connections with other things is to identify knowing with merely having some object of perception or in feeling...."[11]

But knowing, or the exercise of intelligence, involves more than tracing connections and recognizing relations that make problematic the individual's course of action; it also involves formulating a new plan of action that reconstitutes relationships. The exercise of intelligence, when based on the scientific method of problem solving that Dewey equated with the full empowerment of the individual's state of evolutionary development, involves surveying the conditions of lived experience, formulating hypothetical ideas or plans of action, and assessing their consequences. Thinking, which combines an experimental approach both to ideas and values (both aspects of plans of action), leads to "a question answered, a difficulty disposed of, a confusion cleared up, an inconsistency reduced to coherence, a perplexity mastered."[12] The exercise of intelligence within the matrix of connections and interactions that represent the conditions of the natural world does not lead to knowledge that can be applied in recipe fashion to new situations; rather, it serves to resolve an immediate state of doubt or impediment to action and, when viewed from a broader perspective in time, leads to growth in the capacity of problem solving.

Although Dewey did not return to the problem of reformulating his views on education as a process of growth in the scientific method of intelligent participatory decision making, the explanation of the human-nature relationship presented in *Knowing and the Known* will likely be viewed by educational theorists in the future as evidence that

Dewey is a forerunner of ecological thinking. Before turning to an explanation of why Dewey would be miscast in this role, consider Dewey's apparently nonanthropocentric formulation of the human-environment relationship:

> What is called *environment* is that in which the conditions called physical are enmeshed in cultural conditions and thereby are more than "physical" in its technical sense. "Environment" is not something around and about human activities in an external sense; it is their *medium*, or *milieu*, in the sense in which a *medium* is *inter*mediate in the execution or carrying *out* of human activities, as well as being the channel *through* which they move and the vehicle *by* which they go on. Narrowing of the medium is the direct source of all unnecessary impoverishment in human living; the only sense in which "social" is an honorific term is that in which the medium in which human living goes on is one by which human life is enriched.[13]

In the same chapter, which Dewey wrote himself, for *Knowing and the Known*, he strongly criticizes the connection of the scientific method with mastery over nature. "What 'understanding' nature means is dogmatically assumed to be already known," he noted, referring to the mastery-of-nature line of interpretation, "while in fact anything that legitimately can be termed *understanding* nature is the outcome of scientific nature, not something established independent of inquiry and determining the course of science."[14] Again, in this last formulation of thinking as the application of the scientific method to the "concrete reconstructions of antecedent conditions of existence," Dewey unconsciously retains his life-long commitment to a specific cultural view of knowing as, in his own mind, a natural capability, like breathing and seeing.

There are two issues that need to be considered here. The first has to do with why Dewey, when he is found later to be an ecologically oriented philosopher, should not be so regarded. The second issue relates to why emancipatory educational theorists are attempting to re-establish Dewey's position as a founder of a radical theory of education. The two issues are connected in a rather strange yet important way. That is, part of the cultural baggage Dewey failed to recognize in his own formulation of a natural method of intelligence—that everything is in a state of change and that the process is progressive—is also basic to thinking of education as an emancipatory process. But first, why do Dewey's ideas, on the whole, not provide an adequate basis for evolving an ecologically sustainable culture?

The philosopher George Santayana identified the Achilles Heel of Dewey's naturalistic interpretation of experience—that matrix of connections, relationships, and problematic situations that prompts humans to think and to formulate values. The crux of the problem, according to Santayana, is that Dewey's naturalistic philosophy is subverted by his commitment to what Santayana termed "the dominance of the foreground." "In nature," Santayana observed, "there is no foreground or background, no here, no moral cathedra, no centre so really central as to reduce all other things to mere margins and mere perspectives." And "if such a foreground becomes dominate in a philosophy, naturalism is abandoned."[15] The foreground, the sense of time-space perspective in Dewey's thinking, is central to his view of thinking as problem solving. Aside from Dewey's more direct statements, as when he states that "change is associated with progress rather than with lapse and fall," the formulation of plans of action, the experimental approach to values, and the assessment of consequences that follow from directed action, all point toward the validation of thought and action at some future point in time. Because the process is continuous, with movement always being forward from problematic situation to temporary resolution and then starting all over again with a new problematic situation, there is only foreground in Dewey's philosophy, with only temporary resting places. For Santayana, the sense of temporality built into Dewey's way of understanding the process of thinking represents a specific cultural orientation that Dewey was not able to recognize because he interpreted change in nature as always moving forward toward cumulative improvement.

Culture was not one of Dewey's strong suites. Although he used the word on occasion, it was never with the recognition that culture refers to all human activity—including the patterns encoded in the language processes that are largely part of the taken-for-granted aspects of daily experience. He

was more at home with the words "society," "social," and
"individual" (which he understood as socially constituted). A
partial explanation for Dewey's lack of sensitivity to the cultural dimensions of experience, including ways of knowing,
is that his three key generative metaphors for understanding
human problem solving were derived from natural biology,
the scientific method, and the democratic process. The process of analogic thinking, when framed by these generative
metaphors, does not lead easily or naturally to a view of culture where the encoding and re-enactment processes are
part of the person's natural attitude. These generative
metaphors, however, do allow for discussion of individual
action, such as thinking and acting on the basis of habit
(which Dewey likened to a mental engine in an idling state),
and for consideration of how social ends can be attained
through a more collective approach to decision making. His
concern with achieving a more socialist form of democracy,
for instance, involved arguments about how the individual
should be viewed; but the arguments did not address the
interconnections between ideology and cultural patterns of
thought, or between his culture and the "scientific" method of
intelligence he extolled.

Education as growth in the reconstruction of experience
and participatory decision making that pulls everybody
affected by a problematic situation into the process of scientific thinking fits Dewey's metaphor of the "garden of nature"
and how humans must think and relate with each other if
they are to be in harmony with it. Education, participatory
democracy, and growth in the method of intelligence, to
quote him again, is an expression of "nature realizing its own
potentialities." Beyond Santayana's criticism that Dewey's
view of humans as living "forward" reflected a metaphysical
position, and not part of the garden, one can point out that
Dewey's thinking also reflected the dominant cultural themes
of Western Enlightenment thinking. To put it more succinctly, Dewey was unconsciously working within a specific cultural tradition; his achievement was in helping to further hide
his own cultural orientation, and that of his followers, by
using the metaphorical language of natural biology, the scientific method, and participatory democracy. But unlike the
Social Darwinists who based their political extrapolations on
the metaphors of nature as an arena of competition and sur-

vival of the fittest, Dewey stressed cooperation and collective growth.

It is Dewey's hidden cultural agenda that disqualifies him as a thinker who can guide us out of the ecological quagmire of which we are now becoming aware. Three aspects of his cultural orientation seem especially critical to making the point that Dewey, for all the attractiveness of his position when compared to the existing alternatives in early twentieth-century American educational and social thinking, is part of the ecological problem, and will not be part of the solution.

The first has to do with Dewey's failure to recognize the culture-language-thought connection that Edward Sapir made the central part of a paper presented in 1929, which was also the time Dewey was doing his most important writing on the nature of thinking. Language, according to Sapir,

> is a guide to "social reality." ...The "real world" (as people experience it) is to a large extent unconsciously built up in the language habits of the group.... The worlds in which different societies live are distinct worlds, not merely the same world with different labels attached.... We see and hear and otherwise experience very largely as we do because the language habits of our community predispose certain choices of interpretation.[16]

That different language communities organize and experience "reality" according to different root metaphors was not part of Dewey's awareness; thus he could not see his own epistemological preferences in terms of its culturally specific nature. Being a "modern, progressive, intelligent" thinker (the metaphors are nearly interchangeable) meant adopting the method of intelligence (i.e., the scientific method of problem solving). As Dewey viewed them, cultural differences and limitations kept immigrants from participating fully in the communicative and problem-solving processes he associated with a democracy that fostered the growth of all its members.

Dewey would have viewed as backward and prescientific the cultural ways of knowing that are distinctly different from the Western anthropocentrism he unconsciously retained in the privileged status he gave the scientific method of problem solving. Jamake Highwater's observation that for

American Indians, "images are a means of celebrating mystery, and not of explaining it" contrasts sharply with Dewey's method of intelligence.[17] Nor would Dewey be able to accept as credible John Tanner's experience among the Ottawa and Ojibwa where he learned the power of dreaming from the old chieftainess, Net-no-kwa, who on several occasions saved her little band of people from starvation through her ability to communicate with the Great Spirit.[18] The Navaho use of curing rituals, including the sand painting that identifies the patient with the Holy People and thus with the cosmic order, would also not fit Dewey's view that empowerment comes only from the use of the scientific method. The list of alternative cultural epistemologies could be vastly extended. One aspect of what Highwater termed the "primal mind" that separates Dewey's position from the epistemological mainstreams of human history (which makes the tradition of Western Enlightenment thinking look like a cultural experiment that is still in process) is the lack of an anthropocentric view of the universe.

In spite of Dewey's emphasis on connectedness and transactions, the scientifically based method of intelligence is a distinctly human capacity; that is, the meaning and values that give experience its fullness reflect the process of problem solving from a human perspective. Dewey's anthropocentricism can also be seen in that other aspects of the environment are not given a voice, as is the case with cultural groups that evolved a more spiritual and poetic (metaphorical) form of consciousness. The deer, trees, and mountains are not the source of analogic knowledge in Dewey's world, nor do they share in the sacred unity of the universe. Communication, for Dewey, is reduced to what the physical senses of "scientific man" can cope with. Although Dewey would argue that the individual–environment relationship involves interdependency, it is still the Enlightenment hubris of rational thought ("the method of intelligence") making sense of a material world of flux and indeterminacy. In short, Dewey understood that the individual always operates within an environmental context, but he could not recognize other ways of knowing and communicating that more ancient and ecologically oriented cultures have developed.

Dewey's view of knowledge, with its built-in anthropocentrism, is also profoundly different from that of Islamic cultures, as well as those built on the foundations of Buddhism and Confucianism. No case is being made here that these non-Western cultural/epistemological traditions were as ecologically advanced as the original North American inhabitants of Turtle Island, the name they gave to their continent. Rather, they are mentioned here as further evidence that Dewey completely ignored the "realities" constructed by the great language communities of the non-Western world. A case could also be made that large segments of American society that were part of his own language community did not share his scientific/experimental model of decision making, but relied instead on a stock of tacit understandings and analogues that had been handed down from generation to generation—in preparing food, celebrating human events and changes in seasons, planting the seed and harvesting the crop, spiritual practices.

The paradox of Dewey's position is that the more he succeeded in articulating a way of knowing that took account of the dynamic nature of knower/known relationships, the more he lost touch with the constitutive role culture plays in human experience. But culture does not just disappear because the theorist (Dewey) leaves it out of the picture. Humans are esssentially cultural beings (in thought, communication, and behavior), and it is as cultural beings that they interact with the larger biotic community. Thus, the human practices contributing to the degradation of the environment are largely guided by the shared symbolic systems of a cultural group; and it is this cultural dimension of the ecological crisis that represents the greatest challenge for the educational reformers who attempt to build upon Dewey's ecological model. Given his silence in this area, it seems the following questions are essential for assessing the future relevance of Dewey's thinking: What is the form of culture that would emerge if Dewey's epistemological orientation could be made the basis of everyday life? Would Dewey's "method of intelligence" allow for taking seriously the ecologically sustainable practices of traditional cultural groups? Is there any basis in Dewey's dynamic model for forms of moral authority that would frame human actions in terms of self-limitation for the sake of future generations of the biotic community, and how would these forms of moral authority be symbolically grounded? My own judgment is that when the answer to the first question is adequately worked out, the limitations of Dewey's thinking will become clearer.

This brings us to the second aspect of Dewey's thinking that, in my opinion, disqualifies him as a forerunner of ecological thinking. The past, or what others term "tradition," is an integral aspect of experience as Dewey understood it. But tradition was not viewed by Dewey as being a legitimate source of authority in guiding human practices and beliefs. Rather, its value is instrumental to the process of problem solving, and for the individual whose conceptual orientation is toward the future it is to be judged when the consequences of the thought-action process can be sorted out before launching into a new problem-solving situation. Thus, for Dewey the essential attitude toward life is not that of preserving living traditions that have insured communal survival in a limited habitat, but an experimental attitude, framed in terms of the perspective of the single individual or social group, and guaranteed by the belief that each scientifically grounded plan of action represents the outward expansion of human empowerment (Dewey termed it "growth in problem solving") and progress. Dewey's understanding of tradition was framed by the restrictive view of knowledge that the scientific method demands. The forms of knowledge that could not easily be accommodated by Dewey's "method of intelligence" have been referred to by a variety of terms: tacit, implicit, analogue, taken for granted, cultural unconsciousness, and so forth. According to Shils, when these forms of knowledge have survived as patterns handed down over at least three generations they can be understood as traditions. As these patterns are often what gives authority to human action, they are then part of the person's natural attitude, like driving on the right hand side of the road, using the personal pronoun "I" as a means of referring to the self as an autonomous being, and responding to kinesic patterns of communication. Aside from Dewey's failure to understand tradition as encoding other appropriate forms of shared knowledge, there are implications in his thought that relate more directly to the ecological crisis.

In his book, *Pig Earth*, John Berger observes a basic distinction between peasants, who are aware they lack a margin of economic security, and urban peoples who take their affluence for granted. In addition to noting that it is "a commonplace that change, questioning, experiment flourished in cities," Berger brings into focus the basic difference in attitudes toward tradition that separates what he terms "cultures of progress" from "cultures of survival." The former envisage future expansion of freedom and affluence fueled by technological change; the latter "envisages the future as a sequence of repeated acts of survival." In recognizing scarcity (which is artificially hidden in cultures of progress), the members of survival cultures recognize that "the future path through future ambushes is a continuation of the old path by which the survivors from the past have come.... The path is tradition, handed down by instruction, example and commentary."[19] This view of change as a re-enactment of a cycle that is both natural and "in part the result of the ceaseless turning of the millstone of the economy within which they live," to quote Berger again,[20] is echoed in Joseph Epes Brown's explanation of how the view of time experienced by primal peoples leads to experiencing traditions. "Events and processes transmitted through oral traditions," Epes Brown writes, "tend to be recounted neither in terms of time past or time future in the lineal sense. Indeed, most native languages have no such tenses to express this. They speak of the perennial reality of the now."[21]

Wes Jackson, writing from his experience on the land, identifies the problem of losing traditional knowledge in a way that relates this to our scientific approach to agriculture. For him, traditions have to do with the long-term recognition that a knowledge of sunlight, moisture, and soil, and not the use of petroleum-based technology, is the basis of a sustainable food supply. But this form of knowledge is disappearing, largely without even being noticed, because we continue to be awed by the science-based knowledge Dewey was so comfortable with (which is not to say Dewey would have supported the political economy that has evolved with this new "cost-effective" and experimental approach to agriculture). According to Jackson:

> Farm families who practiced the traditions associated with planting, tending, harvesting, and storing the produce of the agricultural landscape gathered information, much of it unconsciously, from the time they were infants: in the farm household, in the farm community,

and in the barns and fields. They heard and told stories about relatives and community members who did something funny or were caught in some kind of tragedy. From these stories they learned basic lessons of agronomy. But there was more. There was the information carried by the farmer who looked to the sky and then to the blowing trees or grasses and made a quick decision as to whether or not to make two or more rounds before quitting to do chores. Much of that information has disappeared.... It is the kind of information that has been hard won over the millennia, from the time agriculture began.[22]

It is easy to romanticize these views of tradition, as they are often associated with a past that was simpler and less ambiguous than today's society. Dewey himself harked back to his own upbringing in mid-nineteenth-century Vermont for his metaphorical images of a participatory community. The purpose here, however, is to point out that, while Dewey understood experimental problem solving as re-working and advancing patterns from the past, he was unable to acknowledge that the scientific model of decision making is only one of many valid forms of knowledge, and that valuing substantive traditions is not always a betrayal of human intelligence.

The final criticism of Dewey relates to the manner in which his "method of intelligence," combined with his fusing of the educational with the process of democratic decision making, politicizes all aspects of cultural life, insofar, that is, as culture can be made problematic. The process of politicizing involves recognizing that some aspects of social life, including shared cultural patterns, are problematic and that the problem can no longer be resolved by relying on traditional forms of authority. Language, for example, becomes politicized when it is recognized that its encoding processes and social usage maintain male domination over women. A food item becomes politicized when a scientific study claims it is a causal agent of a disease. Deauthorizing traditional practices and beliefs, as well as simply making them explicit, creates a condition of liminality, a period of conceptual openness that allows for new definitions and relationships to be established. In a very real sense, the political process involves naming old practices and beliefs in new ways, and then establishing a basis of authority for the newly constituted way of thinking. The politicizing process is one of the ways in which traditions are modified, renewed, and, in some instances, totally discarded.

The central role Dewey gave the politicizing process in his educational and social theory is thus not the main problem; both cultural stability and change are the outcome of the exercise of power, which may take many political forms. The problem with Dewey's position is that he maintained that the only legitimate approach to the politicizing process involved the use of the scientific method of inquiry. The politicizing process, for Dewey, begins with a state of doubt, a sense of indeterminacy. Assessing the nature of the problematic situation, formulating a plan of action, and evaluating the consequences of acting upon the ideas and values formulated as a part of the plan of action were, for Dewey, both educational and political if they met the test of representing a communal approach to reconstructing some aspect of social experience. On the other hand, knowledge and values that do not emerge from this inquiry process had, for Dewey, no legitimate standing.

In terms of considering the contribution Dewey makes to an ecologically responsive approach to education or, more generally, to a sustainable form of culture, this fusing of the educational, political, and inquiry process becomes especially problematic. Briefly, the first and perhaps overriding difficulty with Dewey's position is that there is no way to limit the politicizing process. Every aspect of culture that is or can be made to be experienced as a source of doubt and existential uncertainty should, according to Dewey's narrow view of what gives authority to knowledge, be politicized and reconstructed through the use of the scientific method of problem solving. Secondly, Dewey assumed, by equating knowledge with the "consequences of directed action," that there would be a basis for a new social consensus. But he overlooked the historical evidence that points to the deeper psychological forces that enter into the inquiry process, even among scientists, that lead to the manipulation of the data, widely divergent interpretations of what the consequences mean, or even, at the most basic level, disagreement over the nature of the problem that is to be resolved through the inquiry process. In short, Dewey was optimistic about the efficacy of the political process when guided by scientific reason and democratic practices. What he did not recognize was that the method of thinking itself is a powerful means of deauthorizing traditional sources of authority, but weak in providing the basis of new forms of authority, especially those forms of authority that serve to limit the emergence of an anomic form of individualism.

Dewey's view of the politicizing process can also be seen as the expression of a modernizing form of secular consciousness, expansive in defining human wants, nihilistic in its emphasis on individuals making up their own minds and selecting their own values (Dewey would make the social group the basic unit of authority), deeply committed to viewing science as the only reliable source of nonpersonal knowledge and as the guarantor of progress. It is this modern form of consciousness, with its vision of continued progress in technology and personal freedom, that is now exceeding the life-sustaining capabilities of the natural systems that constitute our habitat. Thus the real test of the adequacy of Dewey's ideas would be to compare his conceptual orientation with that of a cultural group that lives in relative balance with its habitat. Viewing the consequences of his ideas for achieving an ecologically sustainable future, in a time frame that must necessarily exceed what is allowed for in Dewey's "method of intelligence" would be the real test of his ideas.

Ironically, the emancipatory educators who are attempting to restore Dewey as the icon he was before an earlier group of emancipatory educators criticized him as an apologist for capitalism find appealing the very ideas and values that disqualify him as an ecologically oriented theorist. Dewey's emphasis on the progressive nature of change, the need to engage in the continual struggle to escape from forms of knowledge and values that have not been validated within the context of the individual's experience, and the desire to reorganize society in a way that eliminates class divisions and unequal power relationships, all have deep appeal to the emancipatory educators who also share Dewey's penchant for fusing the educational and political process. When they finally become aware of the ecological crisis, it will be interesting to see if they view Dewey as a forerunner of deep ecological thinking or as a liberal thinker who framed the problem of modernization and social justice in terms of the Western assumptions we are now beginning to recognize as part of the problem.

Paulo Freire: (1921–)

The same day I sat down to summarize the role of Paulo Freire in redirecting emancipatory educational theorists there was a newspaper account of the International Workshop on Environmental Pollution in China, held in Beijing. Evidence of environmental degradation in China during the last decade of economic growth was dwarfed by projections for the 1990s, which will witness a population jump from 1.1 to 1.25 billion people and a 40 percent increase in energy consumption, produced primarily by using heavily polluting soft coal. Already, according to the report, eighty percent of China's 532 rivers are polluted, with scientists estimating that seventy percent of all fresh water in China may be fouled by the year 2000. Air and noise pollution, plus the 6.6 billion tons of untreated solid waste (some containing hazardous chemicals) buried in landfills and dumped on unused fields, add to the tragic irony of economic "progress" turning China into a toxic wasteland. Earlier in the week came reports about the severity of water pollution in the Baltic states, and the decision of a Latin American country to reject millions of dollars offered if it would turn itself into a landfill for the solid waste of New York City.

With these daily reminders that human progress, in the long run, is an illusion of our own rhetoric and selective perception of economic practices, I began to reread the writings of the most influential educational theorist today. While Dewey's ideas are being rediscovered, Freire's ideas occupy a position of authority that only a few people have dared to criticize openly. Although much about Freire's thinking should be taken seriously, his followers have adopted the role of uncritical disciples—even while they write about using education to liberate the student's consciousness from all forms of domination. But as an examination of Freire's ideas will show, they are marching to the same anthropocentric drum beat that has drowned out the voices of the larger biotic community. In effect, Freire is seen as giving voice to the socially oppressed; but neither he nor his followers have noticed that his writings do not even mention the ecological crisis. The really difficult task of reframing how to deal with the educational aspects of social justice issues in a way that contributes to long-term sustainability of cultural practices thus remains unaddressed.

Freire shares many of the cultural assumptions that give Dewey's educational and social theories their special appeal to liberal thinkers. But he differs from Dewey in one important respect; where Dewey modelled the "method of intelligence" on the scientific method, Freire uses, without really acknowledging the lineage, Martin Buber's distinction between dialogue and monologue. Although a few of Freire's former followers recognize that the process of dialogue, which is the central feature of the teacher-student relationship, is based on Western assumptions, the idea of dialogue is interpreted as a way of communicating between culture groups which is free of domination. Freire's educational theory leads to an ecological double bind where specific forms of injustice are to be ameliorated through education (such as overcoming illiteracy), while at the same time the subjugated people are being urged to adopt a package of anthropocentric beliefs about the nature of "man," freedom, and what constitutes authority and empowerment. Understanding how this is so will require an examination of his philosophical anthropology, and not the literacy program upon which his earlier reputation deservedly rests. Besides, Freire's understanding of what it means to be human seems now to occupy a more critical place in the thinking of his followers who are attempting to articulate what they call a "critical pedagogy" for society.

Over the 20 years of his most seminal writings, Freire has steadfastly held to the view that there are essential qualities that must be realized as aspects of everyday life if people are to achieve their human potential as free beings. In understanding these qualities it is essential to recognize how certain background categories shape Freire's way of thinking. Although he has, on occasion, referred to "culture," he either equates the term with the outcome of human action (like the artifacts and symbolic constructs of humans) or treats it as synonymous with "limit situations," where the socially constituted culture is a source of domination. Human nature, as he sees it, is universally the same; but humans may express their essential nature in culturally distinct ways. Unlike Confucian thought, for example, which understands human possibilities in terms of the Tao and thus not in terms of individual freedom and responsibility, Freire holds that freedom is the essential human characteristic, realized through a process of critical reflection. Again, this process of reflection, or what he terms "conscientization," which most thoughtful people would recognize as a Western interpretation of the rational process, is viewed by Freire as a universal characteristic of all people who move from a state of domination ("semi-intransitive consciousness") to a state of freedom ("critically transitive consciousness). For Freire, culture is not understood as providing the conceptual templates for organizing social, psychic, and thought patterns, including how the self is understood in relation to others. Thus he never addresses culture in terms of the beliefs and practices of a specific cultural group, like the Hopi, Chinese, or French. Rather, the basic ontological unit is the individual as a conscious agent and, Freire hopes, a reflective self-directing individual. Like Dewey, Freire recognizes that culture is humanly created but he tends to view it as a source of alienation from the active expression of critical thought.

Before citing the evidence of Freire's penchant for treating as a universal a distinctly Western view of human nature, the second taken-for-granted aspect of his thinking must be mentioned. The human condition, including educational processes, is understood in binary terms that echo the earlier theological categories of salvation and sin: freedom or domination, dialogue or monologue, conscientization or a "banking" approach to education. This pattern of thinking is critical to understanding both the appeal Freire has for emancipatory theorists (his position is never complex enough to be ambiguous) and his inability to relate his philosophical anthropology to the distinct patterns of those cultural groups whose thought and cultural patterns are inextricably bound together even when they make innovative reinterpretations of traditional patterns.

The essential ideas of Freire, as well as his reliance upon Western cultural assumptions, are represented in the following statement:

Human existence cannot be silent, nor can it be nourished by false words, but only by true words, with which men transform the world. To exist, humanly, is to *name* the world, to change it. Once named, the world in its turn reappears to the namers as a problem and requires of them a new *naming*. Men are not built in silence, but in word, in work, in action-reflection.

But while to say the true word—which is work, which is praxis—is to transform the world, saying that word is not the privilege of some few men, but the right of every man. Consequently, no one can say a true word alone—nor can he say it *for* another, in a prescriptive act which robs others of their words.

Dialogue is the encounter between men, mediated by the world, in order to name the world. Hence, dialogue cannot occur between those who want to name the world and those who do not wish this naming— between those who deny other men the right to speak their world and those whose right to speak has been denied them. Those who have been denied their primordial right to speak their word must first reclaim this right and prevent the continuation of this dehumanizing aggression.[23]

The world (the context of daily life) named by others thus is a continual source of alienation from the individual's authentic existential self as a being who must name the world anew. As Freire put it in *The Politics of Education*, "conscientization (critical reflection) thus involves a constant clarification of what remains hidden.[24] This process of critical reflection, which leads to a new bases of action that grows out of a dialogical form of communication with others, represents the making of authentic human history. This is the vision of the Western humanist who views change as progressive when guided by the de-mystification process of critical intelligence.

It is difficult to take a critical stance against applying this Western philosophical anthropology to education, particularly when education is represented as an alienating and disempowering experience. Who is willing to challenge the language of emancipation, particularly when there are so many real forms of exploitive relationships and outmoded traditions? Yet for all of the positive dimensions of his thinking—

like reinforcing the importance of dialogue and the use of critical reflection (qualities that good teachers have always attempted to exhibit and encourage)—questions must be raised about Freire's silence on the ecological crisis. The deeper questions relate to whether naming the world from the perspective of an individual who must continue, through the critical reflection—praxis dialectic—to rename the world is an appropriate way of understanding the proper relation of humans to the ecosystems. The hidden Eurocentric assumptions that are fundamental to his thinking—the progressive nature of change, the view that only critical reflection can be the source of legitimate knowledge, the view of "man" as the central actor in the universe—have already been pointed out to be ecologically problematic. Although he would not admit it, these are the same cultural assumptions that undergird and give legitimacy to the development of environmentally exploitive technologies. The only elements not reinforcing this Western mind set are Freire's concern with exploitive human relationships and with basing communication on dialogue.

Another basic problem is Freire's narrow view of knowledge which, in effect, delegitimates the forms of knowledge within the dominant culture that are ecologically responsive (the tacit forms of knowledge identified by Jackson) as well as the myriad forms of knowledge of groups that have evolved habitat based cultures—like the Hopi, the Australian aborigines, and the others. Freire's insistence that all knowledge be made explicit and judged in terms of the existential time frame of an individual (or the group, if dialogue is possible) leads to viewing traditions as a source of domination. He does not recognize that in the broadest sense tradition and culture are nearly interchangeable terms that refer to complex message systems and artifacts whose use, and thus whose value as a source of empowerment, are largely taken for granted. To recognize traditions as a source of authority in people's lives does not have to lead to the claim that all traditions must be uncritically accepted. Traditions cannot be adequately understood in the binary categories Freire uses; nor is there in his system any way of assessing the worth of traditions overturned as his idealized individual continually renames the world. Our understanding of tradition (as opposed to the static image of the past that should more properly be called "traditionalism") is critical to understanding how to live in an interdependent relationship with the habitat. Being able to take seriously forms of knowledge of more ecologically balanced cultures, which we have given the pejorative label of "traditional societies," may even enable us to recognize more clearly our own cultural patterns that are getting us into difficulty. It may also help us recognize and even learn from groups outside the dominant culture who have developed ecologically sound traditions, in technology, communal/ habitat relationships, and psychic/spiritual development.

The anthropocentrism of Freire's position can be seen in the statement that "as active participants and real subjects, we can make history only when we are continually critical of our lives."[25] Aldo Leopold's statement that "an ethic, ecologically, is a limitation on freedom of action in the struggle for freedom" and that we need a land ethic that "enlarges the boundaries of community to include soils, waters, plants, and animals, or collectively: the land"[26] points to our need for learning from the experience of others, including our own traditions, those of other people, as well as the ancient information encoded in the biota.

Critical Pedagogy

In the 1970s spokespeople for the emancipatory tradition in education identified themselves with various schools of Marxist thought: first the economic determinist (structuralist) position given prominence in *Schooling in Capitalist America*, by Samuel Bowles and Herbert Gintis, followed by the attempts to use the ideas of Antonio Gramsci and then Jurgen Habermas for illuminating the interplay between culture, education, and class domination. With the growing ascendancy of Freire's influence among educational theorists concerned with radical reform of the schools, the interest in using a Marxist framework and language waned until only the general targets of capitalism and class domination appear visible in their literature. The new arenas for "resistance" (to use Henry Giroux's phrase) added to the past concern with class domination include race and gender. But the most important development, particularly since the emancipatory educators followed Giroux's lead in using the label "critical pedagogy" to designate their movement, has been the emphasis on using the classroom to liberate students from all cultural traditions. While Freire, in his most recent statement, acknowledges that "only political action in society can make social transformation, not critical study in the classroom," and that there "must be limits on behavior" in the classroom, his followers are propounding a view of education that makes the autonomous individual the epicenter of the universe. Ironically, the deterioration of the environment continues to remain off their list of educational and political concerns.

The spokespeople for a critical pedagogy are important for two reasons: The first is that they now have a large following among educational theorists who represent an alternative to the technocratic educators who largely dominate the professional development and training of new teachers. The second is that both their theory of a critical pedagogy and its conceptual basis represent the celebration of a form of nihilism that will intensify the more ecologically damaging aspects of modernism.

Following the lead of Freire, Giroux, Peter McLaren, and Ira Shor, the critical pedagogues are building a theory of education upon the Dewey/Freire assumption that the educational process is inherently political, and that teachers, as "transformative intellectuals," must align themselves against all forms of injustice and cultural domination. The critical pedagogues have dropped Dewey's concern with the scientific method of intelligence as well as his argument that the socially constituted nature of intelligence should lead educators to reject the goal of individual autonomy in favor of group consensus and interdependency. But the nihilistic elements in Dewey's theory, that the purpose of thought and values is to reconstruct experience in a never-ending process and that critical thought is free of cultural influence, still appear to be part of the intellectual baggage of the critical pedagogy theorists.

In sorting out the distinctiveness (and ecologically problematic nature) of the educational and social vision of critical pedagogy, it is important to set aside the binary categories they use to represent themselves as the only group concerned with issues of gender, race, and economic poverty. Giroux, McLaren, Shor, and Freire, who set the example that the other critical pedagogues follow, always deal with social justice issues at an abstract level, and thus never engage the cultural complexity of specific political issues, like how to deal with a group that may be the victims of racial prejudice and economic discrimination but who largely adopt the "right to life" stance on the abortion issue. Nor do they deal with the social class and cultural aspects of issues that are at the center of the feminist movement. As slogans intended to provide a general focus of messianic energy, "resistance," "emancipatory power," "transformative intellectuals," and so forth, must remain ethereal and thus avoid the contradictions and splintering effects of the real world of politics.

The role of the teacher, the nature of the curriculum, and the political role of the school in freeing society of all forms of domination are framed by the critical pedagogue's philosophic anthropology; that is, the image of the emancipated individual they borrowed directly from Freire's notion that freedom requires each person continually to rename the world. They also retain the binary categories of domination and liberation that are the hallmark of Freire's thinking. Empowerment, according to the critical pedagogy theorists, is associated with the autonomous individual; in fact, Shor represents it as the outcome of an education that "desocializes" the individual. For Shor, education is either "socializing students into the status quo" or a matter of challenging the dominant myths.[27] Giroux's way of understanding the ideal connection between the autonomous individual and the political process is reflected in the following statement: "It is important to acknowledge that the notion of democracy cannot be grounded in some ahistorical, transcendent notion of truth or authority."[28] In a more recent book, *Schooling and the Struggle for Public Life* (1988), he urges radical educators to develop a "defensible view of authority based on a provisional morality that promotes individual autonomy."[29] This view of democracy as incompatible with culturally shared moral norms and traditions (what would happen to the Constitution in Giroux's ideal political world?) is equalled, if not surpassed, by the vision of autonomy presented by McLaren and Rhonda Hammer. In an article on "Critical Pedagogy and the Postmodern Challenge," they urge educators to work out a liberating pedagogy that recognizes that "to *live life as if it generated meaning* is to live within the contingency and uncertainty of the present, a present in which ethics, tradition, and agency are revealed to be social constructions or cultural fictions."[30] Thus, the always critical judgment of the individual becomes, according to the philosophical anthropology of the critical pedagogy theorists, the momentary authority for the ideas, values, and other cultural patterns that give substance to experience.

This view of individual autonomy goes beyond Dewey's idea of the individual as a problem solver. A state of doubt that reflects the breakdown of traditional patterns initiates the inquiry process for Dewey—presumably the nonproblematic background of cultural patterns is beyond the scope of reflective action. The view of the individual central to the position of critical pedagogy requires that all aspects of culture be subjected to critical appraisal by each individual. As McLaren puts it, "*a student's voice* is not a reflection of the world as much as it is a *constitutive force that both mediates and shapes reality within historically constructed practices and relationships of power.*" Teachers facilitate the emancipatory process "when a student's voice is allowed to assert itself so as to be both confirmed and analyzed, in terms of the particular values and ideologies that it represents."[31] One last statement helps establish the extreme nature of their formulation of how far emancipation (or "desocialization," to use Shor's term) is to be carried. The task of critical pedagogy, writes McLaren and Hammer, is "deliberately designed to rupture the unitary fixity and cohesiveness of social life and resist attempts at asserting the homogeneity of the social and public sphere."[32]

Out of this "pedagogical negativism," which leads students to doubt everything except their own voices, they will experience "a state of collective autonomy in which they have the power to determine rationally and freely the nature and direction of their collective existence."[33] Thus the social world is reconstituted as free of cultural traditions, social infrastructures, and the psychological complexities that have transformed similar utopian visions (justified in similar rhetoric) into police states that serve the interests of the ideological visionaries. Ironically, if emancipation were to be carried far enough to rid each student from the historical patterns of thinking encoded in the language, the new society would indeed provide the conditions of absolute and final liberation—for there would be no basis for communication and thus no means to carry out "symbolic violence"!

Given their view that "culture is never depoliticized," the curriculum would be whatever students and teachers experience as a source of external constraint on their own autonomous actions; it is the latter that the critical pedagogues view as always contributing to a "qualitatively better world for all people." The curriculum thus becomes viewed as "contested terrain" where students achieve the Deweyian and Freireian vision of uniting education and politics, and the teacher plays the role of "the transformative intellectual."

There are indeed forms of injustice in the world; and few people, even conservatives like Adler and Bloom, would argue that the educational process should foster the blind acceptance of past cultural practices and beliefs. Most thoughtful people would also acknowledge that one of the possible purposes of formal education is to contribute to the renewal and, in many areas of social life, the radical transformation of social institutions and beliefs. The political problem lies in agreeing on the nature of the renewal and radical transformation processes—a problem that becomes even more exacerbated as the voices of people become more assertive. Given the radical populist stance of the critical pedagogues, it would be interesting to see how different ethnic groups—particularly those who do not share the tenets of that stream of Eurocentric thought which represents the individual as the basic social unit, change as inherently progressive, and critical thought as the basis of authority— would react to having their children guided by a "transformative intellectual" (presumably one who would also be certified by the state) into the "contested terrain" of everyday culture where all existing "relations of power and privilege" would be subjected to a "counterhegemonic" critique. This is the road, I suspect, that will only be taken by theorists who enjoy the security of university tenure. Few parents and people who have played critical roles in recent social reform movements would be willing to support the critical pedagogues' vision of education—even if enough "transformative intellectuals" could be found to guide students in this nihilistic journey into individual autonomy (or even "collective autonomy").

Like the technocratic educators who enthrall their audiences with the latest techniques derived from brain research or the latest developments in pop psychology, the theorists of critical pedagogy also provide an opportunity for like-minded people to meet and share in an uplifting vision of empowerment. But unfortunately their vision and rhetoric promote those aspects of the Western mind set that is contributing to the degradation of the environment: the individual or group of individuals who would constitute the "state of collective autonomy" is still viewed as independent of the natural environment; critical reflection remains the only legitimate expression of intelligence, which excludes both traditional cultures and the complex information exchanges that characterize an ecology; change is still understood in human and culturally specific terms that equate progress only with an expansion of the individual's sense of freedom. Understanding the interdependence of the human culture/natural habitat relationship in terms of what is sustainable over the long term, now the bottom line in the political process, is simply not part of the Enlightenment vision of emancipation uncritically accepted by the followers of Dewey and Freire.

In effect, the scale of the ecological crisis challenges us to become radical thinkers in reconsidering all the foundations of our own culture, and to study the paths taken by other cultures more aware of the dangers of exceeding the sustaining capacity of their habitats. The advocates of critical pedagogy, unfortunately, are not radical enough to reconsider the ideological framework they inherited from Dewey and Freire, who in turn were indebted to earlier generations of Western thinkers equally caught in the myth of an anthropocentric universe. And because they use the highly privileged language of Western humanism, they are likely to continue dominating the limited discourse within the field of education which addresses social and political issues in a critical manner. Meanwhile, we continue to learn of new oil spills, solid waste disposal problems, depleted traditional fisheries, and toxins in our water supply. The avalanche of information on the human impact on the environment is now so great that it is almost inconceivable that it is still being ignored by people who represent themselves as the leaders in education. But unfortunately this is the case.

It is now time to turn our attention to another aspect of public education—textbooks. This will help put in clearer focus whether the content of textbooks complements the efforts of teachers attempting to include environmental education in the curriculum. Bringing the discussion down to the classroom, we may see both the true scope of the problem and, we may hope, ways in which genuine educational contributions to ameliorating the ecological crisis can be made.

4

Anthropocentrism in Textbooks

Conservative and emancipatory critics of education seem to have had little direct influence on the process of classroom socialization. This is not to say that public education is immune to shifts in ideological orientations. At some point, however, arguments about what needs to be changed in education require consensus if ideas are to become the basis of reform. But achieving a consensus on what new guiding ideas should be embraced is becoming increasingly difficult. These days everybody is supposed to make up her or his own mind, and the problem of consensus is now being made even more difficult by the increasing awareness that proponents of educational change are often unconsciously spokespeople for some specific cultural group—or a particular gender. Yet the increasing impotence of ideologically driven criticisms of public education does not mean that the classroom is a neutral arena where students have the opportunity to learn in an objective way what the world is really about.

Indeed, the classroom can best be understood as an ecology of cultural patterns. These patterns are the basis of thought processes and communication about relationships; they are also basic to how the more physical aspects of the classroom are utilized as part of the educational process. But this ecology of thoughts, relationships, and communication, which make up the living reality of a classroom, does not reflect a single cultural orientation. Ethnicity, gender, age, social class, and the media give the classroom a heterogeneity that may be missed by teachers or observers, who often tend to see only what their own cultural orientation allows. Acknowledging both the limited influence of educational criticism and the culturally diverse influences in a classroom, it is important to recognize an aspect of the classroom that has an element that appears to transcend the political and cultural complexity of the classroom, namely the textbooks that are the backbone of the curriculum supposed to be the basis of formal education for all students. The main concern here about the content of textbooks has to do with whether the "factual" knowledge, as well as hidden assumptions and values, reinforce the mind set that assumes a continuing expansion of material well-being

Part of the folk knowledge about schools is that textbooks are generally inadequate on a number of counts, and thus should not be accorded too much significance in the education or indoctrination of students. To understand how schools are responding to the ecological crisis, this line of folk thinking would hold, attention should be given to whether students are learning about climax forests, wetlands, and the myriad ways that people can soften their impact on the environment, such as learning how to recycle and to avoid the use of polystyrene products in the lunch room. These educational activities are indeed important, but they seem more peripheral to the core cultural issues raised by the current decline in the sustaining capacities of the natural systems. These issues relate to the belief and value systems of the dominant culture, which are communicated through textbooks. How students learn to think about success, progress, individualism, community, technology, science, and so forth, is more critical to ameleriorating the ecological crisis, because these are the beliefs that guide our social behavior, including our use of technology. They are also the beliefs that many people in Third World countries associate with becoming "modern" and "progressive," thus adding to the potential human impact on the ecosystems.

Focusing on the cultural orientations reinforced in textbooks does not preclude recognizing other aspects of the curriculum that may, to some critics, be viewed as more powerful influences on the students' thought processes. The impact of television and computer games on students has long been recognized as pre-empting the importance of what students are encouraged to think about in the classroom. But even within the classroom there is a wide variety of curriculum resources, from film and computer software to supplementary readings assigned by teachers who, in many instances, regard textbooks as dull and oversimplified.

The range of intellectual qualities that teachers bring to the educational process is even more varied. But given the limited characteristics of their university education, and the even more narrow approach to their professional education, it seems safe to make the generalization that few teachers understand the most critical aspects of cultural transmission in the classroom, particularly how language encodes earlier thought processes, the way in which most of the particular culture learned is taken for granted, and how cultural assumptions underlie the structures of knowledge that constitute the subject areas of the curriculum. This is not to say there are no bright and intellectually stimulating teachers: Indeed, there are very many. Rather, the point is that neither the university nor professional education of most teachers provide an adequate basis for understanding the interconnection of culture, language, and consciousness—which, ironically, is at the heart of the educational process.

The hidden dynamics of how the culture that is part of the textbook writer's and the teacher's natural attitudes, their sense of unexamined reality, becomes shared with students and taken for granted gives textbooks their important role in the educational cultural transmission process. By not understanding this process, even the most gifted and environmentally conscious teachers take on a more marginal importance, thus leaving unchallenged the way in which textbooks (actually, the mind of the textbook writers) reproduce the conceptual templates of the dominant culture in the next generation of adults.

The questions that need to be asked about the conceptual building blocks of mainstream Western culture reinforced in textbooks must be framed in terms of the newly recognized realities of a limited habitat. These include: What is the image of the individual that is represented, and how is success understood? What are represented as the most central activities in people's lives, and how are these activities related to the nature of power? What forms of knowledge are represented as important, and what is the basis of their authority? How is community represented? What is given as the primary basis of human relationships, i.e., is it primarily economic or political in nature? How is the nature of tradition understood, and which forms of tradition are represented?

How are humans viewed in relation to the natural environment? What is the role assigned to science and technology, and are they treated as synonymous with social progress? What is the nature of the limits that humans face? What are the basic human values and what is the basis of their authority in people's lives?

As in any form of communication where foreground messages (explicit and "factual" information) are always embedded in an equally powerful background message system (the domain of implicit cultural assumptions), textbooks are more than repositories of multiple and often hidden cultural forms of understanding. They are also representative of a political consensus in that they must survive a series of political decisions that begin with an editor's judgment about what will be accepted in the regions in which the book will be marketed, and culminates with the decision of a state or local textbook selection committee. As controversial images, facts, and interpretations will lead to exclusion from the list of state approved adoptions, the content of textbooks tends to represent the stock of knowledge, assumptions, and patterns of thinking shared by the politically and culturally dominant in society. The political process that influences every step of their creation, from selection of authors to placement in the classroom, insures as we all know that controversial content will be omitted or rejected . But the characteristics we tend to ignore have to do with the underlying beliefs and values that, by virtue of their being taken for granted, tend to be invisible to students, teachers, and the more vigilant members of the community.

Before we begin the task of making explicit the mind set reproduced in elementary and secondary textbooks, it may be useful to reiterate the culture-language-thought connection, and why it is so difficult to recognize. Understanding this aspect of the student–culture relationship, particularly the influence of textbooks on consciousness, will also help clarify in later chapters how the educational process can be given a more central role in changing those aspects of the culture that are ecologically damaging.

In framing our analysis of the cultural messages communicated in textbooks it is important to keep in mind that teachers may use them in a variety of ways, from treating them as a source of objective information to using them as examples of taken-for-granted beliefs that need to be examined critically. Given the wide range of perspectives that teachers bring to their interpretation of textbooks, influenced by their own patterns of socialization, there are formative processes that have an influence on the student's thought patterns. In the influence of language on thought, three characteristics of language stand out as critically important to any consideration of the content of textbooks. To summarize the essential points: (1) language is not a neutral conduit through which ideas are communicated to others, but plays a constitutive role in organizing the thought process itself; (2) just as language enables us to think about experience (to name it and to think about its patterns and relationships), the lack of language can leave areas of experience unreflected upon and unarticulated—that is, unrecognized; (3) the metaphorical nature of language involves, as can be seen in the process of analogic thinking—which may have been carried out by earlier generations, encoding a schema of understanding that, in turn, influences current thought processes.

Cultural knowledge that becomes part of the natural attitude of the teacher and students may represent the most formative and powerful aspect of the educational process. Yet it is the least understood, partly because its very nature precludes easy recognition and partly because of the long-standing Western cultural tradition of associating knowledge with the outcome of a rational process performed by individuals. In analyzing textbooks, we want to reverse this Enlightenment prejudice by recognizing the pervasive and formative nature of unrecognized cultural patterns and assumptions. In effect, we will be attending to the unexamined messages as well as the explicit explanations. The variables still beyond the reach of our analysis have to do with the stock of implicit beliefs that students and teachers bring to the curriculum. This is where the cultural backgrounds of the students and teachers become especially important.

To eliminate confusion about what can be learned from an examination of textbooks, it is necessary to emphasize several points. The first is that students and teachers do not encounter as blank slates the content of textbooks. Every person brings a set of preunderstandings that reflect the interplay of his or her own interactions with the hidden cultural patterns acquired through socialization to the primary culture. These preunderstandings constitute the person's natural attitudes which, in turn, exert a powerful influence on future learning. The cultural assumptions and analogues taken for granted by the textbook writer may correspond to the natural attitude of some students, which may result in further learning within a shared framework of understanding—and the further reinforcement of the student's particular attitudes. The textbook writer's stock of taken-for-granted knowledge may also diverge significantly from the patterns of thought and values of other students, which may result in a wide range of responses, from doubt about the adequacy of their own beliefs to an awareness that the textbook has a definite cultural bias.

The second point is that the content of textbooks reflects both the dominant culture's patterns of resilience and its areas of resistance to change. On one level, textbooks are changed to take account of what publishers perceive as shifts in the public consensus. Minorities and women are now given greater visibility, and words like "environment" and "ecology" appear more frequently, which gives the casual reader the sense that the textbook is current. On a deeper level, however, textbooks reproduce patterns of thinking that extend back to the beginnings of the Industrial Revolution, and beyond, to the Judeo/Greek/Christian foundations of Western thought. This substratum of cultural beliefs, which has recently been given visibility by feminists and deep ecologists, changes much more slowly. It is this dimension of textbook content, rather than the cosmetic level, that we shall be examining. Thus we will not be dealing with so-called "factual information" so much as the cultural assumptions and analogues that frame how the "facts" are to be understood and establish the boundaries of understanding.

Although the textbooks examined here are representative of cultural reproduction in American schools, the same questions could (and should) be asked about the cultural assumptions and analogues being communicated to youth in other countries. Our patterns may contribute to a disproportionate part of the ecological crisis, but it must be recognized that they are not essentially North American. Rather, the origins are European, and they are now associated with being modern and progressive.

Textbook Representations of the Anthropocentric Universe

The Western myth that humans have a privileged status among the forms of life making up the biotic community is one of the central cultural messages students encounter in schools. Textbook titles and chapter headings in the early grades rather innocently announce that humans are the reference point for making sense of the world. "The Earth You Live on," "Our Regions," *Our World: Our Land and Heritage,* "What Do You Want in Your Environment?" and "Our Resources" are typical textbook examples of the unexamined conceptual order that mirrors what most students will have already encountered through television and the consumer emporiums that are the end point of technological/ economic activity. The use of pronouns, it might be argued, are intended to help students identify personally with the content of the textbooks. In a sense, each student is being invited to consider the features of the earth that she/he lives on. But here the textbook writer's concern with capturing the students' interest (the old concern with relevance, again) gets mixed up with cultural myth whereby students are further reinforced in thinking that humans are separate from nature. That humans are interdependent with other life forms (that is, the latter are not "our" resources) and that the person can be understood as giving individualized expression to cultural patterns are not part of the conceptual mapping process that characterizes textbooks. But chapter titles are not the only means of keeping alive the Western dualism of "man" and nature.

The sense of separation that leads to thinking in terms of "our environment," to experimenting with animals in order to advance our knowledge and life expectancy, and to fouling the environment with toxic wastes and chemical interventions—to cite a few of the many human practices symptomatic of the current crisis—cannot be traced back to a single cause, like the Biblical account of creation or Francis Bacon's injunction to learn the secrets of nature in order to better control it for human purposes. Here we shall be considering the multiple ways that textbooks, as one aspect of the curriculum, contribute to the cultural orientation toward the environment increasingly recognized as pathological.

One of the most intriguing ideas to emerge from recent

scholarship is that literacy contributes to (but does not cause) a form of consciousness that views separation as a source of empowerment. Although the debate is still ongoing, it is possible to summarize the more essential differences that separate a literacy based consciousness from the characteristics of oral traditions. The discussion can be framed in terms of the school curriculum if we keep in mind that children move from a home environment that is primarily oral to a classroom environment where academic success depends upon learning to think and communicate in the patterns associated with literacy.

Literacy allows for communication across time and space in a way not possible in spoken discourse. Authors, for example, may be ahead of their times, and thus may be able to communicate with future generations who discover their books on a library shelf; similarly, computers now make communication through print nearly instantaneous between vast distances. These characteristics of print-based communication are seen, according to conventional wisdom, as one of the signs of the progressive nature of technology. But this empowerment also involves changes in thought patterns and forms of relationships that have been largely ignored until recent years. Briefly, in print-based communication the emphasis is on the message to be conveyed, generally to an abstract audience. The process of composing the message—writing the memorandum, book, TV script, and so forth—requires the solitude necessary for reflective thought. It also involves a sender-receiver model of communication; that is, it does not evolve through a participatory process, as is the case in most spoken discourse.

Just as we can see that print communication fosters individualism and abstract, decontextualized thinking on the part of the writer, the standpoint of the reader reveals a similar form of reinforcement. Reading is always individualistic (even when carried on in groups), and it fosters an abstract way of thinking where the printed word becomes more real than its experiential referent. The reader's ability to compare two or more written accounts, and to analyze the development of the ideas and arguments put forth by the author, points to how the stability that print gives to ideas fosters an analytical way of thinking.

Although other cultural patterns and values must be

taken into account when assessing the importance that a society accords to one form of discourse over the other, it is nevertheless possible to see how spoken discourse reinforces a different form of consciousness. As Deborah Tannen points out, speaking generally involves an emphasis on negotiating an interpersonal relationship, where contextual cues and multiple channels of communication make it a participatory process.[1] The use of social space, voice (pitch, rhythm, pauses, etc.), and body as part of the message exchange brings together the body's activities as a medium that connects otherness and thought. Writing and reading, on the other hand, involve a relationship between the mind, the eye, and the printed (now electronic) word, and a limited range of motor skills.

The cultural orientation fostered by the privileging of print-based knowledge in schools (books, educational software, and class discussions that lead to some form of print-based evaluation) has a direct relationship with cultural patterns we now recognize as contributing to the long tradition of taking the environment for granted. Ron and Suzanne Scollon summarized the essentials of a print-oriented culture: "The word comes to take precedence over situation, analysis takes precedence over participation, isolated thought takes precedence over conversation and storytelling, the individual takes precedence over community."[2] The use of words to express rational thought, which can then be universalized, and the emphasis on individualism, which is a distillation of the Scollons' statement, are basic to the Western approach to technologically based progress. They are also the cultural patterns that have contributed to devaluing the importance of context, relationships, and an enlarged sense of community. To put it another way, the characteristics of thought associated with the privileging of written discourse as the source of knowledgement are also the essential characteristics of an anthropocentric universe.

Textbook Images of the Individual

In all public education students encounter in textbooks an image of the individual as an autonomous agent engaged in social and technological activities. The pronoun "you" is ubiquitous from grade one through grade twelve. It is typical for the primary student to read "You live on Earth" and "What do you want in your environment?" and for the high school student to encounter a similar image of the autonomous individual. In the opening chapter of *Creative Living: Basic Concepts in Home Economics*, "Focus on You," students read, "You probably spend a lot of time thinking about how other people see you. Maybe you have a hard time figuring out who you are and how you should act.... One way to help yourself make these decisions is to discover what's important to you."³

This use of the pronoun "you" is an example of how a cultural orientation reflecting the taken-for-granted beliefs of the teacher and larger public goes unnoticed. Yet its significance exceeds the use of pronouns as part of a linguistic grid for maintaining gender stereotypes, a process that has received extensive attention in recent years. In the examples cited above the pronoun "you" is used in a way that encodes some of the most deeply held assumptions of Western thought. The primary school student, for example, is learning to think of self as living on the earth, and will later read about nature as "wilderness." That is, students are learning to think about themselves in terms of these most fundamental human–nature relationships. As they come to see themselves as self-contained entities distinct from other things by virtue of having thoughts and feelings, it is natural to think in terms of "What do you want in your environment?" The natural environment is thus no different, in terms of this pattern of thinking, from other aspects of the environment—where the students are encouraged to think about the kinds of friends, consumer choices, and physical aspects of the community they want. The self is thus not understood as the individualized expression of interdependent patterns and relationships that collectively constitute an environment. This would require using terms such as "part of" or "interdependent with" to express the self–environment relationship.

The preposition "on" ("The Earth You Live on" in the chapter heading) expresses the form of relationship that is consistent with the verb to "see" as the way of knowing about relationships. This reference to vision, which involves a viewer relationship, where the "outside" world is seen as a picture, further strengthens the sense of self as separate and self-contained.

To avoid the criticism that too much is being made of a

limited number of examples, I will cite examples from a broad range of textbooks. In one of the leading art textbooks, *Discover Art*, students find "You can create art. You can create artworks about things you see and remember.... Think of an original idea for a picture. An *original* idea is different from the ideas of other people."[4] A high school text on economics, *Understanding Economics*, states that, "Everyone faces the problem of scarcity. Consequently, all individuals must make *choices*. In fact, some economists define *economics* as the science of choice. Since all individual wants cannot be satisfied, each of us must choose which ones to satisfy."[5] The theme of individual autonomy is often given as an ideal. Witness the explanation given students in *Teen Guide*: "To become truly grown up, a person must gain independence. Achieving independence is a process of separating what is you from what is your family.... To achieve independence, you must first recognize your basic needs and then find ways to meet them." But the authors warn against carrying this ideal too far by posing the question: "Do you want total independence? Since we depend on our environment for survival, we can never be completely independent of each other. Nor is total independence desirable. Think about the emotional, mental, and social needs in this chapter."[6] It is important to note that "environment" is used here to refer to society, not the rest of the biotic community. Drawing upon Abraham Maslow's hierarchy of human needs, another textbook, *Housing Decisions*, explains to students that, "if you can meet the final need of *self-actualization*, you will have developed your full potential as a human being." And on the potentially perplexing problem of how autonomous individuals decide what values to hold, students read "What is important to you? What do you like? Your answers to these questions tell you what your values are. Your values are different than those of anyone else."[7]

To summarize the distinctiveness of the thought patterns encoded in the language given students for thinking about who they are in their most basic relationships: thought and values, while initially determined by society (during stages of immaturity), are freely chosen by mature and autonomous individuals; the highest form of thinking and expression involves original ideas; the autonomous individual lives in a social world (but not to be carried too far), and it is in this domain that relationships must be nurtured; and the individual lives on the earth, which can further be understood as the source of natural resources. The metaphor "natural resource," like the metaphor "you," must be understood here as encoding the deepest cultural assumptions for understanding relationships.

Basis of Human Relationships

Through the use of analogues, formal explanations, and photographs, U.S. textbooks provide students with models of human relationships and activities. What students encounter are representations meant to be understood as factual and objective, but in reality represent the conscious and unconscious understandings of the author. For our purposes here, the critical issue has to do with the textbook representations of human activities relating to three questions: What activities do humans engage in? How do these activities influence the way in which individuals relate to the environment? How do these human activities frame what constitutes the basis of community?

In textbooks, human activities seem to fall into two categories: social and technological. Often the nature of technological involvement influences the nature of the social relationships. Less frequently, depending on subject area, the social relationship revolves around the activities of conversation, play, and even intimacy—like in the chapters on "Boy/Girl Relationships" and "What Is a Family?" in one of the social psychology textbooks. Even in textbooks having as their main objective the fostering of self-understanding within a variety of social relationships, another set of cultural themes are reinforced at a subliminal level. These themes have to do with consumerism and physical space organized according to the taken-for-granted patterns of white middle class society. And these cultural themes point to the most important category of human activity, which involves the uses and benefits of technology.

Before considering how technological activity is represented, it is important to explain how human relationships are framed both through pictures and descriptions within a more subtle message system in the United States that equates consumerism with happiness and success. In the chapter on "Boy/Girl Relationships," for example, there are two photographs where adolescents are represented in two different situations—casual relationships and "first romantic feelings." In one photograph well-dressed adolescents are standing by their new bicycles, and in the other the human relationship centers around a stereosystem. Although corporation logos are never shown, each textbook picture represents people as consumers—always dressed differently and always surrounded by the artifacts of a consumer culture that look new and neatly organized, like a display window.

The cultural message in the picture is often supported by textual explanations. In a section on "What Do Your Clothes Say?" students encounter the following: "Clothes tell a lot about what you think of yourself. They also help others decide what to think about you.... Real maturity is knowing how to dress for different occasions." And on the economic treadmill that reflects our resources-don't-matter approach to fashions, students encounter such vacuous statements as "Fashion is big business. Without new styles each year, people would probably buy less clothing. Often a style becomes popular because it is the only one people can find in the stores."[8] A primary grade textbook, *Understanding Communities*, provides a somewhat more expanded view of the main human activities: "Suburban communities have places where people can fill their needs and wants. But people in suburban communities often travel to nearby large cities to work, to shop, and to have fun."[9]

Aside from history and civics textbooks, which largely tell the story of the evolution of current social and political developments but are silent on the impact of these developments on the life-sustaining capabilities of the habitat, textbooks in the social sciences project an image of the person as a user of technology. This image complements the idea that consumerism is a primary basis of human relationships. For example, in one primary-level textbook the pictures of airplanes, logging equipment, roads, and factories (which appear under the heading. "The Earth We Live On") prepare the student for a later section of the book entitled "Shopping Center." In another textbook, *Communities and Resources*, students encounter explanations of all the technologies essential for transportation, and an equally detailed explanation of the different forms of natural resources—coal, oil, natural gas, etc.—essential for sustaining this technology. The message communicated to students is that our technologies determine which aspects of the habitat have value: that is, viewed as natural resources. But the continual representation of technological activity does not, as we shall see later, provide students with an understanding of human–environment relationships and how technology mediates human experience. Rather, the message students are supposed to come away with is that all forms of technology are a natural and essentially nonproblematic aspect of human activity.

Relation to Environment

Anthropocentrism is perhaps the most important feature of elementary textbook explanations of our relationship to the environment. But students in a high school biology class will encounter, if the teacher follows the textbook, the scientific paradigm that treats humans as just another species that contributes to the diversity of ecosystems. However, this shift from the anthropocentric framework to the reductionist account of human behavior in a food chain is not explained. Students are simply expected to make the mental leap.

One of the central conceptual building blocks of Western thought is reinforced in the early grades with explanations such as the following. Under the heading of "Conserving Our Natural Resources" students read: "The earth is full of natural resources that we use every day. However, we have to be careful how we use these *valuable resources*. If we cut down too many trees, the forests will disappear. Then there will be no trees to use to build houses or to make paper."[10] Typically, textbooks represent natural resources—that interesting metaphor that encodes so many cultural assumptions—as the "property" of a political unit. But since people make up the political unit, human needs remain the determining factor in what aspects of the environment are considered a "natural resource." Witness this explanation: "Every country has natural resources. A natural resource is any part of nature that people have found a way to use.... Different parts of the country have different resources.... Because people in the United States trade with each other, they can use each part of the country for its best purposes."[11] Another primary grade textbook acknowledged only part of what every student who reads newspaper headlines or hears the TV newsbite on the latest environmental disaster already knows. But the textbook account of change suggests only the positive aspects of the relationship between humans and the environment: "People change the environment all the time. When people cut down trees, clear the land, and make a field into a farm, they change the environment. All people need food, a place to live, or shelter, and clothing. Food, shelter, and clothes are basic needs.... People change their environment so they can meet these needs."[12] Although young students are daily caught up in a intellectual atmosphere where "needs" are being continually expanded by competing media voices and images, the textbook ignores this Babylon of consumerism by maintaining that human actions derive from the basic needs connected with human survival. As the account is both so simplistic and grounded in beliefs that most teachers take for granted, it is unlikely to be examined more critically.

Textbooks that provide examples of what happens when the sustaining capacities of natural systems are exceeded by human practices stop short of a suggestion that the root of the problem can be traced back to cultural beliefs and values. The closest they come to identifying a cause is usually the suggestion that people need to use more appropriate forms of technology. That environmental problems are merely anomalies is strengthened through the presentation of numerous examples of human activities that appear to be successful. The textbook, *Self*, a book in the American Book Social Studies series, is a good example. Following pictures of new housing developments and well-irrigated crops in what had been a desert ecosystem, students are presented a picture of a parched, deeply fissured, and essentially barren landscape. They are asked to reflect on what might have caused this condition, and to consider what might happen to a farm when water is scarce. There are also pictures of dust storms, city traffic that has reached gridlock, and homes inundated by floods.[13] The questions accompanying the pictures direct thought to technological considerations and not to the deeper cultural beliefs and practices that lead to thinking of the environment as a resource and technology as guaranteeing progress even when conventional natural resources fail to meet human demand.

High school texts on subjects most directly related to human interaction with the environment do not even mention that these activities—for example, in chemistry and economics—can only be carried on within a physical habitat. For example, the 1990 edition of *Chemistry* and *Chemistry: A Modern Course* contains no reference to the role that chemical technology has played in exacerbating certain dimensions of the ecological crisis. But there is a discussion of problem solving through the use of a scientific knowledge of chemistry. The technique of problem solving, according to the textbook, includes the following steps: identify the unknown, identify what is known or given, plan a solution, do the calculations, finish up. But this explanation of problem solving is presented without any cultural-environmental context. In effect, it is a set of abstract procedures. That the knowledge of chemistry is always utilized in a social context involving the influence of cultural values, beliefs (including mythic elements on the nature of progress and empowerment), economic practices, and so forth, apparently is not considered relevant. In effect representing an area of human knowledge like chemistry without situating this knowledge in a habitat seems an extreme expression of anthropocentric thinking.

But chemistry textbooks are not unique in maintaining this silence. High school economic textbooks also perpetuate this silence, even though they proclaim that "economics is the social science that deals with how society allocates its scarce resources among unlimited wants and needs." Scarcity may be the basic economic problem, but students are not given any indication that scarcity, in its deepest sense, is related to how the sun's energy is stored in the natural systems that constitute our habitat. Rather, the true source of energy as found in various parts of the ecosystem is hidden by the special conceptual categories of the economists, which students are expected to utilize as the basis of their economic decisions. Thus, after the statement that people face choices because "our resources are scarce," they are given an explanation of how to think about resources: "*Resources* are the basic ingredients used to produce what we want. They are often called *inputs* or *factors of production*. Resources are *land* (our soil, water, minerals, and other natural resources), *labor*, and *capital* (our buildings, machines, and tools). *Management* is the ability to organize the factors of production, and it, too, is a resource." Although the degree and form of scarcity, when considered historically, have been influenced by the particularities of cultural practices, students are given a more culturally neutral way of thinking about it. As the textbook puts it, "scarcity is the fundamental economic problem people have always faced."[14] The ways proposed for dealing with this aspect of the human condition is to think "rationally" in terms of the vocabulary and conceptual categories provided by the textbook. Unfortunately, few teachers will be able to recognize that this rational process is embedded in the very set of culturally based assumptions that are contributing to the ecological crisis. Aligning economic decision making with the supposed objectivity (and thus cultural neutrality) of the scientific method further undermines those remaining traditional moral analogues that promote self-limitation as a virtue.

History textbooks also promote a basic misunderstanding of the human–environment relationship. Although the chronologies are used to weave together a complex set of events, ideas, institutional and social developments, the dating system (the use of the Christian calendar) and the linear sense of time serve to reinforce the Western myth of human progress. The symbols of progress—evolution of democratic institutions, technology and science, and literacy—serve not only to legitimate the Western mind set, but to build a set of prejudices that will insure few students will think seriously about why traditional, more biocentric cultures were able to survive without the tools of technological domination. Nor do these textbooks provide for understanding the impact of Western societies, at various critical stages of development, on their respective habitats. As in chemistry and economic textbooks, human historical activities are represented against the background of an environment that needs to be considered only in the most tangential manner, as when the features of the environment influence the course of a military campaign, disrupt or facilitate economic strategies, or provide the basis of a dispute over national boundaries. The most important historical process, namely, the impact of the modern industrial society on the world's ecosystems, is not even mentioned in history textbooks published before 1985. While students will be confronted with an overview of other seemingly intractable problems—nationalism, threat of nuclear war, and so forth—totally missing is a historical perspective on how we evolved forms of Western culture that ignore the most fundamental questions about long-term sustainability.

Forms of Knowledge

Everyday activity involves the re-enactment of a wide range of cultural patterns. The patterns—use of body to communicate relationships, organization of space in buildings, metaphors used for thought and communication—encode the thought processes of earlier periods in the development of the culture. It can be said that students (as well as everybody else) exist in a multi-dimensional symbolic world. Clothes, car design, tone of voice, data, print—all aspects of culture—stand for something; that is, at some point in the past, they were created and modified as response to a human problem. And the response was based on an interpretation that had its own geneology in earlier thought patterns. The patterns, in turn, are reinterpreted by succeeding generations. The essential point that relates to our discussion is that students, by virtue of being socialized to the patterns that others take for granted, rely upon, re-enact, are empowered by, and are sometimes dominated by—depending upon the specific cultural pattern—the forms of encoded understandings that constitute the shared culture. The authority of these patterns in the lives of students (like writing from left to right) is largely unconscious; that is, it is mostly when other people have different taken-for-granted patterns that individuals become aware of their own patterns.

Textbook representations raise the question: What are the forms of knowledge that the authors of textbooks uphold as legitimate? A second question that necessarily follows from the first one is: What forms of knowledge are ignored in textbooks, and do these omissions have any bearing on addressing the cultural dimensions of the ecological crisis?

The very nature of textbooks influences the forms of knowledge that will be highlighted as exemplary for students. The use of print as well as the practice of keeping the author invisible has the effect of amplifying the authority of print-based knowledge. This applies to both textbooks and educational software. An example is the student who reads, "*market demand* is a list of the total quantities of a product that all individuals would buy at different possible prices."[15] This type of statement, which suggests factualness and objectivity, is typical of the style of writing in textbooks in all areas of the curriculum, except literature, where students often consider the distinctive traits of the author. Besides the amplification of the sense of factualness and objectivity, textbooks also strengthen a dominant orientation within mainstream culture which equates knowledge with the explicit aspects of rational thought.

Beyond the amplification processes fostered by print, textbooks strengthen the widespread belief that experts' knowledge has greater authority (that is, it more accurately represents the true nature of whatever is being described) than the tacit forms of knowledge of people who do not have the linguistic ability to make explicit and give propositional form to what they know. Pictures of scientists, technicians, and other adults who symbolize a form of expertise are more likely to appear in textbooks than people who base their daily practices on knowledge largely acquired through oral traditions.

Scientific Knowledge.   People rely upon many forms of knowledge in daily life in order to participate in social processes and to give meaning to these experiences. But the impression they will receive in school, particularly if they take a course in the sciences, is that the way of thinking associated with the scientific method is not only the most legitimate, but also the most powerful. Textbooks provide straightforward explanations of how a scientist obtains knowledge, but these explanations nearly always involve examples of the interconnection of science and technology. As the authors of *General Science* put it: "The relationship between science and technology is a continuous cycle of discovery and development. Advances in science and technology have made everyday life much easier than it was in the past."[16] Following this framing of the union of science and technology, students are then presented with examples of technological advances in electronics, industry and transportation, medicine, space, and the arts. The coupling of the first systematic explanations of a way of knowing (most other ways of knowing are learned in context and at a tacit level) with examples of cutting-edge technology serves to represent the scientific method as the pre-eminent form of knowledge and thus the leading cause of human advancement.

The authority of the scientific mode of thinking is further strengthened by the range of phenomena that it purports to explain: the origins of life, the properties of matter, the nature of energy, the animal and plant kingdoms. In the textbook, *Biology: A Journey into Life* (itself an encompassing title) students read that "aging is the sum of changes that accumulate with time and make an organism more likely to die.... Aging and death are genetically programmed."[17] Of the number of science textbooks examined, this was one of the few that provided students with an acknowledgement of those domains of human experience that science cannot explain. But even this admission of the limits of scientific knowledge is framed in a way that communicates the prejudice that what can be known and measured through observation is superior to the claims of other forms of knowing. Witness: "Science is only one way of exploring the world around us; history, religion, and philosophy are others. Science deals only with things that can be experienced directly or indirectly through the senses (sight and hearing, for example). By definition, science has nothing to say about the spiritual or supernatural.... Although science does not deal with the supernatural or with the illogical, scientists themselves may be just as emotional, political, or illogical as anyone else, and this may affect their scientific efforts."[18] Put another way, scientists are human and thus may exhibit the same irrational traits as the rest of us, but when these human failings are not present then the scientist, as a rational-logical being, can present us with knowledge that is objective and factual. That is, strict adherence to the scientific method of thinking can provide knowledge free of the influence of culture, ideology, and prejudice. In effect, the acknowledgement of human weaknesses that prevent strict adherence to the method of scientific inquiry further strengthens the hierarchy of preferred modes of thought implicit in this attempt to help students understand that there are these other less valid forms of knowing.

Not all science textbooks provide students with an explanation of the scientific method. In textbooks written for middle level grades, students may encounter factual information about different aspects of the world, ranging from "Sun, Water, Soil, and Air" and "A Seashore Community," to "Learning about the Earth" and "World Climate," to cite chapter headings from three different textbooks. As students read the factual explanations, they are being exposed to the conceptual orientation of the scientist who supposedly maintains the separation of fact and values, and prevents cultural beliefs from influencing the data. But there is no explanation of the scientific method of thinking. In *Life Science*, which appears to be one of the first encounters students will have with an explicit discussion of what constitutes the mode of knowing connected with science, students read the following answer to the question, "What Is Science?":

> Fact or fiction? Turtle eggs develop into males in cold temperatures and females in warmer temperatures. Insect-eating bats can eat as many as 3,000 insects in one night. The average American teenager eats about 825 kilograms of food a year. Believe it or not, all of these statements are true. They are all facts. The study of science involves the discovery of facts about nature.
>
> The word *science* comes from the Latin word *scire*, which means 'to know.' Scientists seek to know more about nature by uncovering facts. However, science is more than a simple list of facts. Science involves a constant search for information about the universe. A famous nineteenth-century French scientist, Jules Henri Poincaré, said, 'Science is built up with facts as a house is with stones. But a collection of facts is no more a science than a heap of stones is a house.'
>
> Not only do scientists find facts, they try to tie the facts together to explain mysteries of nature. For example, scientists may try to determine how a particular disease is caused. After they determine what causes the disease, they will try to determine how the disease can be cured.[19]

The authors then go on to explain that a theory based on factual data derived from observations must be tested experimentally before it is accepted as the "most logical explanation of events that happen in nature." Although students encounter more extended explanations of how a scientist states a problem, gathers information, forms a hypothesis, and so forth, one of the more interesting characteristics of the public school view of science is that facts and information (recall the "fact or fiction" dichotomy at the beginning of the explanation) are the true building blocks of thought. If thought, in other words, does not start with facts, information, data (these terms tend to be used as interchangeable), then it must be considered as fiction—a word that carries about the same connotation as "speculation" and "myth." What students encounter in the textbook explanations of computers will further strengthen the belief that data and information are the basis of thought.

In the science texts used in the secondary schools where students study chemistry, biology, and physics, the explanations of how the scientist "knows" are presented in a matter of fact manner. The following explanation from a chemistry textbook is typical:

> Like most fields of human endeavor, science has evolved formal and time-tested methods to solve problems. The scientific method is one important approach. It was through the scientific method that many of the chemical elements were first discovered. *The scientific method incorporates observations, hypotheses, experiments, theories, and laws. Scientists make observations when they note and record facts about natural phenomena.* They try to explain their observations by devising hypotheses. *Hypotheses are descriptive models for observations. A hypothesis is useful if it accounts for what scientists observe in many situations.*[20]

In all the explanations of the scientific method, the distinction between a theory and a scientific law is mentioned. But only a few textbooks explain that "one peculiarity of the scientific method is that a hypothesis can never formally be proved but can only be disproved."

None of the textbooks address what seem to be the more critical issues surrounding the privileged status given in Western societies to this form of knowledge, nor do they illuminate the irony that a mode of inquiry that is supposed to be free of cultural and ideological influences may actually be contributing to the cultural orientations that are damaging the life systems of the earth. This comment is made with the full recognition that science is used now to understand the changes taking place in the biosystems.

As we address the broader question of how textbooks, in the different subject areas, reinforce an anthropocentric view of the universe, we can touch only briefly on the consequences of ignoring how far more complicated, culturally and politically, is the use of the scientific method than is acknowledged in textbooks. The people who write science textbooks always make an effort to situate a particular body of scientific knowledge in real world situations. Unfortunately, their knowledge of the culture they introduce in this process of contextualizing too often reflects a surface level of understanding. In effect, the cultural myths that they take for granted as their natural attitude are reinforced in the presentation of scientific findings. For example, the connection always made between scientific discoveries and the development of new technologies (computers, genetic engineering, telecommunications, etc.), further strengthened through use of appropriate visual images, further promotes the cultural myth that change is linear and progressive in nature. Most students, in considering the changes in technology over the last 100 years, would have difficulty challenging this—though the myth is beginning to unravel as the media present incident after incident of the ecologically disruptive effects of technology (oil spills, toxic wastes, pollution, and so forth).

The enfolding of scientific inquiry and findings within the myth of progress has another effect; namely, it makes it even more difficult to recognize that technologies based on new scientific knowledge represent a form of experimentation with the culture—which involves a longer time frame than is usual in scientific experiments. To put this point more succinctly, the development and introduction into society of each new technology based on scientific knowledge also represents the initial stages of a cultural experiment. Changes within the culture that would result from the introduction of computers, for example, were not known at the time they were introduced into the work place and the classroom and proclaimed a great leap forward for humanity. We are just now beginning to recognize the unforeseen consequences of this technology in introducing new forms of dehumanization into the work place and increasing surveillance of people's activities by employers and the state (a threat to traditional civil liberties). The introduction of television represents another experiment with the psychic-social-political-educational patterns of the culture. Like every new technology and scientific discovery, its introduction was heralded as a human advance. But the scientists tend not to recognize that the larger experimental arena is the cultural setting into which the new technology is introduced. This confidence (hubris?) in how science and technology will transform human life (to put it into a new orbit, so to speak) is expressed by Paul G. Hewitt in *Conceptual Physics: A High School Physics Program*:

> We seem to be at the dawn of a major change in human growth, not unlike the stage of a chicken embryo before it fully matures. When the chicken embryo exhausts the last of its inner-egg resources and before it pokes its way out of its shell, it may feel it is at its last moments. But what seems like its end is really only its beginning. Are we like the hatching chicks, ready to poke through to a whole new range of possibilities? Are our spacefaring efforts the early signs of a new human era? The earth is our cradle and has served us well. But cradles, however comfortable, are one day outgrown. With inspiration that in many ways is similar to the inspiration of those who built the early cathedrals, synagogues, temples, and mosques, we aim for the cosmos. We live at an exciting time![21]

It is difficult not to read this as a statement that the next stage in human development will be to leave the earth behind—with its cathedrals and synagogues—to go wherever in space science and technology can take us. Earlier in the discussion of the difference between science and technology, Hewitt stated that "science excludes the human factor." His statement about outgrowing our need for planet Earth shows how this disregard of the "human factor" leads to such a naive understanding of the enormity of the cultural experiment he represents as the inevitable next step in human (now "scientific") progress. A more likely scenario is that as people experience further declines in the life-sustaining capacities of natural systems (that is, when people realize they are dying from chemical poisons in the food chain and from a shortage of food caused by the loss of fertile soil) they are likely to turn on the scientists and technologists with a vengeance that could be Biblical in scale. When the myth of progress ceases to be part of people's natural attitude, the claim that science can be viewed as separate from human concerns (and cultural beliefs) will be likely viewed as basically irresponsible and self-serving. But we are perhaps three or four decades away from any real testing of the myth that gives Hewitt such confidence in the future.

By giving the scientific approach to knowledge the privileged (and largely unquestioned) status that it now enjoys among very powerful social groups, Western society itself seems to be engaging in a long-range cultural experiment. Before the advent of the scientific way of knowing (and thus of an increasingly scientifically based culture) cultures evolved many different ways of understanding and responding to their world. Less prejudiced studies of nonscientifically based cultures are beginning to reveal that a common feature shared by most of these diverse and complex symbolic constructions of reality was the unity of practical knowledge with the moral analogues rooted in the narrative consciousness of the people. As Robert Redfield noted, these cultures had "a moral order to which the technological order was subordinate."[22] That is, the value system served to limit the use of technology—almost the opposite of our situation. New technology helps to establish what we should value by making progress synonymous with the highest good, which in turn encourages technological growth and thus the cultural experimentation that we tend to recognize only in hindsight.

A second characteristic found in pre-modern cultures is that the "man"–nature distinction did not exist. Humans and nonhumans (plants, animals, earth, etc.) were bound together in a shared moral universe. This, in turn, led to a more interdependent sense of all life, rather than to the Western view of nature that it is to be understood, mastered, and exploited as a natural resource. Science, as it is explained in textbooks, reinforces a spectator and an instrumental relationship between humans and the environment. Observation leads to factual knowledge, which then leads to more rationally based ways of intervening in the natural world for the purpose of serving human needs. But the person is separate from what is being observed and, eventually, technologically manipulated. This sense of separation, or spectator relationship, became part of the mind set that produced the Industrial Revolution with its vision of growth in material well-being and technological control over nature. Representing a new symbolic and technological order, it can also be viewed as an experiment on the sustaining capabilities of the ecosystem. Textbooks are totally silent about this aspect of science, and thus leave students with the idea that scientific knowledge provides for a more secure and predictable future.

The spectator relationship to nature and the separation of facts from values can be seen in the statement that, "The universe around you and inside you is really a collection of countless mysteries. It is the job of scientists to solve these mysteries. And, like any good detective, a scientist uses special methods to find truths about nature. These truths," conclude the authors, "are called facts."[23]

Paul Feyerabend, a maverick philosopher of science, points to the danger of viewing science as being the only legitimate approach to knowledge. "At all times," he observes, using the culturally conditioned vocabulary of his time, "man approached his surroundings with wide open senses and a fertile intelligence, at all times he made incredible discoveries, at all times we can learn from his ideas."[24] Feyerabend's warning is particularly germane today, as we observe the special irony in our scientifically and technologically based culture being threatened by its environmentally ruinous successes over a mere couple of hundred years while the Hopi and its predecessor cultures, based on "prerational" forms of understanding (e.g., myth and superstition), has survived in a more spartan habitat for several thousand years. This more complex information chain of human history, as Feyerabend observes, cannot be tapped by students if they accept the limited view of knowledge mandated by the rigid empiricism of textbook science.

To state the problem somewhat differently, accepting the view of knowledge legitimated in the public schools would make it difficult for students to recognize that patterns of thinking of more ecologically balanced cultures can lead to socially useful and accurate forms of understanding and technological achievement. As Feyerabend notes, primitive tribes developed exceedingly detailed classifications of plants and animals, and they accumulated an important body of medicinal knowledge. Other achievements included an internationally known astronomy that solved both social and physical problems (with observations in England and the South Pacific), an ability to navigate across large expanses of ocean, and the domestication of animals, to cite just a few examples. Ironically, scientific knowledge, with all its hidden cultural categories for making sense of reality, serves to hide the achievements of these nonanthropocentrically based cultures, and to promote our own nonecologically sustainable myths.

Values

The descriptive content and the pictures in textbooks tend to emphasize the more positive aspects of social life. History texts largely represent achievements in social life: in the evolution of political institutions, technology, social values, the nation state, and so forth. Science textbooks, as we just saw, are also about successes—the ever increasing ability to explain, predict, and control natural phenomena through the use of the scientific method. Although textbooks are written in a style intended to convey that the content represents an objective explanation, they nevertheless serve another function in the students' socialization. The underlying theme of social progress, which frames the supposedly factual content, communicates what students are expected to value.

An earlier theme of this book was that expectations in consumerism and meeting personal needs can be represented in terms of the dominant culture, in an upward curve, while the life-sustaining capacities of natural systems are represented in a downward curve. From this we can obtain the necessary perspective for asking a fundamental question about value orientations communicated through textbooks. Beyond obtaining a better sense of the values themselves, the most important question is whether students are presented with a way of understanding the limitations and consequences of embracing certain values and of continuing to embrace others beyond a certain point. To put it another way, do textbooks contextualize the values in a way that enables students to consider how they relate to the ecological crisis?

Elementary textbooks utilize a great many pictures, along with more simplified explanations. The pictures now include a better balance in terms of ethnic and gender representation, though the social setting in which people are represented is always that of the middle class. If one just considers the pictures, where the complexity of the vocabulary is not an issue, it is possible to recognize the cultural message that equates human values with material things. In the Heath Social Studies series, *Homes and Neighborhoods*, the pictures of the countryside, urban neighborhoods, shopping centers, and interior of houses represent technological production and consumption as the central activities.[25] Just as a comparison of an early Chinese painting with the work of Thomas Gainsborough discloses profoundly different cultural orientations toward what should be in the foreground and what constitutes the background (a distinction that encodes the deepest cultural assumptions), the pictures in elementary textbooks put in the foreground what is central to the dominant cultural group. Pictures suggesting the consumer-oriented plentitude of middle class life, in effect, help to establish what is real, or at least what students should strive to achieve. The pictures also fuse the "real" with what is to be valued. The ecological consequences of everybody, the world over, living in proximity to such material plentitude is, of course, not discussed in the narrative that accompanies the pictures. Rather the message students are left with is "you can have it all," that is, if you become a member of middle class society.

Self illustrates this equating of basic values with the economic activities of the middle class. The unit on communication shows pictures of people using telephones, television, radios, satellites, road signs, and various nonverbal communications. But the basic form of communication is through the use of technology. Under the heading of "How do people meet their needs?" students find the answer in pictures of people engaged in various forms of work where again technology is the central theme. The answer to the question "Why do people work?" is that people have needs, followed by pictures of food, clothes, and a house that would cost at least $150,000 in most regions of the country. Human "wants" are represented in terms of entertainment and play-things.[26]

High school textbooks contain fewer pictures and more explanations reflecting the thinking of economists, historians, sociologists, and scientists—all still deeply influenced by their respective disciplinary knowledge formed before there was any awareness either of an ecological crisis or an anthropocentric view of the universe. The result is that students encounter the value orientation of a technological culture. Represented as the leading edge of a progressive process, the values are further masked as simply the next inevitable stage of cultural development. Witness the values embedded in the following statement, which appears to mix technological futurism with democratic decision making:

> Today we have throw-away bottles, paper clothes, and plastic knives and forks. Tomorrow we may be able to dispose of the damaged parts of our bodies and get new parts to replace them. Actually, this is already being done....
>
> It may be possible to grow another human being from a single cell of a living person. The second person would be an exact duplicate of the first person. This process is called *cloning*. Very primitive organisms have been cloned in laboratory environments. In the future, human beings may be produced in laboratories. Sex, color of skin, intelligence, height, weight—every aspect of a person may be determined by lab scientists. Robots and computers may have five (or more) senses and act in very "human" ways. If all this happens, will it change the ways we view ourselves as human beings? Who should have the power to make the decisions concerning cloning, laboratory births, and the programming of robots and computers? What do you think?
>
> Through improvements in medicine, *aging* and *death* may take on new meaning. Some scientists and doctors believe that your generation may see an end to sickness. In the future it is possible that death may be avoided for centuries. It is also possible that people may be returned to a physical and mental condition of youth."[27]

What student would be able to give serious consideration to a fundamentally different scenario, one that is based
on values that take into account living in ecological balance
over the long term? The promise of a rationally engineered
life, one free of all the imperfections that make the world so
troubling—differences in color of skin and intelligence, as
well as sickness, aging, and even death—makes both personally appealing and intellectually reassuring the belief that
scientists are helping everybody achieve the highest values.

The influence of the scientific method on how values
are represented to students can be seen in a high school
sociology text. Although there is a strong current of thinking
among teachers in the lower grades that values are to be
chosen by the student on the basis of what feels right, secondary level textbooks tend to represent values in more
functional and utilitarian terms. The influence of science is
manifested in the taxonomic treatment of values. In *Sociology: A Study of Human Relationships*, students learn that
there are different forms of values, such as norms, folkways,
and mores. The section on "Forming Relationships" extends
the taxonomic approach by identifying "trust," "flexibility," and
"availability" as values.[28] But the discussion stops short of
suggesting the kinds of acts that are to be supported by
exhibiting trust, flexibility, and availability; nor is there any
mention of when acting on these "values" might actually reinforce behaviors that, seen from a less relativistic framework,
are immoral. What is the social function of values? What are
the different types of values? What values enable you to feel
good and authentic in your relationships with others? While
this approach appears on the surface to leave real moral
decisions up to the judgment of the students whose func-
tionalist and taxonomic knowledge of values is supposed to
correspond to a similar way of understanding the natural
world, textbooks are not, in actuality, value free.

As pointed out earlier, values associated with technological progress, consumerism, and even "natural resources"
are presented as what successful people take for granted.
This orientation toward educating students to values is further reinforced by the complete silence in textbooks on what
Leopold referred to as a "land ethic"; that is, that a person's
relationship to the environment ought to involve moral judgments and not just the economic judgments that accompa-

ny the practice of viewing the environment as a "natural resource."

Concluding Observations on
Anthropocentrism in Textbooks

In understanding the content of textbooks, it must be kept in mind that they are written for a national market, and thus are largely devoid of anything viewed as controversial by the social groups who have political clout in local and state arenas of public education. The second thing to remember is that teacher use of textbooks varies greatly, from slavish dependency to using them as infrequently as possible. This last variable leaves us with the question: what significance do textbooks have in a discussion of the educational/cultural/ecological problem? The answer must be qualified by all the variables that enter into any generalizations about what goes on in classrooms; but there are still some generalizations that seem to hold up, as long as one is focusing on the dominant or mainstream educational practices. The generalizations are, in part, based on taking into account the recent history of educational reforms (accountability, effective schools) and pop innovations (learning styles, autonomous learning model, lateral thinking), and the Cartesian thinking that continues to dominate teacher education and most university classes. The continuing influence in other parts of the Western world of Cartesian thinking, where the individual is understood as a culture-free being who makes observations and utilizes the results of these "objective" observations as the basis of rational thought, make these generalizations applicable to the educational process in more than the United States.

What is left out of textbooks, it could be argued, is as important as the cultural patterns of thinking that are presented to students. The omissions are not, however, simply a matter of oversight. They result from the anthropocentric mind set, buttressed by the myth that human decisions (particularly when based on the canons of scientific inquiry) are progressive in nature. That is, the anthropocentric way of thinking cannot be reconciled with the ideas that are not presented to students. But this may be putting the cart before the horse. A better explanation is that the conceptual framework of the people who write the textbooks leaves out of focus fundamental characteristics of human existence; thus they are not even aware of what is being left out. If they were aware of the silences, they would then face the problem of reconciling the counterevidence with mainstream cultural orthodoxies—but they do not even get to this stage. Unfortunately, many teachers share the same cultural patterns of thinking that constitute the anthropocentric orthodoxies, with the result that most attempts to supplement a textbook-centered curriculum will leave intact the core body of cultural assumptions. Let's be more specific.

One of the silences in all the textbooks is that the ecological crisis is a symptom of a deep crisis in human values and beliefs. The population explosion has its roots in cultural beliefs and practices, as does the way in which we are altering the chemistry of the biosystems. Cultural beliefs that influence how human wants and needs are worked out in technological practice, and influence how humans understand their relationship to their habitat, are the wellspring for the demands humans place on the environment. Yet this connection, which might involve at some point a recognition that the profit motive, personal vanity, and other sources for these demands might be the basis of decisions that have an adverse effect on the environment, is never presented in textbooks. Instead, the anthropocentric myth is sustained by referring to the environment as a natural resource (for humans) and ecological problems as merely indicators of bad technological practices. The following example is from an otherwise exemplary textbook that teaches chemistry as part of the process of solving environmental problems like water and air pollution:

> Can we keep from doing this? Nature conserves automatically at the atomic level. Let's look at what conservation means in human terms.

> How can we conserve our resources? That is, how can we slow down the rate at which we use them? The "three R's" of conservation are replace, reuse, and recycle. To replace a resource requires finding substitute materials with similar properties, preferably materials from renewable resources.

Gathering, processing, and using resources gener-
ates unwanted materials. We must also manage these
materials. The waste and dispersion of nonrenewable
resources may eventually pose serious threats to the
well-being of our society. It is preferable that the by-
products of what we use be gathered and stored or disposed of wisely.[29]

At first glance this appears an enlightened and responsible
statement that clearly identifies the problem, and provides
an effective way for resolving it (i.e., the three Rs of conser-
vation). But framing it as a technological problem maintains
the silence on the cultural aspects of the problem. Cultural
beliefs and values, such as our view of time, efficiency, freedom of choice, wanting conveniences, using consumer
goods as a mark of social status, and so forth, do not lend
themselves to a technological solution, so they are ignored.

There are other areas of silence in the content of textbooks, and, because of the ideological orientation of the university education most teachers undergo, few of them are
able to present students with an alternative way of thinking.
Unfortunately, these areas of silence are particularly critical
in addressing the deeper, nontechnological dimensions of
the ecological crisis. One of these has to do with textbooks'
image of the individual. Textbooks that introduce concepts
from anthropology provide explanations about how differences in people's behavior and thought reflect cultural differences. But this "let's learn to appreciate differences" message does not really challenge the main orthodoxy. While
others may be influenced by culture, students must learn to
think of themselves as the author of their own choices, rationality, and behavior. In effect, they must view their particular
thought process as having the potential of freeing them from
their embeddedness in culture. The goal is to confront the
data, evidence, information with one's own mind and to
reach an objective conclusion. The testing process that utilizes "objective information" reinforces this, as does the practice of presenting explanations and information in textbooks
in a manner that hides that it is a process of interpretation all
the way along.

The emphasis on students "doing their own thinking,"
that oft-repeated cliche of the classroom, also suggests that

the educational ideal is the autonomous, self-directing individual. If textbooks presented the truth, that we give individualized expression to shared cultural patterns, the notions of "objective fact" and "unbiased information" would go out the window. The notion that students read "what's in the text," as though they are objective observers of the author's thought process, also would have to be fundamentally altered. The reader's cultural knowledge is as critical to understanding as what the author writes. It is the Cartesian view of the culturally autonomous individual that leads to the public school notion of reading or doing an observation of an experiment, where the reader or observer adopts the stance of objective observer.

A third area of silence has to do with the metaphorical nature of language and thought, discussed earlier. The view of language presented to students, if it is presented at all, is typified in the following explanation: "A *language*, such as English, is simply a system of symbols used to communicate ideas and thoughts to others. These symbols may be letters or numbers or sounds. Whether the symbols are written or spoken, they are arranged in a certain order to convey meaning. You think, read, and talk every day by using the symbols of a language."[30] The key point here that most students will take away from their reading of this passage is that they, as autonomous individuals, use the language to convey their ideas to a listener. That language encodes the thought process (analogic thinking) of earlier generations, and now helps to organize the thought processes in terms of the encoded schema of understanding, is hidden by the textbook representation of language merely as a conduit for ideas.

The critical issue relating to the ecological crisis is that, as students develop a set of unexamined attitudes toward this fundamentally incorrect view of language, they will find it more difficult to become aware that the belief system contributing to the ecological crisis is encoded in the language that tacitly influences their patterns of thinking. Each one of them thinking of themselves ("I" is an iconic metaphor that encodes earlier ways of understanding what it means to be an individual) as separate from nature reflects a conceptual mapping process that has its roots deep in Western thought. Similarly, thinking of science and technology as the primary means of resolving the ecological crisis reflects our tendency to generalize to other areas successes in certain aspects of experiences; but this process of metaphorical thinking (the ecological crisis "is like" other problems requiring scientific understanding that, in turn, will lead to better technological solutions) leaves out human values and beliefs—because science cannot deal with them. Textbook silence on the metaphorical nature of language and thought thus serves to hide the cultural/conceptual roots of the vision of progress that must now be reframed.

A fourth area of silence has to do with the nature of tradition in people's lives. Textbooks provide students with a way of thinking about the past, present, and future; but the central organizing concept is that change is linear and inherently progressive. Thus students learn about the past to understand the advances in current thought, technology, and social values. But students are not given a complex view of tradition, which includes everything from the past that continues to be a living aspect of today's experience: road systems, keyboards, body language, political institutions and norms, spelling of words, and so on. Understanding the pervasive nature of tradition, as well as how living traditions differ from traditionalism (which involves the desire to maintain or recover lost or dead traditional patterns) is also an important aspect of healing our relationship with the earth.

Even the use of the word "tradition" in a conversation with people who view themselves as followers of Enlightenment thinkers (itself a tradition) can cause unbelievable misunderstanding. This suggests that the view of tradition that continues to be presented in schools distorts how human existence is understood. My using the word in conversation, has led many people to automatically assume I was making a plea for the status quo or even from going back to the patterns of an earlier time. They did not recognize that their own taken-for-granted patterns involve the re-enactment and reinterpretation of traditions and that we tend to become aware only of traditional patterns, norms, and technologies as they become no longer suitable to present circumstances. Tradition, in its broadest sense, is nearly synonymous with culture. But this view of tradition cannot be reconciled with the dichotomous pattern of thinking that represents progress as overcoming and transcending traditions.

How traditions change from within and are changed by

outside social forces, how new ones come into being, and how they can become outmoded, are all important for understanding the person–culture relationship. But the ecological crisis provides other reasons for understanding the complex nature of tradition. Cultures that lived in ecological balance appear to have had a very different way of understanding the nature of tradition. That is, tradition appears to have been the thread of continuity that helped insure that social practices attuned to the characteristics of the habitat were slowly modified over time, as opposed to overthrown by new experimental approaches. Secondly, as we shall see in the final chapter, the sense of tradition enabled people to live in time-space relationships that were symbolically far more rich and complex. Through dance and song, tradition filled the human need for meaning in and transcendence over the mundane routines of daily survival in a way very different from our society, where we escape by moving physically through space— in the process contributing to pollution, depletion of nonrenewable resources, and the spread of our freeway systems. These are very complex issues that need to be laid out with more care, so we shall later return to them.

Lastly, textbooks are silent about alternative ways of knowing. This criticism should not be interpreted to mean that students are not exposed to explanations of the norms of other cultural groups. What they do not encounter, however, is any in-depth account of other cultural ways of knowing. The evidence of our own technological, scientific, and political achievements is arranged to suggest that we are the most progressive society in existence, thus making it difficult to take seriously any suggestion that we could learn from less "advanced cultures." Individual conveniences, happiness, and technological control, however, must be judged by the ultimate test that in the recent past we assumed would not apply to us: namely, whether the cultural beliefs and practices are environmentally sustainable over the long run. That we are failing this test suggests the need for taking seriously other belief systems, both to learn how other peoples have evolved ecologically sustainable forms of existence and to recognize our own taken-for-granted beliefs and practices.

Unfortunately, a concern with understanding the metaphorical nature of the language-thought processes, the nature of tradition, and other cultural epistemologies does not fit the ideological orientations that drive the curricula of most colleges and universities where teachers receive their education. That most teachers are not able to compensate for these areas of silence in the curriculum or, for that matter, to recognize the dominant ideology that frames the entire curriculum, suggest the primary areas of reform that need to be addressed if public education is to be part of the long-term solution to the double bind of an anthropocentric view of the world.

5

Toward Deep Changes
in the Educational Process

Legislative action alone will not be adequate to alleviate
the impact of humans on the environment, although it is an
essential and perhaps the easiest step to take. We must also
consider the nature of the culture being passed on to the
next generation. Culture, to recall Clifford Geertz, provides
the "template or blueprint for the organization of social and
psychological processes."[1] Others have referred to culture
as providing, in part, the collectively shared schema or patterns for making sense of the flux of experience, and for acting to solve problems and maintain relationships. What the
ecological crisis has done is to bring into question the adequacy of the shared templates or patterns being communicated and reinforced as part of youth's natural attitude. When
we focus on the interrelation of culture and youth, we enter
the arena that includes media pop culture and public and
university education. Although the influence of the media is
not being discounted here, our attention will be focused on
the formal educational processes that occur in American
public school and university classrooms. Our primary concern will be to identify general principles that might serve as
a more adequate basis for transforming formal education in
a way that contributes to better environmental citizenship,
as opposed to the current view of citizenship in a consumer-
oriented society.

By making the ecological crisis our most important pri-
ority, particularly in reforming how we think about formal
educational processes, it should be kept in mind that social
justice issues relating to ethnicity, gender, poverty, and the
widespread sense of anomie that now fuels the drug crisis

should be understood in a new way. As we attempt to resolve the sources of inequity within society, in basic human rights, in living personally and socially meaningful lives, and in the use of our national wealth, it will be necessary to frame the solutions in terms of cultural values and practices that will not contribute further to the overuse of nonrenewable resources and to the pollution of the environment. One can hope that the mainstream of American society will begin to realign its priorities and practices to more sustainable levels; this may have implications for redefining the social goals to be achieved by the reform efforts of marginalized groups. For example, if the feminist movement succeeds primarily in achieving equality in the work place and as consumers, but does not help to transform both areas in ways that are more ecologically sustainable, it will be a reform that failed to take the larger picture into account. Like other political reforms that bring more people into the modern, consumer-oriented society (estimates now are that the world economy will be five to ten times larger in the coming century than its present size) the problem of the diverging trends, where cultural demands exceed the sustaining capacities of natural systems, will be exacerbated. We need to begin to evolve, as cultures, into new directions that do not involve the need of individuals endlessly to pursue conveniences and personal meaning through consumerism. This means that many of our guiding ideals will need to undergo change, particularly as the extent and immediacy of our collective environmental situation rises into conscious awareness.

As pointed out earlier, neither liberal nor conservative political/educational agendas can serve as a guide for achieving the fundamental reforms now needed in public school and university education. The different streams of educational liberalism share the assumption that progress is attained either by maximizing the freedom of the individual (the emancipating and neo-romantic tradition), by increasing the ability to unite the process of participatory decision making with the scientific method of problem solving (the Deweyan tradition), or by using the techniques of scientific management and behavioral reinforcement to improve the individual's behavior (the technicist tradition). But it is a view of progress that is based on the myth of an anthropocentric universe. How humans might live lightly within the web of the biotic community is still not part of their vision.

The same criticisms apply, as we have seen, to conservatives who want the present generation to follow the model of past great thinkers who demonstrated the power of rational thought to clarify the problems surrounding the human situation. Conservatives have maintained a more complex view of human possibilities, thus avoiding the escalator view of progress that characterizes the various forms of educational liberalism. But their commitment to a narrow interpretation of the rational process has made them vulnerable to the view that scientists are somehow free of traits that make progress in other areas of human endeavor more problematic. Like the educational liberals who share in more attenuated form a common intellectual tradition, educational conservatives would not share Aldo Leopold's view that, "A thing is right when it tends to preserve the integrity, stability, and beauty of the biotic community. It is wrong when it tends otherwise."[2]

Bateson's Analogue of a Mental Ecology

In the past, philosophers have suggested powerful analogues that have become the basis of thinking about the nature and purpose of education. Education as the process of bringing forth what is latent in the mind of the individual (Plato's notion of the teacher as midwife), education as an outgrowth of direct experience (Locke's view of the teacher as facilitator of experience), education as growth in reconstructing experience (Dewey's naturalistic image of the collective process of using the "method of intelligence"), have each exerted a powerful influence on how education has been understood. But what now seems most appropriate both to understanding the complex cultural processes we now recognize to be part of the educational process and to preparing students to be more responsible citizens of a community that includes trees, grasses, birds, and all other life forms, which make up the energy and food chains of life, is the analogue of an ecology. Gregory Bateson uses this metaphor as a way of understanding human thought processes, as well as our prospects for long-term survival. This iconoclastic thinker made lasting contributions in the fields of anthropology, linguistics, ethology, and psychiatry, but will likely have his greatest influence not on present but future generations of thinkers. His understanding of how humans participate in life as part of a larger mental ecology provides a general conceptual framework that can be supplemented by recent developments in the social sciences that have particular significance for understanding education as a cultural process. Bateson's use of ecology as the analogue for understanding the mental processes we associate with education also leads to reframing how we understand the nature of community, freedom, tradition, science, and technology.

It would be correct to say that Bateson's primary interest in *Steps to an Ecology of Mind* (1972) and *Mind and Nature* (1980) is to demonstrate that the foundations of modern Western thought are based on basic misunderstandings about the nature of the individual. Of particular concern to him is the way in which Cartesianism continues to exert an influence on how we understand the relationship between the knower and known, which Bateson saw as embodied in such everyday expressions as "I am thinking about the problem," "I see the tree," and "I am driving the car." As these commonly used expressions suggest, the same way of understanding the process of thinking frames how individual actions are viewed. Bateson considered the epistemological orientation embedded in these common expressions to be both conceptually incorrect and a partial cause of our environmental difficulties.

Basically, when a person speaks or thinks in a way that identifies the self as "I," an autonomous actor who may be thinking, feeling, walking, and so forth, a relationship has been formed that separates the person from the context. In effect, the personal pronoun "I" is a metaphor that encodes a sense of separation: the knower from the known and the actor from the context. The sense of separation is strengthened by a particular way of seeing that has its roots in the Italian Renaissance, namely, the sense of perspective, where the individual viewer becomes the vantage point used to give objects in space a sense of a linear depth. This sense of vantage point becomes in the Cartesian mind set a view of the individual as the source of rational thought and the observer of an external world. The critically important point, in terms of Bateson's concerns, is that the person is represented as thinking about something, moving through space, and acting upon something.

The epistemological problems associated with the sense of relationship framed by these expressions are not just part of an academic battlefield that Bateson wants to explore; rather, they go largely unnoticed in public school and university classrooms (as well as on the streets and in the hallways of American corporations) where the personal pronoun "I" continually signals that sensate awareness, physical actions, and thoughts are individually centered. The dualisms of mind and body, knower and known, and "man" and nature, while not maintained only by what we now recognize as more than a mere figure of speech, are continually reinforced by this grammatical/epistemological convention, even as we expand our knowledge of the world through scientific discovery and scholarly insight.

The challenge Bateson faced was in explaining to Cartesian thinkers—who take for granted thought patterns that organize phenomena into discrete entities—how the person (or other organism or object) and context in fact go together. Just as he recognized this problem—and even admitted to his own difficulty in avoiding slipping back into the Cartesian way of thinking—we must also acknowledge it. The motivation for taking seriously a radically different and, some would say, difficult way of understanding the individual as part of an ecology where the old hierarchy of man over nature disappears, is the environmental crisis that is now beginning to disrupt our tacit patterns. Unless we are prepared to make immediately the epistemological leap demonstrated by others who have achieved a sense of wholeness through a variety of spiritual disciplines, we had better take seriously whatever intermediate steps are available to us, within the context of our culture, for transforming the cultural myths now deepening our difficulties.

One of Bateson's more important insights is that an individual (or any other organism) never simply acts in a unilateral way upon the environment, like one billiard ball hitting another. Rather, there is always a context and an interacting relationship. The context, or "system" to use Bateson's metaphor, involves relationships, and these relationships involve an ongoing exchange of information taken into account in the subsequent behavior of the participants. Viewed in this way, we would know another person only in context, and only in terms of her/his relations with other things. The relationships involve the exchange of information through different pathways that depend on the complexity of the interacting elements. To use Bateson's words, the relationships (like a person greeting a stranger) involve eye contact, body posture, tone of voice, spatial distance and so forth—an ongoing series of "difference which makes a difference," which he considers to be the most basic and elementary unit of information or idea.[3] Like a cybernetic system, information is exchanged as a difference (the person directing speech to the stranger, like "hello"), followed by a response (a new difference that provides the information for a change in response). If the stranger continues to look away, that becomes the new "difference which makes a difference," leading to a subsequent behavior, like proceeding on without attempting further conversation. The ongoing "difference which makes a difference" is like a dance that connects the participants in a larger system or whole. To use the language of the Chilean biologist, Humberto Maturana, the perturbations (difference which makes a difference) "can be understood as a process of structural coupling," where the behaviors are interlocked.[4]

The following example brings out how Bateson's focus on the information exchanges that characterize relationships leads to recognizing that actions are always collaborative; that is, expressions of interacting systems, and not individualistic:

> Consider a man felling a tree with an axe. Each stroke of the axe is modified or corrected, according to the shape of the cut face of the tree left by the previous stroke. This self-corrective (i.e., mental) process is brought about by a total system, tree-eyes-brain-muscles-axe-stroke-tree; and it is this total system that has the characteristics of immanent mind. More correctly, we should spell the matter out as: (differences in tree)–(differences in retina)–(differences in brain)–(differences in muscles)–(differences in movement of axe)–(differences in tree), etc. What is transmitted around the circuit is transforms of differences. And as noted above, a

difference which makes a difference is an *idea* or unit of information.[5]

This example of a system includes, if we use the Cartesian categories, both human and nonhuman elements. By reframing how we understand the relationship in terms of the information flowing through the pathways that are the points of contact within an interactive system, Bateson overcomes the long-held Western bias that represents humans as the source of mental activity, and the nonhuman as essentially material and nonintelligent. His example of the coupling of tree and man as an interdependent mental system overturns this bias. To use Bateson's own words, "in no system which shows mental characteristics can any part have unilateral control over the whole. In other words, *the mental characteristics of the system are immanent, not in some part, but in the system as a whole.*"[6] And in another passage from *Steps to an Ecology of Mind* he writes: "The total self-corrective unit which processes information, or, as I say, 'thinks' and 'acts' and 'decides', is a *system* whose boundaries do not at all coincide with the boundaries either of the body or of what is popularly called the 'self' or 'consciousness'"; and it is important to notice that there are *multiple* differences between the thinking system and the 'self' as popularly conceived."[7]

The use of such metaphors as "mind," "intelligence," "information" to describe the communication essential to the life of an ecological system, and to locate humans as interactive members of this larger system, will appear strange and even unwarranted to Cartesian thinkers. But the same Batesonian way of understanding mental characteristics as immanent in the entire system was expressed by Gary Snyder in a manner more difficult to dismiss out of hand. Writing about the pioneering work of Eugene Odum, Snyder notes how Odum equated life with biomass as "stored information"; "Living matter is stored information in the cells and in the genes." The human/habitat relationship is brought further into proper perspective as Snyder elaborates on Odum's view that "there is more information of a higher order of sophistication and complexity stored in a few square yards of forest than there is in all the libraries of mankind." But as Snyder writes, "it is a different order of information. It is the information of the universe we live in. It is the information that has been flowing for millions of years. In this total information context," concludes Snyder, bringing humankind down from the various pedestals erected as part of the myth of an anthropocentric and progressive destiny, "man may not be necessarily the highest or most interesting product."[8]

Understanding biomass as stored information seems today, particularly among many scientists and the remaining primal peoples, as little more than common sense. Bateson's way of thinking of the patterns that connect (the tennis player continually adjusting to the "difference which makes a difference" in the patterns of the other player, the ball, and the physical characteristics of the court, or students who are part of the equally complex ecology we know as the classroom) simply shifts the focus, but does not change the framework of understanding. It is still the context or the interactive system that is the unit of mental activity, the person being only part of the process of information exchange.

In the previous quotations, however, both Bateson and Snyder give important clues to the distinctive way in which humans are part of a larger ecology of information and communication. Bateson's reference to differences between the "thinking system" and the popularly held view of the self, and Snyder's reference to the "different order of information" that characterizes a biomass, are critically important if we are to avoid a source of confusion that might turn away many readers. What is not being suggested here is that the tree and the person are engaged in the same order of mental process; that is, that a tree "thinks" in the same way as the person. The interactive parts of a system exhibit mental characteristics because collectively the "difference which makes a difference" are the bits of information that lead to changes in different parts of the system. But Bateson holds that humans make sense of differences in a distinctive way—they think metaphorically, and their metaphorical constructs are built up over time as part of a collective way of making sense of experience, like using a linear pattern to organize our sense of time.

Bateson uses the distinction between the terms "map" and "territory" to illuminate why humans may not take account of all the information being communicated through relationships, and how they may impose on the information exchanges an interpretation that is destructive over the long-term—like responding to pests by applying stronger doses of insecticides and to a declining water table by drilling deeper wells. The metaphor of a map, for Bateson, suggests how the prefigured mental schema of a person influences what part of the territory (the domain of impacts, events, and relationships that constitute the information exchanges within the system) will be recognized. Like a road map that indicates the system of roads and services available to travellers, what is not included on the map may often go unrecognized—like places of historical significance, distinctive flora and animal life, important geological formations, and so forth.

Our conceptual maps, as Bateson warns time and again, may not be adequate for understanding important changes taking place in the territory. Yet the survival of humans is dependent upon making decisions that take account of the complexity and viability of the territory. His warning about the dangers of any system's members assuming they can control the whole is echoed in his statement that "the unit of survival is not the breeding organism, or the family line, or the society.... The unit of survival is a flexible organism-in-its-environment."[9] And in another place he urges us to recognize that "*the unit of evolutionary survival turns out to be identical with the unit of mind.*"[10]

Bateson's way of understanding the map–territory relationship connects directly with what has been identified earlier as the person's culturally derived framework of understanding. Two features of a person's conceptual map that correspond most closely to that earlier discussion include the way in which, as Bateson claims, most of "the mental process is unconscious," and its becoming part of the "determinative memory" influencing what aspects of the web of information the person will respond to, and how. Although Bateson does not deal directly with culture in the essays where he most fully articulates his understanding of mental processes, this is really the area of human experience he is pointing to when he warns of the danger of an ecology of bad ideas. The following statement seems to summarize Bateson's ecological model of understanding and provides a bridge to our concern with establishing the conceptual underpinnings for a more adequate approach to formal education.

When you narrow down your epistemology and act on the premise "What interests me is me, or my organization, or my species," you chop off consideration of other loops of the loop structure. You decide that you want to get rid of the by-products of human life and that Lake Erie will be a good place to put them. You forget that the eco-mental system called Lake Erie is a part of your wider eco-mental system—and that if Lake Erie is driven insane, its insanity is incorporated in the larger system of your thought and experience."[11]

He does not, of course, mean "your" in the sense of individual authorship, but is referring here to a shared set of cultural thought patterns.

An Ecologically Based Approach to Education

The previous examination of cultural myths contained in textbooks, as well as in the thinking of educational liberals and conservatives, brought up a set of beliefs that now need to be reconsidered in light of an ecological model of existence. The most important of these includes how we think about the nature of time, knowledge, freedom, change, community, science, and technology. There are other aspects of our guiding beliefs—how we view success, our dichotomy between "man" and nature, our tendency to use mechanistic models for understanding everything from the "functioning" of the brain to such other basically human/cultural processes as education. But the latter beliefs seem to be framed by the mythic dimensions of these more fundamental metaphors. The speeches of university presidents seldom leave out references to the empowering nature of certain forms of knowledge, and to the necessity of bringing our individual and social practices into line with a particular way of thinking about freedom, change, community, and the fullness of human existence. These dimensions of the thought process of mainstream culture are also distinctively framed by social reformers, manipulated by hucksters who want to create the illusion their product is connected to higher purposes, and encoded in the activity of artists. The context and form of representation varies widely, but the symbolic content—the conceptual images evoked by the words—is fairly orthodox across many (but not all) strata of society.

The generative metaphors used to frame our way of

understanding knowledge, freedom, change, and the rest, have been used to reinforce both the process of analogic thinking and an attitude taking for granted the individual as the basic social unit. That is, learning to think within the epistemic traditions certified by public education is viewed as creating more opportunities for the individual, just as science and technology are interpreted as benefitting the individual and through the individual collectively the society and state. These culturally specific metaphors are also fundamental to the culture represented in the curricula of our public schools and universities. Indeed, influencing the thought process of the individual who is represented as a culture-free being is one of the central purposes of education.

In some parts of the curriculum individual empowerment ("competency" is often used as an equivalent term) is attained by learning a body of factual information—often framed in a way that emphasizes an upward ascent of humankind—and in others it involves learning methods of inquiry, analysis, data collection, and now deconstruction. But the linchpin is the individual who must use the knowledge within the competitive social arena of interest group politics, which is now how "community" is primarily understood by people who have acquired a university education—including public school teachers. For the reader who may think these are unfounded generalizations about the dominant conceptual orientations reinforced through the curricula (the mind set of teachers and professors as part of the curriculum), they have only to examine the books read, the courses offered, and the general lack of deviation from the mainstream orthodoxy on the part of administration and faculty. Put another way, the curricula and the people who oversee how it is to be interpreted reproduce the conceptual templates that have guided our approach to a modern, technologically based, consumer-oriented society. Although there are intense sources of conflict and alienation, and even genuine iconoclasts, among faculty at all levels of formal education, the process is that of cultural reproduction, and thus development along a pathway dictated by the cultural root metaphors encoded in the language.

Bateson's understanding of humans as interdependent with the life processes of larger systems undercuts, as we have seen, the conventional image of the individual; it also leads to reframing how we think about freedom, change, and the other basic conceptual building blocks of the dominant American culture. This reframing process, in turn, suggests a fundamentally different approach to certain areas of formal education, even though for the immediate future education will continue within schools and universities in the form we know today. But it has been nearly impossible to get academics (regardless of level of institutional affiliation) to agree that different cultural groups have their own epistemological orientations, Therefore, achieving agreement on replacing the myth of an anthropocentric universe with the root metaphor that represents life as a mental ecology might revive our belief in the existence of miracles. If evidence of a stressed environment were less prevalent, one suspects that the process of educational reform suggested here would founder over disagreement on the nature of metaphorical thinking—if it got even that far.

The future direction of cultural development must be, if we are to believe the evidence on environmental deterioration, in the direction of a more benign relationship with the habitat. To recall the statement by Lester R. Brown and Sandra Postel that could serve as a guiding moral maxim, "a sustainable society satisfies its needs without diminishing the prospects of the next generation."[12] This suggests a shift from a culture of progress, with continual experimentation with new ideas, values, and technologies, to a survival-oriented culture, one that puts more emphasis on constructing a rich symbolic world to sustain its members over the long-term. As current language legitimates experimentation by enveloping it in the myth of progress, we must reconstitute our guiding metaphors, with some given a different emphasis and others replaced entirely.

The following reworking of our master metaphorical templates would seem to move us in the right direction in terms of revitalizing the curriculum. Suggesting changes in our language may sound naive in the face of the immediate environmental challenges we face. But if we consider how the feminist movement focused attention on the importance of realigning the language with analogues that now seem more appropriate, we can see that long-term solutions involve changes in consciousness, which means changing language.

Guiding
metaphors of a culture of
progress and environmental
exploitation

New (and ancient)
guiding metaphors for a
sustainable culture

Change (Innovation,
Experimentation). Belief that
change is progressive. Being
new (in ideas,
values, products), is an
expression of progress.

Tradition. An awareness of
continuities with the past.
Valuing traditions (cultural
patterns) that contribute to
long-term sustainability. But
redirecting or discarding
traditions that threaten survival.

Freedom. Choice of ideas
and values by the
autonomous individual.

Freedom. "Restriction of self
for sake of others"
(Solzhenitsyn). Self as a cultural
being whose individualized
needs and forms of expression
are part of a larger mental ecology. Interdependence.

Community. A geographical
area, a collection of common
interests. Humans only.

Community. An ecology of life
forms. Energy and information
webs that include humans as
dependent members. A source
of analogue thinking.

Science. The way to explain,
predict, and control
natural phenomena,
the culture-free way of
knowing. Associated with
progress and rational
understanding. Value-free.
Mastery of nature.

Science. One of many forms
of knowing. A way of
understanding relationships,
patterns, and processes.
Observer influences how
phenomenon is understood.
Wholeness. No clear edges.

Technology. Rationally
formulated procedures,
designed to be context-free.
Concerned with improving
efficiency, which must be
measurable. Part of a
mechanistic mind set.
The expression of progress
and modernization, and "Man's"
power to control nature.
Experimental.

*Environmentally Sensitive
Technology.* Sensitive to
environmental/cultural context.
Contributing to sustainable
community delelopment, based
on an ecological model of
understanding. Built upon
traditional technologies. Using
local sources of energy and
skill. Decentralized.

| *Knowledge.* From rational thought and observation. Explicit. Basis of generalizations across cultures. Contributes to freeing individual from the hold of tradition. Acquired mainly through books or scientific observation. Elevates "man" over other forms of life. The basis of human progress. Secular. | *Many forms of knowledge.* Thought process influenced by epistemological orientation of cultural groups. Many forms: tacit, theoretical, critical, technical, folk, encoded (in genes, language, cultural artifacts, plants, animals, etc.), poetic, spiritual, bodily. Continuities with the past. Responsibility for not diminishing future prospects. |

An ecological model for educational reform is appropriate for a number of reasons. But the most important is that as an analogue it aligns our approach to public education with a pattern of thinking that takes account of the relationships that bind our destiny to that of the environment. It also helps place in the foreground Bateson's concern that the symbolic maps we inherit from the past are increasingly poor guides for understanding the territory we now find ourselves in. The problem, to use Bateson's metaphor of an ecology of bad ideas (like an "ecology of weeds" that overwhelms the natural diversity), is to take a fresh look at how we are connected to the past, and to current information and energy webs. This leads to a reconsideration of what we regard as useful knowledge for guiding our own lives and for passing on to the next generation.

John Berger's distinction between cultures of survival and cultures of progress takes on greater meaning today as the myth of unending progress begins to unravel. Although our technological ability and the dominant ideology governing economic and political relationships still sustain the illusion of continued growth and prosperity, we are all cultures of survival now, although some are likely to survive on more generous terms, perhaps bordering on luxury. To recall part of Berger's discussion, one of the distinguishing characteristics that separates the two types of cultures, which could also be called "modern" and "traditional," is that the narratives and practices of the former are framed by the belief that the expansion of material opportunities is ever outward, while the latter, in recognizing the limits of nature's bounty and the threat from natural cycles, are framed by a reliance on past practices and beliefs. That is, cultures of survival rely more on the proven traditions of the past as a guide to what has enabled them to survive while others disappeared. This does not mean these cultures are against change. Rather, it suggests a sense of caution toward innovation. Put another way, the analogues used to judge the prospects of an innovation are rooted in a "community of memory," the phrase used by Robert Bellah and his co-authors.[13] But the final standard is its meeting the collective obligation to future generations.

If we can avoid misinterpreting the recommendation that we adopt a more thoughtful attitude toward that part of the past–present–future continuum that has to do with what has been proven (i.e., living traditions) rather than the quest to control the future, we would then have one of the elements of an ecologically oriented conceptual framework that will help us recognize the changes in educational priorities we need to make. What is not being suggested here is that we adopt the specific beliefs, values, and technologies of a particular survival-oriented culture. But a sense of where we are in the flow (or cycle?) of time seems more prudent than the rush to experiment, particularly since the unanticipated consequences of many current technological innovations now verge on the catastrophic.

It may be that the patterns now used to transmit culture in a classroom setting are suited only to fostering an individualized approach to the rational process and to decontextualized forms of knowledge. Reliance on encoding knowledge in print makes it very difficult to avoid presenting students with anything other than abstract knowledge. The other extreme of having students rely upon their own feelings and thoughts for making sense of experience, which is more characteristic of the elementary grades than universities, also seems to ignore the essential elements of an educational process where a mentor shares the skills, tacit patterns, and verbal guidance in the context of a real problem-solving or ceremonial situation. Ivan Illich envisaged a "convivial" form of education that avoids both shortcomings in our approach to schooling, by maintaining a balance between personal choice and mentoring.[14] But his arguments for deschooling are not likely to be taken seriously—at least in the immediate future.

The changes suggested here are not intended to divert attention from the possibility of considering more fundamental changes in the future. Rather they reflect changes in the conceptual frameworks used to make judgments about what should be included in public school and university curricula, and how they are to be interpreted. Essentially, these changes involve a process of reframing what constitutes the knowledge being passed on to students, and thus do not require massive government grants to carry them out. But they will involve the ability on the part of public school teachers and university faculty to bring into question attitudes taken for granted about the conceptual building blocks upon which many academic disciplines now rest. The following proposals, it must be remembered, are not the threat; rather, the real threat has to do with the scale of natural consequences that follow from continued cultural mistakes.

Changing from an Anthropocentric to an Ecological Model of Historical Understanding

Currently, presentations of history involve putting humans in the foreground—their thoughts, artistic achievements, wars, political struggles, technological developments, and so on. This anthropocentric bias is further strengthened by representing social change as the expression of progress. This narrative tradition seldom gives an adequate account of how different aspects of cultural development—political and religious ideas, arts, technologies and economic practices, etc.—were influenced by the unique features of the local ecosystems. Nor does it provide an adequate understanding of the culture's impact on soil fertility, wildlife, and the nonrenewable elements of the environment. Historical understanding should situate humans in the context of natural systems, and it should avoid anesthetizing students with the myth of progress. Examples of how history can help illuminate the interplay between cultural practices and local habitat include William Cronon's *Changes in the Land: Indians, Colonists, and the Ecology of New England*, Carolyn Merchant's *The Death of Nature: Women, Ecology, and the Scientific Revolution*, and Frederick Turner's *Beyond Geography: The Western Spirit Against the Wilderness*.

Giving More Attention to the Development of
Ecologically Sound Folk Practices and Technologies

Accounts of the past too often have focused on exemplary individuals in politics, philosophy, science, and other fields of endeavor. Recently, the experiences of common people, as well as marginalized groups like women, have been given greater attention. This now needs to be supplemented by giving more emphasis to the development of technologies and folk practices that minimize disruption of the environment. This history of sustainable practices should also take into account the achievements of non-Western peoples. By shifting the emphasis from the development of energy-intensive and high-prestige technologies to technologies that are refinements of historically rooted practices, students may begin to recover part of the knowledge built up over millenia of environmentally responsive practices.

Learning How Guiding Conceptual Frameworks Altered
the Way the Human–Habitat Relationship Was Understood

Such areas of inquiry and expression as philosophy, religion, political theory, science, and art (now itself heavily supported by a body of theoretical writings) originated in the West partly as a reaction to earlier stages of cultural development, variously perceived as barbaric, pagan, primitive. These new developments can also be viewed as attempts to turn consciousness in new directions promising greater human understanding and control of life processes. The other pathways of cultural development, particularly primal cultures whose members viewed themselves as participants in the natural system, thus became part of the past that had no place in the memory of rational people. The conceptual building blocks put in place over the past twenty-five hundred years have walled Westerners off from so-called "primitive" forms of consciousness that had evolved a complex "land ethic" going, in terms of spirituality, far beyond Aldo Leopold's more recent formulation. The consequences of environmental degradation caused by Western technological practices also was ignored. How this happened needs to be understood. These conceptual building blocks, continually relativized by the drive to acquire new ways of thinking, are a constitutive part of the mental ecology students take on, often in attenuated form, as their own modes of thinking. To understand themselves as well as the form of consciousness that will allow them to re-connect with the larger mental ecology of plants, animals, soil, and the rest of nature, it is essential to reframe the development of Western ideas from a self-congratulatory history of progress to a reconsideration of influential thinkers' assumptions about what can be termed, in all its complexity, the "man"/nature relationship. Herbert N. Schneidau's *Sacred Discontent: The Bible and Western Tradition*, Morris Berman's *Coming to Our Senses: Body and Spirit in the Hidden History of the West*, and Ellen Dissanayake's *What Is Art For?* are examples of the radical reframing process suggested here.

Changing the Guiding and Legitimating Ideology of Science and Technology

When students learn about the methods and achievements of science, a taken-for-granted attitude toward the most basic tenets of modern liberal ideology is also being reinforced. Liberalism, with its assumptions about the progressive nature of change and of rational understanding as the source of empowerment and self-direction, is like an aura that surrounds the activities of the scientist. It also surrounds and gives legitimacy to technological innovation. Although technology, now largely inseparable from science, has become a dominant aspect of Western cultures, the underlying assumptions and long-term consequences of technology have seldom been studied directly in American universities; and its treatment in public schools seldom goes beyond a listing of the latest technological marvels.

Both science and technology need to be studied in a systematic manner, but within the ideological framework of what might best be called ecological conservatism. This form of conservatism, as pointed out earlier, takes account of the interdependence of cultural practices and the life-sustaining characteristics of natural systems. It also recognizes, in a way that liberalism does not, that the margin of surplus that previously allowed for failed cultural experiments, like the use of DDT as a pesticide, has largely disappeared. Whereas liberalism lauded contributions to progress as the highest human endeavor, ecological conservatism emphasizes the importance of understanding human culture as part of a larger self-correcting system, as Bateson suggested. Consequently, cultural hubris and narrowly conceived experiments would be considered as inappropriate.

In addition to learning, without the overlay of liberal ideology, the basics that now constitute scientific knowledge, students should also study the history of science and technology, particularly their interaction with other cultural developments. This would help students recognize the shaping influence of culture, and how culture has, over time, been altered by scientific and technological developments. Students should also learn to examine closely advances in scientific understanding and technological control, as well as their unintended consequences, like the hole in the ozone layer and the loss of genetic diversity in plants. Lastly, reframing our approach to teaching the next generation of scientists and technologists, as well as citizens who will be concerned with the politics of the biotic community, should include learning how to assess the influence of scientific/technological developments on cultural patterns—such as how to do a cultural impact study. For example, we know that a technology like the computer amplifies certain characteristics within the culture, and reduces other tendencies. That is, it amplifies the importance of explicit forms of knowledge and the cultural/epistemological orientation that represents all thought as based on data; it reduces by putting out of focus the importance of tacit and metaphoric forms of knowledge. To put this another way, the form of knowledge this technology can "process" is based on cultural assumptions about the irrelevance of tradition. Learning to think relationally about the impact of science and technology on culture—and by extension, on the environment—may lead to asking the question that seemed totally inappropriate in the days of liberal-dominated science. Will this new knowledge, and the technology it fosters, contribute to long-term sustainability?

More Emphasis on Arts, and Less on Areas of Study that Further the State and a Consumer-Oriented Society

Music, dance, art, narrative, poetry, and theatre represent the areas of future human growth and progress (if we even want to keep using these comforting metaphors). Long journeys or short trips through these symbolic landscapes are not dependent upon the use of fossil fuel, nor do they add carbon dioxide to the atmosphere, unless, of course, they are presented as consumer experiences like a rock concert. The arts represent areas of opportunity for creative expression, and for connecting with realities symbolically represented by other peoples. They can be the medium for community participation, where shared experience elevates and transforms. The arts are also metaphorical languages, sources of challenge for reflecting on the kinds of experiences that could become the analogues upon which collective experiences are to be based.

But in the area of art, the approach must be radically different from the current modernist ethos, what Suzi Gablik calls "the retreat into privatism and self-expression, which means that there is no example to follow, no authority to rely on, no discipline to be received."[15] Geertz reminds us that art, even when it has no other purpose to serve than to overturn the authority of tradition, is an expression of the deepest guiding beliefs of a culture; this suggests a partial way of redirecting the human need for giving symbolic expression a transformative power. If culture—the sign system and conceptual categories that give texture and definition to everyday life—is the invisible presence that guides the artist's hand and sense of vision, the characteristics of the larger biotic community influence the evolution of cultural patterns and determine which patterns will survive over the long-term. The challenge now is to move away from the relativism that characterizes the dominant culture by developing art as a spiritual language that allows for experiencing the deeper connections of person, culture, and physical habitat.

Learning About the Bio-Region

The current ethos that determines much of the curriculum from elementary through graduate school is predicated on representing the student as a rootless individual. The legitimating metaphors for disregarding both the student's traditions and bioregion include "individual empowerment," "rational self-determination," "social mobility," and "citizen of the world community." When filled with the right form of abstract knowledge, including data gathering and processing techniques, the individual is then presumed to be capable of living successfully anywhere, which also means frequent changes in geographical location. This ethos of the rootless but rationally armed individual is supported by an economic ideology that views consumer markets, technology, and exploitation of "natural resources" as part of a worldwide system. A consequence of the mind set fostered by this approach to education can be seen in the current situation where highly educated people view with nearly total indifference the rapid depletion of the nation's petroleum resources. Knowing about the existence of adequate reserves in other parts of the world provides all the assurance needed for continuing current patterns of life.

This orientation to educating the person to be a participant in a world economy, too often a matter of learning to look elsewhere for scarce natural resources, must be changed for two reasons. First, the economically and technologically powerful will continue to distort the possibilities for local economic and technological self-sufficiency by less powerful and often tradition-oriented societies. Second, the people who participate in the dominant consumer-oriented society need to learn how to live more within the limits of their own bioregions. Failure to begin moving in this direction will result in increasing economic disruption at the local level (witness what has happened to timber employment in the Northwest as a result of log exports and overcutting to meet the demands of outside markets) and more military conflict over access to natural resources.

A curriculum that fosters a knowledge of the student's bioregion seems more consistent with Bateson's insight that the unit of survival is "a flexible organism-in-its environment" and that the ideas that guide human action should come out of the patterns that connect them. Viewing the person as a participant within a larger ecology (as opposed to the invader who exploits the local ecological systems and moves on or now simply orders the resources shipped from afar) leads to a radically different set of curricular priorities, as Gary Snyder and Ron and Suzanne Scollon have suggested. Learning about one's own bioregion involves studying about the plants, animals, soils, sources of water, economic and technological practices, and the community of memory that encodes the collective wisdom about both past mistakes and sustainable practices. How local patterns and practices are affected by those of other regions, as well as at the international level, would also be important to understanding the problem of sustainability. As both Snyder and the Scollons point out, learning about one's own bioregion may contribute to what often is missing in the modern person's relationship to the environment: a sense of care that comes out of experiencing the connectedness within one's bioregion. The questions asked by the Scollons seem especially pertinent to whether knowledge will be used to exploit and move on or to nurture and renew the web of relationships. As they put it: "Learning place also means a commitment to place. What is your commitment? Are you there to stay or just passing through? What's your attitude to those who stay and those who pass through? With whom do you identify and with whom do you connect yourself?"[16]

Teaching, Culture, and Communicative Competence

The suggestion that the forms of knowledge given privileged status in the curricula of public schools and universities be radically changed brings into the open the political nature both of the educational process and the task of reconstituting the root metaphors upon which the culture of modernism is based. Whether we can reach a consensus on the most basic questions surrounding the connections between cultural beliefs and environmentally disruptive practices is in itself problematic. The continuing series of publications dealing with the findings of scientific studies of changes in the environment continues to refer to the actions of people, countries, and generally humankind. But they uniformly ignore the point that people and countries must be understood as embedded in the conceptual orientations of their distinctive cultural traditions. The recent report of the National Academy of Sciences, *One Earth/One Future: Our Changing Global Environment*, is only the latest example. Although practice suggests otherwise, making this connection should be easy compared to overcoming the political impasses that will arise in trying to revamp the curriculum, particularly at the university level. Recent attempts at Stanford University and elsewhere to deemphasize the Western canon in order to provide an increasing multicultural student population with the opportunity to encounter their own cultural traditions suggests how acrimonious the process can become among academics. But it is difficult to envision what an effective alternative to this kind of curriculum reform might be.

There is, however, a basis for guarded optimism that individual school teachers and university faculty will quietly begin to make changes in the content of their courses. Just as achievements of women and other minority groups are increasingly incorporated into course syllabi, the daily account of ecological problems is leading to minor changes in what students are assigned to read, and in class discussions. But when we look back on the length of time it took our society to begin reforming itself in racial and gender practices, and recognize that the same combination of denial and glacial pace of reform is part of how we are confronting the new crisis, we can only hope that the largely invisible efforts by individual educators is widespread and that the cultural maps being made available to students accurately represent the territory that must now be rediscovered.

Educational reform has another dimension related to curriculum reform, but distinctive in several important ways. The actual process of teaching itself cannot be separated from the patterns and epistemological orientation of the culture. That is, the use of the body, paralinguistic cues like voice pitch, social space, and even silence itself involve both teacher and students in a complex ecology of signs that communicate attitudes toward relationships and content. Often what is communicated about relationships, like a tone of voice, body posture, and even where the teacher stands in the room, will influence the student's attitude toward the teacher and thus the content of the curriculum. If students feel they are being talked down to, the subject matter will take on secondary significance, if not dismissed entirely by students as irrelevant. How behavior can be understood as a culturally patterned language system, as well as implications for teacher decision making, have been discussed more fully in *Responsive Teaching: An Ecological Approach to Classroom Patterns of Language, Culture, and Thought.*

The more critical issues, in terms of the culture/ecological-crisis connection, relate to how the process of teaching is based on largely unconscious cultural assumptions that give the dominant culture of modernism its distinctly Cartesian orientation. Recognizing how these assumptions are embodied in the process of teaching, and what an ecologically based model of teaching would be like, are the immediate issues needing to be addressed. Reforming the curriculum along the lines suggested here would be undermined by a Cartesian style of teaching. The analogues have to be consistent all the way around, from passing on the culture to the next generation to living in an interdependent relationship with the environment.

Aspects of the Cartesian mind set can be seen in a teaching style that reduces content to "culture-free" facts and information. It is present when the teacher uses language as though it were a neutral conduit for getting ideas and information across to students. It is present when the teacher associates knowledge and the thought process with the mental processes occurring in the head of a particular individual (teacher, student, author from a specific culture). Finally, Cartesianism is present when the teacher relates to students as autonomous, potentially rational agents. These assumptions lead to a process of teaching-learning where objective examinations are used to determine students' grasp (recall) of factual information presented through lectures and readings. These assumptions also increase the use of lectures where the information and analysis are broadcast, like throwing seeds on a plowed field, to waiting students. A Cartesian style of teaching is visible not only in the tendency to break knowledge into ever smaller components and in a procedural, problem-solving orientation to thinking, but also in the areas of silence it creates. The latter include the metaphorical nature of language and thought, the multiple layers of cultural templates that unconsciously guide human thought and behavior, and the tacit nature of how most of a person's cultural knowledge is learned and practiced. These areas of silence become sources of political conflict for students whose cultural traditions have evolved ways recognizing and valuing the connected nature of knowledge, context, continuity, and practice. For the less semiotically oriented students of the dominant culture, the silences further strengthen their Cartesian mind set, with its mind–body, "man"–nature dualisms.

The purer form of Cartesian teaching, it must be pointed out, is more prevalent in universities than in the public schools, where a variety of ideological genres—which now recognize the multicultural nature of the student population and learning styles—are mixed and stirred into an intellectual soup that can best be called "relativism." But even in public school classrooms and faculty meetings where there is talk about "empowerment," the "autonomous learner," "learning styles," important aspects of Cartesianism continue to serve as the collective schema for understanding. These include the assumption that ideas and feelings (an area where Descartes has had to yield to the insights of Freud and the prescriptions of Rogers) originate with the individual, and the anthropocentrism that is reflected in the image of the individual as a spectator of an external world that can be humanized by choice and technological manipulation. Students are conditioned by years of classroom learning, where they experience the syncretism of often conflicting ideological traditions; this, in turn, reflects the failure of higher education to insure that an understanding of the dominant Western intellectual traditions is part of the classroom teacher's professional knowledge. Students will thus enter the highly politicized world of adults in a nearly complete state of innocence about the metaphorical nature of thought and the shaping influence of culture. Ironically, they will also feel empowered by not being encumbered with either useless historical facts or an awareness that the present, as Edward Shils put it, is in the grip of the past.

What is not being suggested here is that there is a Batesonian style of teaching. But the more modest claim can be made that Bateson's understanding of the interconnectedness of a mental ecology, as well as other insights from the sociology of knowledge and recent work in language/thought relationships, help illuminate how teachers' decisions in the critical area of primary school socialization can help lay the conceptual foundations for students' communicative competence. A further claim can also be made that, when the teacher frames the learning process in terms of an ecological model, students are likely to develop a greater sensitivity to relationships, interactive patterns, and the multiple pathways of information exchanges that connect cultural and natural systems. In short, this will provide students better models for understanding the map/territory relationships, where the awareness of their own connectedness with the fate of the territory causes them to be more concerned with the adequacy of their conceptual maps.

But before explaining what is involved in an ecologically responsive model of teaching, it is necessary to clarify how the phrase "communicative competence" is being used here. The phrase has been used by several authors, each giving it a distinctive meaning. The anthropologist, Dell Hymes, used the phrase to designate the person's ability both to speak the language of her/his cultural group and to conform to the norms that govern its use in terms of social context, status differences, and metacommunication patterns.[17] More recently, communicative competence has been associated with the Critical Theorist, Jurgen Habermas. Framed by the emancipatory interests of this Marxist school of thought, and by Habermas' own penchant for elaborate theoretical formulations free of any specific and in-depth understanding of cultural embeddedness, communicative competence became associated with a form of rational discourse that was to establish social consensus on the basis of truth rather than interests. The complexity of his theory made it possible for academics to build personal careers on the interpretation and criticism of his ideas, but when all the dust has settled from their efforts there is little in his theory of communicative competence that relates to the world of everyday experience.

Communicative competence, as used here, designates not only the ability to speak the language and use it according to the norms of the cultural group (Hymes), but also the ability to participate in (even to initiate) the public discourse about problematic aspects of social life. More simply put, it is being used here to bring out the political potential of language, highlighted by the mainstream cultural ideal of participatory decision making. Communicative competence in some areas of social decision making does not mean that this more fully articulated position will necessarily prevail, but it does mean that a person can at least enter into the discussion, which is not possible if the process of socialization has left her/him with only taken-for-granted beliefs and the limited language code that goes along with them. For example, parents, school board members, and public educators were largely unable to enter into the discourse that represented computer illiteracy as a new form of social pathology. The cost of letting interested experts and corporations establish the language used to frame the public's understanding of the educational empowering characteristics of the computer was a massive outlay of school budget dollars. More recent examples include policies pertaining to toxic waste disposal, protection of old growth forests, drugs, public support of the arts, and reform of public education. With more areas of individual and social life becoming politicized through the breakdown of traditional patterns, the need for communicative competence becomes greater, particularly if we are to avoid the consequences of centralizing political power in corporate boardrooms and political bureaucracies that increasingly have come under the influence of special interest groups.

Not only is the need for communicative competence on the part of citizens becoming more obvious, there is also a need to reframe how the citizen views this source of political empowerment. Communicative competence, when viewed from a more political perspective, could lead to strengthening the cultural orientation toward individual pursuit of self-interest. But if the process of schooling, as well as other sources of socialization, can help establish connectedness and interdependency as a more accurate way of understanding the person–community and, by extension, the human–natural community relationship, communicative competence may increasingly contribute to a form of political discourse that takes account of the problem of long-term sustainability. There is a need to shift the root metaphor, which frames how communicative competence is understood, from Cartesianism, which partly underlies the liberal view of the autonomous individual, to that of a participant in an interdependent ecological system. This must be kept in mind as we begin exploring how the teacher's control over the dynamics of primary socialization influences the form of communicative competence the student develops.

Primary socialization occurs in any situation where a person is learning something for the first time from an already socialized member of society, whom we shall call the "significant other" in the relationship. The child's first encounters with siblings and care givers, where the patterns of appropriate behavior and the first words for thinking and communication are given, are examples of primary socialization. Learning to read, to think about self, to understand the scientific method or what an experiment is, may involve primary socialization, even for people who possess very complex self-images and social repertoires, as in learning how to think about themselves as retirees. A significant other can be anybody who is perceived, for a wide range of reasons, as possessing the knowledge of how to act and think in a particular situation. Not all persons who want to share their way of thinking about a situation are perceived as significant others, and not all significant others have accurate knowledge or are always aware of the unexamined assumptions they pass on to the person undergoing primary socialization. The process is further complicated by the different previous experiences and already built interpretive frameworks the participants bring to the relationship. Ethnic and gender differences between the person undergoing socialization and the significant other can lead to profound misunderstandings, while a shared cultural background between the participants in this relationship may result in a mutual strengthening of behavior already taken for granted.

In spite of these variables and the fact that primary socialization is an ongoing aspect of social life, it is possible to focus specifically on primary socialization in classrooms from kindergarten to graduate seminars. Only the degree of vulnerability to the influence of the significant other varies— which is not to say that graduate students entirely escape the dependent relationship when they are hearing something for the first time. Primary socialization in schools, for the most part, has a distinctive characteristic that separates it from what occurs socially sanctioned in the larger society. That is, the classroom involves acquiring the sanctioned language and theoretical frameworks for how to think about different aspects of experience, and about aspects of the culture (like history, other cultures, what was going on in the mind of an author, and so forth) that will never be part of the student's personal experience. For the most part, primary socialization in the classroom involves the more symbolic dimensions of culture, and often there is little opportunity to test the explanations in real life situations. To put it in Bateson's terms, it is a purer form of conceptual map building, and there is less accountability for whether the maps relate to any territory. In schools where there is an emphasis on equating student experience with education, the conceptual map-building aspects of primary socialization may be minimal.

Bateson's insight that most mental process is unconscious, that the person's (student's) thought process is part of a larger mental ecology that extends both back in time and across the pathways that connect culture and habitat, and that the conceptual maps may incorrectly represent the most important features of the territory (to stay with that metaphorical image), relates directly to what occurs in primary socialization in classrooms. When framed as a mental ecology, the Cartesian tendency to view language as neutral, the student as an individual, and the rational process of individuals as based on data, tend to recede as a useful way of understanding the process of learning. Borrowing from the sociology of knowledge, it is possible to use a new vocabulary that helps illuminate critical areas of teacher decision making within the process of primary socialization. Again, it must be stressed that the essential characteristics of decision making occur at all levels of the formal educational process, but the student's maturity affects which variables appear at a given level.

Regardless of whether it's a complex topic like the causes and consequences of the Civil War or a seemingly simple one like how to take a true/false examination, there seem to be four distinct yet interrelated stages in the movement from the liminality of encountering a new area of the culture to being able to think and act in a way congruent with the patterns shared by the significant other. These stages, or what might better be called "gate keeper" situations, involve what loosely can be termed "defining what is," "implicit/explicit knowledge," the "fact/interpretation distinction," and the "reproduction of the culture's root metaphors." The decisions made by the teacher, when accepted by students as the significant other in each of these gate keeper situations, relate directly to whether the cultural patterns are being learned in a way that contribute to communitive competence, as well as whether communicative competence will be understood within a Cartesian/liberal or an ecological framework of connected community.

The initial step in primary socialization involves the significant other's (hereafter called the "teacher" to contextualize the discussion) providing the student with the words and conceptual framework for thinking about a new area of cultural experience. Because thought is initially organized by the schema encoded in the iconic and generative metaphors, the first words provided by the teacher and textbook may help organize thought in terms of patterns already accepted by members of the language community. Learning something for the first time, like "Columbus discovered the New World," "All social scientists use evidence obtained through observation, documents, surveys," and "1945" means, quite literally, that the student does not have a basis for challenging this initial process of naming, which also establishes how relationships are to be understood. The language and conceptual framework for establishing "What Is" provides, to use Jerome Bruner's phrase, the initial conceptual scaffolding for subsequent thought.

This aspect of primary socialization has a number of dimensions that involve fundamental decisions by the teacher. Often the decisions are unconsciously made, and reflect the teachers' own taken-for-granted beliefs formed by the earlier process of their own primary socialization. In effect, to use Bateson's terminology, when certain variables are present the student is being socialized to the "determinative memory" that has its roots in the metaphorical thinking of people who may have lived centuries ago. When teachers are unaware of their gate-keeper role, and approach teaching as merely passing on knowledge that fits their own beliefs, the students will encounter a language framework that simply reproduces the understanding of the teacher and authors of the textbooks. However, the teacher who is alert to the complexity of the "reality" constitutive moments in primary socialization may make a number of professional decisions that will lead to a fundamentally different form of education.

For example, if the teacher is aware of the metaphorical nature of the language–thought connection, it will then be easier to recognize decisions relating to the conceptual schema encoded in the iconic metaphors (e.g., "New World," "social scientists," and the use of the Christian calendar that leads us to situate events in "1945," to stay with these already used examples). The iconic metaphors given to the student as part of the initial explanation represent what has survived from earlier processes of analogic thinking, which in turn were influenced by the metaphorical language that helped to constitute the sense of reality at that time. In addition to recognizing when it is important to bring out the history of that part of the mental ecology, teachers must also make decisions about the adequacy of the generative metaphors used in the process of analogic thinking when the student is being encouraged to understand the new in terms of the familiar. Is the scientific model of investigation (as a generative metaphor) really adequate for understanding what sociologists, economists, and historians do? Or does it tend to hide how the language, culture, gender, and personal experiences of the "social scientist" enter into the selection and interpretation of the "data"?

The teacher should also be aware of decisions that relate to the complexity of the language framework presented as the initial basis for the student's thought process. Is the vocabulary and conceptual framework adequate for understanding the variegated nature of human experience? Do the explanations of work, technology, and art—to cite examples of primary socialization at both public school and university level—take account of their underlying cultural assumptions and the multiple ways they are woven into the fabric of social and personal life? Or are they presented as ways of thinking that will, if unconsciously accepted by students, serve to block the information pathways connecting students to the changing patterns of social life? For example, how many people working in educational computing reproduce implicit beliefs about the neutrality of technology and the conduit view of language they received from their teachers? There are also decisions to be made about whether the language for thinking about "What Is" relates to the experiences of the students. What students bring to this initial socialization, particularly in terms of personal experiences relating to ethnicity, gender, and social class, are important considerations, if the new language is going to have any real explanatory power.

The interplay of implicit and explicit knowledge is an integral aspect of how "What Is" is represented to students. But in order to illuminate the decisions confronting teachers, we shall focus on it as a distinct aspect of primary socialization. "Implicit knowledge" is used here as nearly synonymous with taken-for-granted belief, and as the person's natural attitude toward cultural patterns. It can also be understood as background knowledge that frames and makes comprehensible the explicit knowledge of which the person is constantly aware. An example of implicit/background knowledge (hopefully, now in the past) are the assumptions and unexamined patterns relating to gender differences and, to use an entirely different example, the way time is understood in the dominant culture. The explicit knowledge that represents the more conscious aspect of primary socialization is embedded in the implicit background knowledge; but the embedded relationships and even the existence of such taken-for-granted background beliefs are often not acknowledged by the teacher, textbook writer, or the student.

There are a number of decisions the teacher makes in this aspect of primary socialization. Whether they are made largely depends upon the nature of the teacher's beliefs. If the teacher is sensitive to the hidden and unconscious nature of the culture being shared in the classroom, three immediate areas of decision making stand out: beliefs embedded in the curriculum materials, in the student's thought process, and in the teacher's own way of thinking. But even being aware of the need to be sensitive to taken-for-granted beliefs (and not all are morally wrong or bad in the sense that they no longer represent an adequate response to present circumstances) does not guarantee that the teacher will be able to recognize even the most critically important background patterns and assumptions. We have only to observe how few public school and university teachers would be able to recognize the many ways in which an anthropocentric world view is represented in the curricula to recognize how complex the problem is.

Beyond the challenge of the teachers' ability to recognize their own underlying beliefs is the difficult problem of knowing which ones to make explicit and which to leave alone. What is taken for granted, like the pattern of writing from left to right, has authority in people's lives. Making explicit involves the relativizing of culturally shared authority, as when the patterns and assumptions of privileged males in a dominant culture were challenged. As pointed out earlier, however, not all fundamental beliefs are wrong, and the political process used within the dominant culture does not always lead to the establishment of a more adequate set of taken-for-granted beliefs. The shift from certain forms of traditional knowledge to believing in the authority of experts is a constant reminder of the danger. An additional issue that makes the teacher's judgment even more difficult is that there may be students in the class whose primary cultural affiliation does not involve a political process where communicative competence, as the phrase is used here, is the norm.

These issues, along with the pedagogical task of dealing with taken-for-granted beliefs in a psychologically nonthreatening manner, make it impossible to resolve the problem through the use of techniques alone. But the presence in the curriculum of so many such beliefs running counter to the evidence of habitat degradation, like the assumptions relating to technology, consumerism, individualism, makes this aspect of primary socialization a most critical challenge.

There is third aspect of primary socialization which occurs as the student is learning from the teacher the language that will constitute thought in a socially congruent manner, and as the explicit explanations play off against, and at other times reinforce, the participant's taken-for-granted beliefs. It has to do with how the explanation is understood by the student. A largely print-based curriculum and the pervasive influence of Cartesianism in the education of teachers have resulted in much of the "knowledge" presented to students being represented as "factual" and "objective." The use of objective tests further strengthens this orientation. When students read or hear accounts that appear to be based on objective observation, there is a greater likelihood, given the cultural backgrounds of the participants, that they will accept these as factual. When this occurs, primary socialization weakens the ability to ask questions and to test the adequacy of explanations against the complexities of experience. Moreover, the factual knowledge may become part of the student's schema of understanding and the authority for future interpretations and actions.

Primary socialization also involves a continuing series of decisions relating to whether students should be allowed to frame the explanations and information in a way that supports the author's misconceptions about factual knowledge, or to help them recognize the metaphorical characteristics of language, as well as how the cultural, gender, and class background of the author are encoded in the descriptions, explanations, and factual information. To put this another way, teachers can let the third-person accounts stand as objective representations of how to think about some area of cultural experience, or they can help students understand them as interpretations and to recognize the cultural forces that influenced them. As not all aspects of the curriculum can or should be put in a cultural/historical context, the teacher has to make judgments about the topics most deserving this more extended treatment, Again, the teacher's own essential beliefs will play an influential and largely unconscious role in the decision-making process.

The last aspect of primary socialization may exert the most powerful influence in blinding students to the mind set of the dominant culture; it may also be the most difficult for teachers and students to recognize. Basically, it is the reinforcment of the root metaphors upon which the culture's values, practices, and ways of knowing are based. In some instances, primary socialization in a classroom setting may actually introduce students to root metaphors not shared by the larger society, like the metaphor of an historical dialectic that leads to interpreting revolutionary change as "progressive." For the most part, however, the curriculum from elementary grades through graduate school reinforces the underlying metaphors of the dominant culture. The earlier chapter on anthropocentrism in textbooks is a good example, in that it demonstrates how "factual knowledge" and values are framed by a deeper set of cultural assumptions— what we are here calling "root metaphors." The use of the pronoun "you," the chapter title of "The Earth You Live On," and the statement, "You can create art," to cite previous examples, make sense to most students who have already been socialized to the root metaphors upon which the mental ecology of the dominant culture is based. The root metaphors are varied; they often are supportive of other basic aspects of our belief system. For example, in American culture our way of thinking about individualism and technology are examples of two deep metaphors that frame the process of analogic thinking, and give us the taken-for-granted schema encoded in our iconic metaphors. But there are other metaphors that provide contradictory maps of everyday reality—like contradictions between the root metaphors of a mechanistic unverse that largely govern the work place and technical problem solving over against the root metaphor of individual equality that appears to govern our political ideals. And at the level of everyday politics and economics a different root metaphor appears to operate, namely, the competitive and unequal pursuit of self-interest.

Recognizing the deep symbolic models that underpin everyday understanding, and knowing when to make them explicit, are two areas of teacher decisions that relate directly to whether primary socialization contributes to the student's communication competence. If the root metaphors are left at the tacit level of understanding, the student's ability to make sense of the "difference which makes a difference" will be limited to their earlier patterns of understanding. That is, the student's ability to understand current relationships and patterns may be limited by a mind set that originated centuries ago and continues to survive in the root metaphors of the culture, like our habit of thinking about time as a measurable unit and of humans as separate from nature.

The process of primary socialization involves teachers performing a gate-keeper role similar to the role that metaphor plays in blocking or facilitating comprehension of the information flowing through the information network that constitutes the student's cultural/natural environment. It can also be understood as constituting the conceptual maps used to make sense of and respond to changes in the territory, to return to Bateson's metaphor. Acquiring the knowledge for communicative competence in negotiating more environmentally sustainable technological practices and ways of thinking will be undermined by teachers who socialize students to the Western canon underlying the modern myth of "progress." Unfortunately, even teachers with good intentions about educating students to becoming better environmental citizens, if they do not understand the culture–language–thought connection, will contribute to the current schizophrenic condition that keeps environmental education from considering the deeper anti-ecological levels of Western consciousness.

An ecologically responsive approach to education requires that teachers recognize the need for reform in both the curriculum and in the process of teaching itself. The two records set in 1989—carbon emissions from fossil fuel use climbing to 5.8 billion metric tons and 88 million people being added to total world population—serve as reminders that the diverging trends of rising human demands on the environment and declining viability of natural systems make the need for radical reform of the educational process, from elementary through graduate school, one of the most urgent problems we face. The challenge for educators will be to assess whether the curricula they teach contribute to the myths of progress and an anthropocentic universe or to sustainable balanced living.

6

The Political
and Spiritual Dimensions of
the Ecological Crisis:
Toward a New Sense of Balance

Implementing any of the educational changes suggested in the last chapter would represent an important shift toward an ecologically responsive form of education. But even if any of the proposals were to prevail over the devotees of the various traditions of anthropocentric thinking—the followers of Bloom and Adler, the advocates of science and secular humanism, and the modernist interpreters of Enlightenment ideology—the change might still be inadequate for reversing the impact of an expanding world population on the environment. Nevertheless, one part of the ecological crisis where we have particular responsibility has to do with an ideology that equates personal identity and success with consumerism, and with possessing the symbols of power and social status. This drive to consume, and to go further into debt, as though it were a sign of success, further strengthens the ecologically destructive practices within our form of economy where the demand for growth in profits leads to creating new markets for a continual stream of technological innovations. The insanity of living in a state of ecological imbalance has been discussed, deplored, and even correctly identified in some quarters for what it really is: namely, a crisis in the direction our spiritual development has taken over the course of the last four to five hundred years.

According to the dictionary, "worship" involves an attitude of reverence, devotion, admiration, and intense love. The dictionary also suggests that worship may take the form of idolizing something—like money, a car, technique, power, social standing. Worshipping the possession of material goods—especially on a scale unimaginable to the Old Testament fathers who constantly warned against the dangers of idolatry before false gods—can be viewed as the modern expression of religion. That is, what is experienced as being the ultimate source of meaning and authority in life are the consumer items that appear to give people in modern society a sense of rich variety and continual excitement. That the experience of the "ultimate" is both as shallow as a mood shift, and as fleeting as the disappearance of newness as the acquired item takes its place in the ordinary patterns of everyday life, does not really matter. The lack of depth appears, to most modern individuals, as an easy trade-off for the increased frequency of momentary "highs" that accompany new purchases. In effect, the credit card has become a religious symbol of the new spirituality. Consumerism as well as other cultural reifications, like the sense of empowerment that comes from using various forms of modern technology, can thus be understood as a cornerstone of today's spirituality.

But "spirituality" is part of a vocabulary that most Americans are uncomfortable using (and it is not really the word of the month in other scientifically and technologically based societies). This is partly a result of the dominance of a secular discourse originally intended to establish a more enlightened way of understanding the sources of human empowerment. Such words as "freedom," "rationality," "progress," "science," and "technology" also now seem to serve the purpose of expressing the modern sense of awe and the ineffable, but they seem to carry a more explicit guarantee of success. We need to begin addressing the implications of both this more limited (even distorted) spirituality and the adequacy of social practices that have evolved as a means of filling the resulting spiritual vacuum.

American social practices and beliefs reveal a deep faith in the efficacy of the political process, particularly when conducted in a democratic manner, to resolve social problems and establish the guidelines for future growth. This increasing dependence upon the political process, it can be argued, is one of the chief ways of expressing our anthropocentrism. By democratizing the political process, we have simply extended to everybody of a certain age the right to participate, which is not the same as prevailing, in public discourse. But it is a political process that represents the individual as the basic social unit; and in its ideal form, it is supposed to be guided by reflective and informed citizens who are able to balance self-interest with that of their larger community. That the ideal is seldom attained, either in terms of genuine reflection or in terms of community-mindedness, is not the main concern here. Rather it has to do with the trajectory we have been following where the political process has been extended into more areas of cultural life.

In order to understand how our increasing belief in the efficacy of the political process has led to more areas of social life being politicized, as well as why this trend is failing, we must examine more closely the connection between public education and the ideology that drives the political process. The deeper conceptual underpinnings of this ideology, it will be argued here, not only have contributed to relativizing American cultural traditions, thus opening them to the nihilism of interest group politics, but are totally inadequate for resolving problems connected with the cultural aspects of the ecological crisis. Important elements of this ideology have played a key role in how we have understood the purpose of public and university education. Indeed, it might be more accurate to say that this ideology has been used to justify the establishment of our system of education. From Thomas Jefferson, Horace Mann, and John Dewey, to current school officials and university presidents, educators used the ideal of a participatory democracy to justify a form of rationalism that was to be acquired through literacy and the privileged knowledge of the curriculum. The form of rationalism learned through schooling, in turn, embodied the cultural assumptions underlying the dominant orientation to politics.

The rhetoric intended to remind the public that an ideal form of a liberal education contributes to an equally ideal form of political democracy usually is presented in ritual settings that make inappropriate an examination of the deeper assumptions that most educators, both out of naivety and (in some instances) self-interest, keep hidden from public scrutiny. These assumptions can be made visible by returning to our earlier discussion of what Alvin Gouldner called the "culture of critical discourse." In recalling the key characteristics

of how the rational process is supposed to be used to establish a new basis of authority upon which belief and social
practice are temporarily to rest, we find the following
assumptions, or what Gouldner calls an "historically evolved
set of rules." Rationally based discourse "(l) is concerned to
justify its assertions, but (2) whose *mode* of justification does
not proceed by invoking authorities, and (3) prefers to elicit
the *voluntary* consent of those addressed on the basis of
the arguments adduced." Other assumptions embedded in
this supposedly open-ended intellectual process to facilitate
the equally open-ended political process are illuminated by
Gouldner's summary:

> The culture of critical discourse [what educators consid-
> er to be the ideal expression of rationally based dis-
> course] is characterized by speech that is *relatively*
> more *situation-free,* more context or field-'independent.'
> This culture thus values expressly legislated meanings,
> and devalues tacit, context-limited meanings. Its ideal
> is: 'one word, one meaning' for everyone and forever.[1]

Our cultural orientation to valuing criticism, as well as
our continual need to re-establish authority on a new rational
basis, suggest that Gouldner has overstated how long the
meaning of words will endure. Nevertheless, his other
observations remain critically important to understanding
how this form of rational thought contributes to a relativizing
process that makes sense within the context of a culture of
progress, but is inadequate for thinking and sustaining the
political process in a culture oriented toward long-term sustainability. As Gouldner notes, the culture of critical discourse "*de-authorizes* all speech grounded in traditional soci-
etal authority, while it authorizes itself, the elaborated
speech variant of the culture of critical discourse, as the
standard of *all* 'serious' speech."[2]
There are several important points that might be lost in a
quick reading of this quotation. The first is that the ground
rules governing rational thought and by extension, the political process, prohibit the acceptance of other forms of cultural authority as the basis of belief and action. This means, as
Gouldner points out elsewhere, that there is no place in the
competitive arena (which has also been referred to as the

"open market place of ideas") for acknowledging the authority of the speaker's experience and status in society. Nor does this form of rationality recognize the authority of a cultural group's symbolic and technical practices, even when they have enabled it to survive in a limited environment. That is, the authority of traditions, which may range from the Austraian Aborigine's songlines, which served over the millenia as both spiritual and geographical maps, to such relatively recent traditions as rotating crops and the design of buildings, have no special standing. The ground rules require that all previous forms of authority be open to critical examination, argument, and the challenge of competing evidence; in a word, the authority underlying all traditions is to be continually relativized, with a new basis of authority continually emerging from the supposedly open competition of ideas.

The second point needing emphasis is that by de-legitimating all other forms of authority only the people who possess the elaborated language code and forms of knowledge essential to this form of rational discourse are equipped to play the game. In effect, the ground rules disqualify everybody except the groups with access to the special form of education essential for this culturally specific form of political discourse.

Although educational and political practices increasingly appear to fall short of being in line with the assumptions underlying critical discourse, the assumptions themselves continue to be held by influential social groups. And they are still invoked to give legitimacy to how political problems are framed, and to provide the authority upon which political decisions increasingly rest (e.g., research reports, surveys, and policy statements). Academics tend to decry the failure to use critical discourse as the means of reaching agreement on political ends. But what they do not understand is that while critical rationalism is a powerful means of making explicit hidden assumptions and social practices, it is particularly inadequate for constituting a new basis of belief and social practice. Its weakness, in effect, lies in the lack of any self-limiting principles, where continued critical analysis would be viewed as inappropriate. Academics also fail to recognize that the guiding assumptions of critical discourse are culturally and historically specific (some would say gender-specific as well).

Politics within the dominant culture are also influenced by the widespread acceptance of the cultural myth that leads people to think of themselves as autonomous individuals. In addition to being caught up in cultural patterns of consumerism, this sense of being an autonomous self leads to the continual quest for a deeper sense of self-expression, authenticity, and personal empowerment. As they attempt to live this cultural metaphor, the surface patterns of critical thought are viewed as complementing the quest to escape the constraints that external forms of authority place on their individuality. Indeed, the cult of individualism (particularly the expressive and utilitarian varieties described in Bellah's *Habits of the Heart)* requires the relativizing process of critical inquiry. But where the root metaphor of the autonomous individual is dominant, politics are circumscribed by what is of interest to the individual. This aspect of the dominant culture also contributes to politicizing more areas of social life, where individual judgment takes on increasing importance and where continual negotiation over the meaning of words, authority for beliefs, and what constitutes appropriate behavior becomes a never-ending treadmill. The energy put into the politics of self-interest, as well as the older variety of interest group politics, becomes important as it erodes the sense of membership in a larger community. When the metaphor of community is extended to include the interdependence of species and other natural systems that constitute the bioregion, we can see the danger posed by increasing our reliance on the use of the political process.

As people begin to recognize that the ecological crisis is more than a newspaper headline and a television "sound bite," and that it has to do with the growing incidence of cancer, as well as the rising prices of food, energy, and disposal of toxic wastes (not to mention increasing international competition for control of increasingly scarce natural resources), we are likely to witness an even deeper weakness in the political process, which has been put out of focus by the ideological lenses of liberalism. This weakness has been identified clearly by a German political theorist who lived at the center of a different period of political disintegration, the breakdown of the Weimer Republic and the rise of Naziism. Although Carl Schmitt's own personal involvement in the events of this period make it difficult to render an overall assessment of his ideas, there is one aspect of his thinking that seems particularly relevant to understanding the emergent features of the political process as we move further into an era of ecological disruption and scarcity.

One of Schmitt's concerns was to identify the basic distinctions that come into play when political action has been reduced to its most basic element, that is, when political action threatens the survival of one of the contending groups. Just as he thought, in the final analysis, that the basic distinction in morality is between good and evil, in aesthetics between beautiful and ugly, and in economics between profitability and unprofitability, so he found the most elementary distinction in the realm of the political is between friend and enemy.[3] That is, the bottom line in the political process is survival as a member of a cultural group. When all the compromises and accommodations have been made short of yielding the beliefs and values on which the group's identity is grounded, this basic political distinction begins to emerge. But Schmitt is careful to specify more precisely how the word "enemy" is to be understood. As he put it,

The enemy is not merely any competitor or just any partner in a conflict in general. He is also not the private adversary whom one hates. An enemy exists only when, at least potentially, one fighting collectivity confronts a similar collectivity. The enemy is solely the public enemy, because everything that has a relationship to such a collectivity of men, particularly to a whole nation, becomes public by virtue of such a relationship.[4]

It is important to understand that Schmitt is not advocating a new set of political categories, but rather identifying one of the most elementary aspects of social existence. The friend–enemy distinction, furthermore, does not carry any prejudgments about which of the adversaries occupies the higher moral ground. Rather, Schmitt appears to be saying that after all the moral rhetoric is cleared away, we find that when a cultural group still has a distinct set of beliefs, and a commitment to perpetuating itself for future generations who will hold essentially the same core beliefs, it will view other groups who threaten it with extinction as the enemy. The Aztecs quickly realized that Hernando Cortès and his army of 400 Spanish soldiers were intent upon their subjugation, and that would mean the extinction of life as they knew it. Similarly, the battles that raged across the North American continent during the nineteenth century had to do with questions of group survival. The friend–enemy distinction was the only political category of thinking at the Battle of the Little Bighorn, and the Native American energy to survive as a distinct cultural way of life was nearly extinguished by the Battle of Wounded Knee. Other groups who currently view themselves as threatened by the democratic process, like the Moral Majority and the religiously based anti-abortion advocates, also appear to use the friend–enemy distinction as the basis of political action. If we can avoid getting into the question of whether their positions are morally defensible, we can more easily recognize the point Schmitt is making about the existential nature of fighting for the survival of group truths and the way of life built upon them.

Schmitt's criticisms of liberalism were directed at what he regarded as the obfuscation of this basic political distinction through an elaborate set of misrepresentations and false promises. The latter are sustained, according to him, by the myth of progress which holds out the promise to the politically vanquished that at some future time they may be able to re-enter the political arena. And if they are able to present compelling ideas and evidence they may, in turn, prevail. If the politically vanquished fail in this attempt, the myth of progress provides a form of cosmic justification for the outcome. Schmitt's insights into the "moral pathos" of liberalism are even more interesting, and deserve to be more fully quoted:

> The political concept of battle in liberal thought becomes competition in the domain of economics and discussion in the intellectual realm. Instead of a clear distinction between the two different states, that of war and that of peace, there appears the dynamic of perpetual competition and perpetual discussion. The state turns into society: on the ethical-intellectual side into an ideological humanitarian conception of humanity, and on the other into an economic-technical system of pro-

duction and traffic. The self-understood will to repel the enemy in a given battle situation turns into a rationally constructed social ideal or program, a tendency or an economic calculation. A politically united people becomes, on the one hand, a culturally interested public, and, on the other, partially an industrial concern and its employers, partially a mass of consumers. At the intellectual pole, government and power turn into propaganda and mass manipulation, and at the economic pole, control.[5]

But beneath the liberal gloss of competition on an even playing field, where the more competitive deserve to prevail, lies the more basic existential issue of group survival.

As the consequences of environmental disruption become more visible, the myth of progress will begin to erode, and with its disappearance will go the sense of hope that sustains the politically defeated's sense of the temporary nature of their situation. Current political etiquette governing how to be a good sport about the outcome of the political game (doesn't a winner always require that there be a loser?) is likely to be jettisoned as cultural groups and nation states face the loss of protein, fiber, and the other sources of energy necessary to sustain themselves. The bottom line, politically, will increasingly become framed by the issue of survival. Then we can expect the friend–enemy distinction to displace more ideologically grounded principles, including the argument that rational planning on a global scale will enable all groups to have a sustainable existence. The current re-emergence of a strong sense of cultural self-awareness sweeping around the world, displacing both Marxism and the liberal view of the autonomous individual, is likely to accelerate the realization that survival as a cultural group is the fundamental issue that frames how all others are to be understood.

Schmitt's insights into the weakness of the political process, exemplified in the violent and uncompromising politics practiced in recent decades in the Middle East, also have implications for another aspect of liberal thought that relates more directly to education. If we sort through the discourse of educational liberalism, we find an interlocking set of metaphors that serve to legitimate each other and, in the process, put out of focus the issue of survival that underlies Schmitt's friend–enemy distinction. Progress, advancement of knowledge, the free marketplace of ideas (freedom of inquiry), scholarship, and so forth, are powerful metaphors— partly because they are considered essential for the unfettered form of thought education is supposed to exemplify. They are also esteemed because of their association with social progress in a wide number of areas. But perhaps the most important metaphor in the discourse of educational liberalism is "academic freedom," and it is this metaphor that is increasingly made problematic by the ecological crisis.

Schmitt's insight that a metaphysical notion of progress obfuscates how the political process is related, most fundamentally, to the issue of survival challenges us to reappraise the special status now given to academic freedom. That is, we need to frame how we think about academic freedom in terms of its contribution to an environmentally sustainable form of culture, rather than in terms of the myth of progress. To state the problem in a more specific way: Should faculty be free (and supported by public resources) to pursue whatever line of inquiry they think important even if their inquiry leads to strengthening the cultural orientation of living beyond what can be sustained over the long-term by the habitat? For example, should academic freedom be used to protect research into how the media can be used more efficiently to create new consumer markets? We can take examples from other areas of the academic community, like the highly esteemed philosopher, Richard Rorty, who uses academic freedom to advance his ideals of relativism (modified by a concern with mitigating the suffering of others) "where we no longer worship anything, where we treat nothing as a quasi-divinity, where we treat everything—our language, our consciousness, our community—as a product of time and chance."[6] His view of the ideal liberal society we should all strive to attain is an interesting example of the point Gouldner was making. Writes Rorty: "A liberal society is one which is content to call 'true' (or 'right' or 'just') whatever the outcome of undistorted communication happens to be, whatever view wins in a free and open encounter."[7] Rorty's use of academic freedom to promote a vision of individual and social relativism is not unique in the academic world, nor is his total disregard for how his ideas, if taken seriously, relate to the ecological crisis. Jacques Derrida is another example of an intellectual who uses the free market of academe to argue that nothing has authority in people's lives except private fantasies and postcards. Other deconstructionists could easily be cited as examples of how academic freedom is used to create a safe haven for intellectuals to build professional careers promoting nihilism and endless word games that can only strengthen the anomic form of individualism upon which our consumer-oriented society depends.

Other areas of the university, particularly in schools of business and certain areas of the sciences, utilize academic freedom to pursue lines of inquiry intended to increase our technological proficiency in areas of social life that seemed essential when framed against the background myth of progress, but seem more problematic when we recognize that the earth's population is now expanding at nearly ninety million people a year. A strong case can even be made that most disciplines within the university are based on an anthropocentric view of the universe, and the more recent assumptions of Western Enlightenment thinking. To return to the question posed by Schmitt's argument that the friend–enemy distinction emerges in the political process when survival becomes problematic for one or more of the contending factions, we can see that this distinction also has relevance for how we think about the consequences and limits of academic freedom. If the achievements of the intellectual process protected by academic freedom contribute to weakening the ecological survival of our own culture, as well as others around the world, should they be viewed as enemies and thus proscribed? This question, in turn, leads to others, such as, "What are to be the guiding principles to replace the old ones embedded in the myth of unending technological and material progress for humankind?" "Can these decisions be made in a way that avoids destroying the positive aspects of academic freedom (that is, the protection academic freedom affords to scholars and others who question current orthodoxies that are contributing to the degradation of the environment)?

Many readers are likely to criticize this line of analysis by arguing that the ecological crisis is now being used to introduce into the university a political element that is foreign to the existing tradition of academic freedom. This reaction ignores, however, that the university is already one of the most highly politicized institutions in society. One of the primary purposes of creating (discovering?) new knowledge and technologies is for the purpose of displacing older ones—which is a political process. Relationships between the university and the many communities affected by its activities are political (often at the friend–enemy level), and relationships both within and between departments are also highly political. In-fighting over budgets, paradigms of understanding, and decisions in the areas of faculty selection and promotion are a common aspect of university life. The current ascendancy of molecular over organic biology is just one example of how academic freedom in the sciences is politicized, not to mention being commercialized by the economic opportunities associated with patenting new discoveries.

Business schools are not likely to hire Marxists, even though the latter subscribe to many of the same taken-for-granted cultural assumptions, and would find a deep ecologist thinker an anathema and a threat to the mind set they wish promoted. Other examples are so numerous and generally recognized within the university that it would not be too far off the mark to say that academic freedom is, for the most part, invoked primarily in situations that have degenerated politically to the friend–enemy distinction, where the survival of a faculty member or academic program is at stake.

Like so many aspects of our guiding beliefs and values now being brought into question by the signs of culture/habitat imbalance, academic freedom should no longer be treated as sacrosanct. Nor is it being suggested here that it should be relegated to the junk yard of outmoded conventions. It may still serve an essential purpose if it can be situated within a moral framework that recognizes the interdependence of natural systems and that human cultures must evolve new or recover older nonexploitive forms of relationships. Even this adjustment in consciousness will involve a political process that may evolve into the politics of survival, or simply be ignored as the intellectual agenda of the Enlightenment continues to frame the process of inquiry within the university. After Rorty and Derrida, it will be interesting to see if academics can take us to new depths of nihilistic thinking. A more likely scenario becoming visible in public school education is a kind of relativism where courses on environmental understanding will be just one part of a diverse curriculum that also includes an emphasis on fostering the autonomous learner. A university counterpart is token support given for a small environmental studies program and more massive support given to a school of business. Pluralism seems to complement moral and intellectual relativism, and as long as most professors and public school teachers share the same illusions of contributing to progress the political issues will remain hidden.

Education and the Recovery of the Spiritual

Any discussion of how public school and university education can contribute to redirecting the form of spiritual development taken in the last several centuries in the West is likely to be misunderstood unless the issues are carefully framed—and even then the word "spirituality" is likely to evoke knee-jerk antagonism from many people who unconsciously support modernism as part of secular humanism. Thus, it is important to summarize the argument being developed here about the spiritual aspects of the ecological crisis. The crucial issue now is not the lack of spirituality in modern society, but rather of having developed cultural forms of spirituality where authority and worshipful attitudes are associated with forms of individualism that lead to treating the environment as an exploitable resource. Thomas Luckmann, a German sociologist, described this form of spirituality in the following manner: "It may be said, in sum, that the modern sacred cosmos symbolizes the social-historical phenomenon of individualism and that it bestows, in various articulations, 'ultimate' significance upon the structurally determined phenomenon of the 'private sphere.'"[8] These "various articulations" include a concern with autonomy, self-expression, self-realization, mobility, sexuality, and familism, all to be fulfilled through consumerism.

The second part of the argument is that the conventional wisdom that the ideal form of rationalism contributes to strengthening a democratic form of politics, to be fostered through public education, ignores how this form of thinking contributes to relativizing other more traditional forms of authority, and that it has proven particularly unsuited for establishing new cultural norms—unless one wants to regard cultural relativism as a new norm. A third part of the argument is that, as the environment becomes more degraded, the basic concern with group survival will become more prominent. Lastly, it is being suggested here that academic freedom, as part of the culture of progress, contributes to new technologies and social expectations that continue to demand more from the environment than can be sustained, and that academic freedom needs to be reframed in terms of a new form of spirituality that takes for granted Bateson's way of understanding that "*the mental characteristics of the system are immanent, not in some part, but in the system as a whole.*"[9] Or as Paul Shepard put it, "ecological thinking... requires a kind of vision across boundaries. The epidermis of the skin is ecologically like a pond surface or forest soil, not as a shell so much as a delicate interpenetration. It reveals the self as ennobled and extended...as part of the landscape and the ecosytem."[10]

The modern ethos of spirituality described by Luckmann, which I have suggested is centered on the fetish of consumerism, has to do with relationships. The quotations from Bateson and Shepard also can be interpreted as framing spirituality in terms of relationships, but of a fundamentally different kind. Thus it is important to recognize we are not advocating forms of spirituality associated with momentary states of ecstasy, awe, oneness with the totality of Being, or peak experiences. Nor is there any intention here to associate the word with the current ethos of spiritual democracy, where individuals choose their own formal religion or personal pathway to cosmic awareness. The latter too often becomes a matter of chemically induced alterations in consciousness or of borrowing a mix of Eastern and Nativist religious practices.

Rather, the form of spirituality being suggested here should be considered as partly rooted in the traditions and patterns of how a cultural group understands relationships. That is, spirituality should not be viewed as separate from other encoding processes of a culture, a point that also applies to the "modern sacred cosmos" of individualism. This is important for two reasons. The first has to do with a characteristic of spirituality still recognizable in the remnants of primal cultures that inhabit large areas of the North American continent and Australia; namely a sense of time that connects the person with both past and future generations as part of a sacred bond. The second reason for considering spirituality as, in part, a cultural symbol system (a language of expression) is that it represents a collective form of knowledge, refined over the centuries it takes to demonstrate that it is more than a cultural experiment with the bioregion. This way of understanding spirituality, it must be emphasized, does not reduce its transcendent and healing potential. Nor should it allow us to adopt a romantic attitude toward all forms of primal spirituality. For example, the Ilongot's practice of using headhunting as a ritual for freeing bereaved persons of their burden represents a form of spirituality, no matter how else it might enable them to live in ecological balance, that would not be considered appropriate—for all sorts of reasons.

The recognition of spirituality as, in part, a cultural phenomenon confronts us with at least as many forms of spirituality as there have been cultures. But as our task is not to provide an inventory that would, like our other religious emporiums, expand consumer choice in a new growth industry, it must be emphasized that any consideration of the spirituality of other cultural groups is intended primarily for the purpose of clarifying how spiritual forms of knowledge serve to fulfill a wide range of human needs, including the paramount need to live in an interdependent relationship with the rest of the biosphere. The more spiritual forms of knowledge, which are primarily ways of understanding relationships, cannot be directly borrowed; nor can they be reduced to techniques that can be superimposed on fundamentally different cultural root metaphors for understanding reality. But they can serve as guides for understanding the various cultural languages especially suited for communicating across generations and between species. In rediscovering these languages, we might have a better sense of the changes we need to make in our approaches to formal education.

The forms of spirituality of primal people are interesting for their sheer diversity, but they also help us put into perspective what is lacking in our own sacred cosmos, with its consumer and technological fetishes. Whether we are considering one of the primal cultures still holding on in the arid Southwest, or living along the coastline of British Columbia, or the interior of Alaska, or the nonurbanized areas of Australia, there appear to be several common features that are especially relevant. These commonalties exist in spite of the profound differences in the root metaphors that underlie the culture's understanding of the origin and sense of order that characterize the universe. In spite of the very real differences among the beliefs and social practices of primal peoples, as evidenced in the design of their dwellings, technologies, and ritual practices, there nevertheless seems to be a shared sense of the wholeness and interdependency of all life forms. That is, to contrast this aspect of primal consciousness with the modern Western mind set, their sense of wholeness means there are no divisions between the cognitive, ethical-political, and libidinal-aesthetic dimensions of experience, to use Terry Eagleton's categories for understanding the fragmented nature of modern life.[11]

This connectedness of a way of knowing and a deep sense of spiritual (and political) being was expressed by a chief of one of the principal bands of the Northern Blackfeet who responded with the following words to the request to sell part of their tribal territory:

> Our land is more valuable than your money. It will last forever. It will not even perish by the flames of fire. As long as the sun shines and the waters flow, this land will be here to give life to men and animals. We cannot sell the lives of men and animals; therefore we cannot sell the land. It was put here for us by the Great Spirit and we cannot sell it because it does not belong to us. You can count your money and burn it within the nod of a buffalo's head, but only the Great Spirit can count the grains of sand and the blades of grass of these plains. As a present to you, we will give you anything we have that you can take with you; but the land, never.[12]

In the *The Spiritual Legacy of the American Indians*, Joseph Epes Brown explains how the experience of sacredness, as evidenced in the Blackfeet chief's refusal to trade land for money, enfolds the person into a larger moral and aesthetic ecology. According to Brown:

> Native American experiences of place are infused with mythic themes. These express events of sacred time,

which are as real now as at the other time. They are experienced through landmarks in each people's immediate natural environment. The events of animal beings, for example, which are communicated through oral traditions of myth and folklore, serve to grace, sanctify, explain, and interpret each detail of the land. Further, each being of nature, every particular form of the land, is experienced as the locus of qualitatively differentiated spirit beings, whose individual and collective presence sanctifies and gives meaning to the land in all its details and contours. Thus, it also gives meaning to the lives of the people who cannot conceive of themselves apart form the land.[13]

Among the aboriginals of Australia the sacred unity of the land, time, and life forms was expressed in what Westerners have referred to as the Dream-Tracks or Songlines. According to Aborigines' creation myth, legendary totemic beings wandered over the continent in the dreamtime singing out the names of everything—animals, birds, plants, rocks, waterholes—that crossed their path. As Bruce Chatwin put it, these Ancestors sang the world into existence. The Songlines, which were a form of spiritual geography, served as a collective memory bank about the characteristics of the land and its inhabitants. As both map and direction finder, the songline enabled a person to "Walkabout" the country and to meet other people who knew the same songline. The Walkabout was a ritual journey in the footsteps of the Ancestors, with the land being sung in its primordial form—as it will be sung by future generations.

The use of song as a spiritual direction finder also had practical consequences for those living in an environment that proved life-threatening to Westerners who put their reliance on their own rational processes and, of course, their technology. Chatwin summed up the encoding characteristics of these musical trails by noting that

certain phrases, certain combinations of musical notes, are thought to describe the actions of the Ancestor's *feet*. One phrase would say, "Salt-Pan," another "Creek-bed," "Spinifex," "Sand-hill," "Mulga-scrub," "Rock-face," and so forth. An expert song-man, by listening to the order of succession, would count how many times his hero crossed a river or scaled a ridge—and be able to calculate where, and how far along a songline he was.[14]

Aside from the way the Songline integrates the person into the larger sense of community, extends the boundaries of space and time (all the way back to the Beginning), having a map of the land, including the location of sacred sites and waterholes, has very practical implications indeed.

To cite another example that will help avoid romanticizing primal forms of spirituality, the Kwakiutl developed an elaborate culture that took account of the sustaining characteristics of their bioregion, which is the coastline of what is now called the province of British Columbia. Unlike the sacred cosmology of many primal cultures in North America, where the world is considered orderly and harmonious, the Kwakiutl cosmology represents the world as discordant, and a source of conflict and self-destruction. It is only the cooperation of all the inhabitants (all forms of life), including the suppression of greed and appetites, that insures the necessary balance required for mutual survival.

The core metaphor used by the Kwakiutl to integrate the different spheres of existence, and to understand the behaviors and attitudes appropriate to each relationship, including the taking of life, is summarized by the anthropologist, Stanley Walens:

> The Kwakiutl moral universe becomes united, not by any vague religious sense but by the fact that the entire universe contains all beings within its bounds, and that all beings are subject to the principle of being both hungry and the food of other beings who are themselves hungry. The Kwakiutl universe is a universe of related beings, all of whom have the moral responsibility to control their eating. Eating is the universal property of the world, and thus it is the basis of morality.[15]

This root metaphor also serves to connect the necessity of taking life in order to live with the need to sustain relationships that characterize the cycles of life in the spiritual world. Thus, animals are viewed as willing to die, because without death they cannot continue in the cycle of rebirth. And if the hunter does not perform the correct rituals, the cycle of rein-carnation will be disrupted. As Gary Snyder puts it, in attempt-ing to call a secular and technologically oriented culture back to a recognition of these primal truths, "There is no death that is not somebody's food, no life that is not somebody's death." But the deeper truth and moral obligation, which the Kwakiutl understood, is that "eating is a sacrament."[16]

One potentially instructive aspect of primal spirituality is that the codes regulating relationships and the psychic space of the individual members of the cultural group appear to be grounded in a metaphorical (mythic) construc-tion that represents all aspects of life as interdependent. The term "metaphor," rather than "myth," is emphasized here because it is easy for the modern mind to dismiss "mythic" thinking as archaic and backward, but when spirituality is understood as grounded in metaphorical thinking, it becomes more difficult to claim that modern people have advanced to a higher stage of thinking. Many modern thinkers may view singing the world into existence with either skepticism or mild amusement. Yet it would not be too far off the mark to claim that the mainstream of Western culture metaphorized the world into existence, and that over time the Western form of spirituality changed to reflect the evolution away from the root metaphor of an interrelated universe (understood as a "Great Chain of Being") to that of a machine, which is to be rationally understood for the pur-pose of making human relationships and activities more effi-cient, predictable, and, now, cost-effective. Modern tech-nocrats are thus no less free of their cultural group's root metaphor than the Kwakiutl hunter.

But there are differences beyond the more obvious one between root metaphors that lead to an exploitive relation-ship (now called "resource management") and primal root metaphors that involve a moral obligation to maintain inter-dependent relationships. One of the most important differ-ences is that primal forms of spirituality, in maintaining a core body of beliefs and values grounded in the authority of a sacred cosmology, validated through centuries of survival, reduce the realm of the political. That is, more areas of social and psychic life are regulated by norms that have either a taken-for-granted sense of authority (it would not occur to people to question them) or forms of authority (like taboos) where the punishment for transgression is known and both feared and understood as a condition of group survival. The symbolic foundations of spirituality meet Michel Foucault's description of power as an "action upon an action," and as "guiding the possibility of conduct and putting in order the possible outcome."[17] Spirituality is thus a form of the political, if we understand the political as involving one's exercise of power where an "action upon an action" changes or governs the other. It may even lead to the friend–enemy distinction that Schmitt considered as underlying the political process when group survival is thought to be at stake.

Viewed in this manner, it appears that the modern Western form of spirituality (what Luckmann describes as the "sacred cosmos of individualism") expands the areas of life that can be politicized by individuals and interest groups. This form of political behavior may be framed by any number of competing ideologies, most of which envision the world as an arena for the expansion of human freedom, material standard of living, and personal wealth. By way of contrast, the political process dictated by primal forms of spirituality do not allow for such a more limited perspective (both in terms of a sense of time and social space) to have as much latitude for expression. Being realists in a way modern industrial cultures are not, the different forms of primal spirituality appear to be oriented more to sustaining the balance of relationships into a future unlimited by an individual's own personal sense of time and immediate need. Ironically, the authority of tradition, to use a metaphor that often causes intense hostility because it is, so misundertood among modern thinkers, appears to allow for a different form of individuality to be more fully realized than what we now witness among the "autonomous" individuals so easily exploited within our consumer oriented culture.

In *The Primal Mind*, Jamake Highwater explains how primal cultural groups oriented more toward relationships and the politics of long-term survival (as opposed to the politics of the short-term, which characterize the liberal tradition of individualism) leads to a different form of individuality: Writes Highwater:

It is through relationships that Native Americans comprehend themselves. Such relationships are richly orchestrated, as we have already seen, by elaborations of language and ritual activities. Underlying the identity of the tribe and the experience of personality in the individual is the sacred sense of place that provides the whole group with its centeredness. The Indian individual is spiritually interdependent upon the language, folk history, ritualism, and geographical sacredness of his or her *whole* people. Relationships between members of families, bands, clans, and other tribal groups are defined and intensified through relational and generational language rather than through personal names, which are considered to be sacred and private to the individual. The relatedness of the individual and the tribe extends outward beyond the family, band, or clan to include all things of the world. Thus nothing exists in isolation. Individualism does not presuppose autonomy, alienation, or isolation. And freedom is not the right to express yourself but the far more fundamental right to *be* yourself.[18]

The form of critical thought Gouldner described as being fundamental in the mainstream culture's conflict model of progress and individual self-determination is not easily reconciled with the form of consciousness that experiences sacredness in a way that reterritorializes the world through interdependent relationships. But this does not mean that the person's world is a primal version of *1984*, as some Western thinkers might be quick to conclude. Rather, a strong case can be made that the form of spirituality, and the norms of behavior that follow from it, allow for a different form of expressiveness, and thus of individualization. What is most important for our discussion, however, is the way primal cultures developed the more aesthetically oriented languages of dance, art, music, and narrative as a means of sustaining their moral/spiritual sense of order. As they view these languages as participatory, rather than as spectator and commercial events, the avenues of individualized expression tend to enfold the person in a larger symbolic reality. As Highwater put it, referring to dance, "The body is the organism in which motion makes visible the sacred forms of life itself. Our bodies live through motion. And thus motion is the most important and pervasive means by which primal peoples celebrate life."[19]

Song and narrative are also prominent aspects of primal spirituality. Like the dance that connects individual participation and expressiveness with the cultural group's deepest metaphorical templates, they serve as pathways to a larger and more interconnected sense of reality. They are both essential aspects of rituals necessary for sustaining the cycles of life, just as our many genres of music and stories serve as metaphors for understanding relationships and purpose in a consumer-oriented society. But when we begin a comparative examination of the deep templates and other metaphorical messages encoded in both primal and modern songs and stories we find a radical divergence.

An example of Highwater's point that primal peoples have a tradition of thinking poetically (that is, metaphorically), rather than in the detached and objective manner associated with Western science and technology, is the way in which many primal cultures view the possession of songs, stories, and the ability to perform them well, as a sign of wealth. For example, Gary Witherspoon notes that the Navajo accompany and enrich both their ceremonial and nonceremonial activities with songs. And the songs reinforce the basic motifs of group life, like the repetition in the First Snake Song associated with "renewal, regeneration, rejuvenation, revolution, and restoration."[20] The Aborigines also view their songs as a kind of property, and thus as wealth. More important in terms of our focus on songs as one of the spiritual languages of primal people is the way in which Aborigines think their songs originated in the spirit realm, and that humans are not the authors of the songs.[21] Again we see how song binds the person to the group's way of understanding the principal relationships in life.

The telling of stories is also a way of reinforcing knowledge for survival, and of connecting the existential world of daily routines with the cosmic order. Like the other spiritual languages, narrative can also be understood as a form of cultural storage. But it has other dimensions relevant to making a cultural shift away from the autonomous and all-too-often driven individual. These dimensions can be most easily and quickly seen by recalling Ron and Suzanne Scollon's comments on the deep differences between print-based discourse (literacy) and narrative-based communication: "The word comes to take precedence over the situation, analysis takes precedence over participation, isolated thought takes precedence over conversation and storytelling, the individual takes precedence over the community."[22] Both the content and the process of narrating is about relationships; it also involves being able to perform well, even aesthetically in participatory relationships.

Whereas we have created categories that allow us to separate art from the other spiritual languages, and even to give it an autonomous existence that we can approach as spectators and consumers, for primal peoples art is an integral aspect both of ceremony and daily relationships. In *What Is Art For?* Ellen Dissanayake suggests art be understood as a behavior involving the intent to "make special;" that is, to give an object like the Dogon granary door or an activity like speech a "specialness" that separates it from the ordinary and taken for granted. As Dissanayake puts it, "one intends by making special *to place the activity or artifact in a 'realm' different from the everyday....* In both functional and nonfunctional art an alternative reality is recognized and entered; the making special acknowledges, reveals, and embodies this reality."[23] This behavior, which Dissanayake regards as a universal human trait like breathing and speaking, results in pots, baskets, spears, dwellings, hairpieces, sacred instruments and objects, and so forth, being given a "specialness" through attention to design and decoration. The refined sense of line and decorative pattern, as well as the ability to carve stone and wood in a manner that brings it alive, are recognized in the art of primal peoples—which makes it so valued by Western collectors.

Although Dissanayake may not be entirely comfortable associating the behavior of "making special" with the spiritual languages, she does suggest that in "making special...reality is converted from its usual unremarkable state—in which we take it or its components for granted—to a significant or especially experienced reality in which their components, by their emphasis or combination or juxtaposition, acquire a meta-reality."[24] This transformative aspect of art, where the artifact or behavior is experienced as part of a participatory relationship within a larger reality, is what is being identified here as a pathway for communicating spiritual knowledge. What is being communicated can also be understood as encoding the cultural group's way of understanding reality; it also establishes the areas of collective silence. This is the point made in Geertz's observation that, "It is out of participation in the general system of symbolic forms we call culture that participation in the particular we call art, which is in fact but a sector of it, is possible. A theory of art is thus at the same time a theory of culture, not an autonomous enterprise. And if it is a semiotic theory of art," he concludes, "it must trace the life of signs in society...."[25] But in understanding spiritual languages as culturally grounded we must be open to the possibility that they may enable individual members to enter another realm of reality not bounded by culture.

So far we have been attempting to understand the spiritual languages of primal peoples as forms of cultural storage, and as pathways for communicating across space and time. It has also been suggested that the enfolding of the primal person within a more complex and interconnected sense of order has contributed, in many instances, to the culture's ability to live in ecological balance. To again use Bateson's language, their form of spiritual knowledge recognizes that "*the mental characteristics of the system are immanent, not in some part, but in the system as a whole.*"

The cost, however, as many modern thinkers would view it, is the reduction of the realm of the political, that is, the realm of individual critical reflection and pursuit of self-interest. The latter point of view, however, avoids considering the possible connection of a culture that discounts relationships in favor of a form of atomistic vitalism (centering life within the individual rather than in her/his relationships) with the pathologies that are now endemic in society—drug dependency, mental illness, violence directed toward children and women, alienation, and so forth. Moreover, this modern attitude about the danger of reducing the realm of the political has not fully awakened to the irony of progressive ways of thinking being blind to the dangers of exceeding the sustaining capacities of the habitat.

It is this latter point that brings us to consider another aspect of primal spirituality, namely, the ways in which the various spiritual languages enable the person to enter a world of meaning and activity that does not require the massive use of fossil fuel, freeways, and a wasteful form of consumerism. To put it another way, growth in the ability to understand and participate in the spiritual languages of music, dance, narrative, and art has only the limits imposed by the organizational characteristics of the cultural group. For primal people the environment, as well as other forms of life, appears to be a reservoir of symbolic possibility for dance, song, and story. Their form of travel is not dependent upon massive transformations of energy, unlike the modern person's intervention in the carbon cycle.

The challenge facing educators at both the public school and university level is to contribute to the transformation of the spiritual languages of the mainstream consumer-oriented culture. As they have been mostly framed by the values of a remisssive form of individualism and the marketplace, the contemporary spiritual languages have become subject to shifts in consumer taste. Their primary messages, particularly in the areas of modern art and rock music, are that nihilism is exciting and profitable and that it is the immediate experience that counts. This expansion of the importance of the private sphere of life, where the need for excitement feeds on the unending quest for a personal sense of identity, increasingly shapes political agendas at the local and national level. But these political agendas have to do with how to cope with the consequences of this spiritual malaise: teen pregnancies, drugs and street violence, the growing number of people sinking below the poverty line. Aside from the human suffering and alienation that seem beyond the mitigating capacity of the political system, attention is taken away from the even more crucial political problems associated with degrading the life-sustaining capacities of natural systems.

Educators cannot ignore the social problems that leave students hungry, without positive parental guidance, and fearful of violence, even death if they happen to be wearing a particular item of clothing or find themselves caught between feuding street gangs. Educators also have to recognize, particularly at the university level, that students may be mesmerized by the materialistic-personal success ethos promoted through the media and shopping malls. But beyond coping with these problems as best they can, educators still have a primary responsibility for the curriculum (i.e., the culture represented in their subject area). And if the content of the curriculum is largely dictated by precedent or outside agency, educators still have a responsibility for determining whether the content is to be taught at a taken-for-granted level, or considered in a more critically reflective manner. There is a vital need to provide students with both knowledge of the world they live in (its history, geography, political economy, expressive arts, and so forth) and an opportunity to consider critically how past and current ways of knowing relate to the current ecological crisis.

As suggested by the previous discussion of the limits of the political process, educators also have a responsibility to help lay new foundations, as well as to recover more attenuated but still existing ones for redirecting our current form of spirituality. It does not take a genius to recognize that the current images of individualism, success, competition, and progress are part of the anthropocentric world view that is deepening the ecological crisis. But what the new vocabulary will be is not entirely clear. Taking seriously the root metaphors of primal cultures that evolved more sustainable relationships with their bioregions might provide a good starting place for beginning the task of reworking our own root metaphors.

Deep cultural changes, at the level that affect the taken-for-granted reality of everyday life, are not effectively achieved through governmental attempts to engineer social change or through a politicized system of signs (as was so well illustrated in the film, *Brazil*). Nor have modern totalitarian regimes been able to deal with the basic problems of our era: human rights and the ecological crisis. The political process has a dismal record, including the squandering of vast material resources on the arms race. The development of the spiritual languages may have the best potential for helping us avoid the political process moving beyond excessive regulation to the friend–enemy conflicts that now seem to be on the increase. The challenge for educators will be to find suitable analogues for the songs, stories, dance, and art, either from the histories of the cultural groups that constitute American society or from the current cultural scene. Help must come from other sectors of society, but this help can only be incorporated into the education of the next generation if educators are receptive, that is, able to understand how the contributions of various cultural groups relate to living in a sustainable balance within the larger web of life. This receptivity will require escaping from many of the prejudices that are now the basis of our modern hubris. This means that reform starts close at home and with the little prejudices, like the beliefs and values that sustain our environmentally disruptive behaviors. Reform does not require a master plan before it begins; but it needs to be guided by a clear sense of the direction in which we must move, and a full awareness of the consequences if we fail.

Notes

Introduction

1. C. A. Bowers. *Cultural Literacy for Freedom.* Eugene, OR: Elan Publishers, 1974.

2. Gregory Bateson. *Steps to an Ecology of Mind.* New York: Ballantine Books, 1972, p. 316.

3. Alexander Solzhenitsyn, A. B. Argursky, Evgeny Barabanov, F. Korkakov, Vadim Borisov, Igor Shafarevich. *From Under the Rubble.* Boston: Little Brown, 1974, p. 136.

Chapter 1. Cultural Aspects of the Ecological Crisis

1. Stephen H. Schneider. "The Changing Climate." *Scientific American,* vol. 261, no. 1 (September 1989), p. 78.

2. William D. Ruckelshaus. "Toward a Sustainable World." *Scientific American,* vol. 261, no. 1 (September 1989), p. 169.

3. *Die Grünen: The Program of the Green Party of the Federal Republic of Germany.* Bonn: Die Grünen, 1989. p. 4.

4. Die Grünen, p. 40.

5. Clifford Geertz. *The Interpretation of Cultures.* New York: Basic Books, 1972, p. 261.

6. Ernst Cassirer. *The Philosophy of the Enlightenment.* Boston: Beacon, 1951, p. 13,

7. Robert N. Bellah, Richard Madsen, William M. Sullivan, Ann Swidler, and Steven M. Tipton. *Habits of the Heart: Individualism and Community in American Life.* Berkeley and Los Angeles: University of California Press, 1985.

8. Martin Heidegger. *The Question Concerning Technology and Other Essays.* New York: Harper Colophon Books, 1977, p. 129.

9. Robin Horton. "Tradition and Modernity Revisited," in *Rationality and Relativism,* Martin Hollis and Steven Lukes, eds. Cambridge, MA: MIT Press, 1982, p. 39.

10. Alvin W. Gouldner. *The Future of Intellectuals and the Rise of the New Class.* New York: Seabury Press, 1979, pp. 28–29.

Chapter 2. Conservative Misinterpretation

1. William J. Bennett. *Our Children and Our Country: Improving America's Schools and Affirming the Common Culture.* New York: Touchstone Books, 1988, p. 165.

2. Mortimer J. Adler. *The Paideia Proposal: An Educational Manifesto.* New York: Macmillan, p. 3.

3. Adler, p. 5.

4. E. D. Hirsch, Jr. *Cultural Literacy: What Every American Needs to Know.* Boston: Houghton Mifflin, 1987, p. 21.

5. Hirsch, p. 24.

6. William J. Bennett. *Our Children and Our Country,* New York: Simon & Schuster, 1989, p. 6

7. Bennett, p. 234.

8. Allan Bloom. *The Closing of the American Mind: How Higher Education Has Failed Democracy and Impoverished the Souls of Today's Students.* New York: Simon and Schuster, 1987, p. 87.

9. Bloom, p. 254.

10. Bloom, pp. 346–347.

11. Quoted in "Back to Eden," by Evan Eisenberg, in *The Atlantic Monthly,* November 1989, p. 59.

12. Lester R. Brown and Sandra Postel. "Thresholds of Change," in *The State of the World,* Lester Brown, ed. New York: Norton, 1987, p. 4.

13. Frederick Turner. *Beyond Geography: The Western Spirit Against the Wilderness.* New Brunswick: Rutgers University Press, 1983.

14. Martin Heidegger. *The Question Concerning Technology and Other Essays.* New York: Harper Colophon Books, 1977, p. 129.

15. Lynne V. Cheney. *50 Hours: A Core Curriculum for College Students.* Washington DC: National Endowment for the Humanities, 1990, p. 43.

16. Rushworth M. Kidder. "Drawing the Human Blueprint." *The Christian Science Monitor,* November 13, 1989, p. 14 (emphasis supplied).

17. Gregory Bateson. *Steps to an Ecology of Mind.* New York: Ballantine, 1972, p. 316 (emphasis in original).

18. Bateson, p. 483.

19. Wendell Berry. *The Unsettling of America: Culture and Agriculture.* San Francisco: Sierra Club Books, 1986. p. 47.

20. Aldo Leopold. *A Sand County Almanac.* San Francisco: A Sierra/Ballantine Book, 1970, p. 239.

21. E. F. Schumacher. *Small Is Beautiful: Economics As If People Mattered.* New York: Harper Torchbooks, 1973 p. 148.

22. Berry, p. 43.

23. Bloom, pp. 381–382.

24. Edmund Burke. *Reflections on the French Revolution.* Chicago: Henry Regnery, 1955, p. 92.

25. Michael Oakeshott. *Rationalism in Politics.* New York: Basic Books, 1962, p. 11.

26. Gary Snyder. *Turtle Island.* New York: New Directions, 1974, pp. 107–108.

27. Wendell Berry. *A Continuous Harmony: Essays Cultural and Agricultural.* New York: Harcourt Brace Jovanovich, 1972, pp. 68–69.

28. Burke, p. 223.

29. Bloom, p. 261.

30. Frederick Turner. "A Field Guide to Synthetic Landscapes: Toward an Environmental Ethic." *Harper's,* April, 1988, p. 49.

31. Ron Scollon and Suzanne Scollon. *The Problem of Power.* Haines, Alaska: The Gutenberg Dump, 1985.

32. Scollon and Scollon, pp. 32–33

Chapter 3. Liberal Impasse

1. Peter McLaren. *Life in Schools: An Introduction to Critical Pedagogy in the Foundations of Education.* New York: Longman, 1989, p. 233 (emphasis in original).

2. Paulo Freire. *Pedagogy of the Oppressed*. New York: Seabury Press, 1974 ed., p. 76.

3. Maxine Greene. *The Dialectic of Freedom*. New York: Teachers College Press, 1988, p. 5.

4. Greene, p. 126.

5. Aldo Leopold. *A Sand County Almanac*. San Francisco: Sierra Club/Ballantine Books, 1972 ed., p. xvii.

6. Jere Brophy and Thomas L. Good. "Teacher Behavior and Student Achievement," in *Handbook of Research on Teaching*, Merlin C. Wittrock, ed. New York: Macmillan, 1986, p. 370.

7. Meredith D. Gall. *Making the Grade*. Eugene, OR: Damien Publishers, 1988, pp. 46, 77, 156.

8. John Dewey and Arthur F. Bentley. *Knowing and the Known*. Boston: Beacon, 1949, p. 121.

9. Thomas Colwell. "The Ecological Perspective in John Dewey's Philosophy of Education." *Educational Theory*, vol. 35, no. 3 (Summer 1985), pp. 255–266.

10. John Dewey. *The Quest for Certainty*. New York: Capricorn Books, 1929, pp. 214–215.

11. Dewey, p. 267.

12. Dewey, pp. 226–227.

13. Dewey and Bentley, 1973, p. 169 (emphasis in original).

14. Dewey and Bentley, 1973, p. 173 (emphasis in original).

15. George Santayana. "Dewey's Naturalistic Metaphysics," in *The Philosophy of John Dewey*, Paul Arthur Schilpp, ed. New York: Tudor Publishing, 1951, p. 251.

16. Edward Sapir. *Culture, Language and Personality*. Berkeley and Los Angeles: University of California Press, 1970, p. 69.

17. Jamake Highwater. *The Primal Mind: Vision and Reality in Indian America*. New York: New American Library, 1981, p. 65.

18. Frederick Turner. *Beyond Geography: The Western Spirit Against the Wilderness*. New Brunswick, NJ: Rutgers University Press, 1986, p. 248.

19. John Berger. *Pig Earth*. New York: Pantheon Books, 1979, p. 203.

20. Berger, p. 203.

21. Highwater, p. 90.

22. Wes Jackson. *Altars of Unhewn Stone: Science and the Earth*. San Francisco: North Point Press, 1987, pp. 11–12.

23. Freire, pp. 76–77 (emphasis in original).

24. Paulo Freire. *The Politics of Education*. South Hadley, MA: Bergin & Garvey, 1985, p. 107.

25. Freire, *The Politics of Education*, p. 199.

26. Leopold, pp. 238–239.

27. Ira Shor, ed. *Freire for the Classroom: A Sourcebook for Liberatory Teaching*. Portsmouth, NH: Boynton/Cook Publishers, 1987, p. 15.

28. Henry A. Giroux. *Teachers as Intellectuals: Toward a Critical Pedagogy of Learning*. Granby, MA: Bergin & Garvey, 1988, p. 170.

29. Henry A. Giroux. *Schooling and the Struggle for Public Life: Critical Pedagogy in the Modern Age*. Minneapolis: University of Minnesota Press, 1988, p. 52.

30. Peter McLaren and Rhonda Hammer. "Critical Pedagogy and the Postmodern Challenge: Toward a Critical Postmodern Pedagogy of Liberation." *Educational Foundations*, vol. 3, no. 3 (Fall 1989), p. 31 (emphasis in original).

31. McLaren. *Life in Schools*, p. 230.

32. McLaren and Hammer, p. 53.

33. McLaren and Hammer, p. 52.

Chapter 4. Anthropocentrism in Textbooks

1. Deborah Tannen. "Relative Focus on Involvement in Oral and Written Discourse," in *Literacy, Language, and Learning: The Nature and Consequences of Reading and Writing*, David R. Olson, Nancy Torrance, and Angela Hildyard, eds. Cambridge: Cambridge University Press, 1986, p. 127.

2. Ron Scollon and Suzanne Scollon. *The Problem of Power*. Haines, Alaska: The Gutenberg Dump, 1985, p. 10.

3. Visual Education Corporation. *Creative Living: Basic Con-*

cepts in Home Economics (Teacher's Annotated Ed.). Encino, CA: Glencoe Publishing, 1985, p. 13.

4. Laura A. Chapman. *Discover Art*. Worcester, MA: Davis Publications, 1985, pp. 6–7 (emphasis in original).

5. Roger LeRoy Miller and Robert W. Pulsinelli. *Understanding Economics*. St. Paul, MN: West Publishing, 1983, p. 5 (emphasis in original).

6. Valerie Chamberlain, Peyton Bailey Budinger, and Jan Perry Jones. *Teen Guide* (6th ed.). New York: McGraw-Hill, 1985, pp. 22–23.

7. Evelyn L. Lewis. *Housing Designs*. South Holland, IL: Goodheart-Willcox, 1984, p. 10 (emphasis in original).

8. Chamberlain et al., pp. 271, 275–276.

9. Frederick M. King, Herbert C. Rudman, and LoDoris R. Leavell. *Understanding Communities*. Irvine, CA: Laidlow Brothers, 1977, p. 102.

10. Richard H. Loftin. *The World and Its People: Communities and Resources*. Morristown, NJ: Silver Burdett, 1984, p. 155 (emphasis added).

11. Gloria P. Hagans. *Regions Near and Far*. Lexington, MA: Heath, 1985, p. 62.

12. John Jarolimek and Mae Knight Clark. *The Earth and Its People*. New York: Macmillan, 1981, p. 37.

13. *Self*. New York: American Book Co., 1979, pp. 65–68.

14. Marilyn Kourilsky and William Dickneider. *Economics and Making Decisions*. St. Paul, MN: West Publishing, 1988, p. 11.

15. Kourilsky and Dickneider, p. 103.

16. Patricia A. Watkins, Cesare Emiliani, Christopher J. Chiaverina, Christopher T. Harper, and David E. LaHart. *General Science* (Teacher's Ed.). Orlando, FL: Harcourt Brace Jovanovich, 1989, p. 25.

17. Karen Arms and Pamela S. Camp. *Biology: A Journey into Life*. Philadelphia: Saunders College Publishing, 1988, p. 553.

18. Arms and Camp, p. 6.

19. Jill Wright, Charles R. Coble, Jean Hopkins, Susan Johnson, and David LaHart. *Life Science*. Englewood Cliffs, NJ: Prentice-Hall, 1991, p. 6.

20. Antony C. Wilbraham, Dennis D. Staley, Candace J. Simpson, and Michael S. Matta. *Chemistry*. Menlo Park, CA: Addison-Wesley, 1990, p. 3 (emphasis in original).

21. Paul G. Hewitt. *Conceptual Physics*. Menlo Park, CA: Addison-Wesley, 1987, p. 7.

22. Robert Redfield, *The Primitive World and Its Transformations*. Ithaca, NY: Cornell University Press, 1953, p. 145.

23. Dean Hurd, Susan M. Johnson, George F. Matthias, Charles William McLaughlin, Edward Benjamin Snyder, and Jill D. Wright. *General Science: A Voyage of Discovery* (Teacher's Guide). Englewood Cliffs, NJ: Prentice-Hall, 1989, p. 14.

24. Paul Feyerabend. *Against Method*. London: Verso, 1978, p. 307.

25. Barbara Rodner Regne. *Homes and Neighborhoods*. Lexington, MA: Heath, 1985.

26. *Self*, pp. 98–101.

27. John Jay Bonstingl. *Introduction to the Social Sciences*. Boston, MA: Allyn and Bacon, 1985, pp. 526–527.

28. W. LaVerne Thomas and Robert J. Anderson. *Sociology: The Study of Human Relationships*. Orlando, FL: Harcourt Brace Jovanovich, 1982, pp. 99–101.

29. American Chemical Society. *ChemCom: Chemistry in the Community*. Dubuque, IA: Kendall/Hart, 1988, p. 115.

30. Bonstingl, pp. 172–173.

Chapter 5. Toward Deep Changes

1. Clifford Geertz. *The Interpretation of Cultures*. New York: Basic Books, 1973, p. 216.

2. Aldo Leopold. *A Sand County Almanac*. New York: Sierra Club/ Ballantine Books, 1970, p. 262.

3. Gregory Bateson. *Steps to an Ecology of Mind*. New York: Ballantine, 1972, p. 318.

4. Humberto R. Maturana. "Biology of Language: The Epistemology of Reality," in *Psychology and Biology of Language and Thought: Essays in Honor of Eric Lenneberg*, G. A. Miller and E. Lenneberg, eds. New York: Academic Press, 1978, p. 13.

5. Bateson, p. 317 (emphasis in original).

6. Bateson, p. 316 (emphasis in original).

7. Bateson, p. 319 (emphasis in original).

8. Gary Snyder. *Turtle Island*. New York: New Directions, 1974, p. 107–108.

9. Bateson, p. 451.

10. Bateson, p. 483.

11. Bateson, p. 484.

12. Lester R. Brown and Sandra Postel. "Thresholds of Change," in *State of the World 1987*, Linda Starke, ed. New York: W. W. Norton, 1987, p. 4.

13. Robert N. Bellah, Richard Madsen, William M. Sullivan, Ann Swidler, and Steven M. Tipton. *Habits of the Heart: Individualism and Commitment in American Life*. Berkley and Los Angeles: University of California Press, 1985, p. 153.

14. Ivan Illich. *Deschooling Society*. New York: Harper & Row, 1971, p. 75.

15. Suzi Gablik. *Has Modernism Failed?* New York: Thames and Hudson, 1984, p. 118.

16. Ron Scollon and Suzanne Scollon. *The Problem of Power*. Haines. Alaska: The Gutenberg Dump, 1985, p. 33.

17. Dell Hymes. *Foundations of Sociolinguistics: An Ethnographic Approach*. Philadelphia: University of Pennsylvania Press, 1974, p. 17.

Chapter 6. Political and Spiritual Dimensions

1. Alvin Gouldner. *The Future of Intellectuals and the Rise of the New Class*. New York: Seabury Press, 1979, p. 28 (emphasis in original).

2. Gouldner, p. 29 (emphasis in original).

3. Carl Schmitt. *The Concept of the Political*. New Brunswick, NJ: Rutgers University Press, 1976, p. 26.

4. Schmitt, p. 28.

5. Schmitt, pp. 71–72.

6. Richard Rorty. *Contingency, Irony, and Solidarity*. Cambridge: Cambridge University Press, 1989, p. 22.

7. Rorty, p. 67.

8. Thomas Luckmann. *The Invisible Religion*. New York: Macmillan, 1967, p. 114.

9. Gregory Bateson. *Steps to an Ecology of Mind*. New York: Ballantine, 1972, p. 316.

10. Paul Shepard. "Ecology and Man: A Viewpoint," in *The Subversive Science: Essays Toward an Ecology of Man*, Paul Shepard and Daniel McKinley, eds. New York: Houhgton Mifflin, 1967, p. 2.

11. Terry Eagleton. *The Ideology of the Aesthetic*. London: Basil Blackwell, 1990, p. 366.

12. Quoted in T.C. McLuhan. *Touch the Earth*. New York: Simon & Schuster, 1971, p. 53.

13. Joseph Epes Brown. *The Spiritual Legacy of the American Indian*. New York: Crossroad, 1985, p. 51.

14. Bruce Chatwin. *The Songlines*. New York: Viking Penguin Inc., 1987, p. 108.

15. Stanley Walens. *Feasting with Cannibals: An Essay on Kwakiutl Cosmology*. Princton, NJ: Princeton University Press, 1981, p. 6.

16. Gary Snyder. *The Practice of the Wild*. San Francisco: North Point Press, 1990, p. 184.

17. Michel Foucault. "The Subject and Power," in *Michel Foucault: Beyond Structuralism and Hermeneutics*, Hubert L. Dreyfus and Paul Rabinow, eds. Chicago: University of Chicago Press, 1982, p. 220.

18. Jamake Highwater. *The Primal Mind: Vision and Reality in Indian America*. New York: New American Liberary, 1981, p. 172 (emphasis in original).

19. Highwater, p. 133.

20. Gary Witherspoon. *Language and Art in the Navajo Universe*. Ann Arbor: University of Michigan Press, 1977, pp. 155–156.

21. Richard M. Moyle. *Songs of the Pintupi: Musical Life in a Central Australian Society*. Canberra: Australian Institute of Aboriginal Studies, 1979, p. 11.

22. Ron Scollon and Suzanne Scollon. *The Problem of Power.* Haines, Alaska: The Gutenberg Dump, 1985, p. 10.

23. Ellen Dissanayake. *What is Art For?* Seattle: University of Washington Press, 1988, p. 92.

24. Dissanayake, p. 95.

25. Clifford Geertz. *Local Knowledge: Further Essays in Interpretative Anthropology.* New York: Basic Books, 1983, p. 109.

Index